German-French Unity

Basis for European Peace

German-French Unity
Basis for European Peace

HERMANN LUTZ

HENRY REGNERY COMPANY
Chicago   *1957*

To all those who are striving for a permanent reconciliation of the French and German peoples as the indispensable foundation for Western European Unity

Acknowledgments

In September, 1948, I left Germany, my native country, to join my wife in New York, and to acquire United States citizenship which was accorded me in June, 1951. An old friend in this country approached me with the suggestion that I write a book on German diplomacy under Hitler, and he kindly obtained a grant for me from an American Foundation.

Since May, 1952, I have had the privilege of doing the required research work at the Hoover Institute and Library on War, Revolution and Peace, Stanford University, Stanford, California. Its unique collection of material relevant to my subject has been invaluable. I am much indebted to Professor Harold H. Fisher, Chairman; Dr. C. Easton Rothwell, Director; Professor Ralph H. Lutz, the former Chairman; Mr. Philip T. McLean, Librarian of the Hoover Institute and Library, for the facilities accorded to me, and for their friendly interest in my work; and to Mrs. Hildegard R. Boeninger, Curator of the Western and Central European Collections of the Hoover Institute and Library, for her help in various ways. I wish to thank also the Staff of the Library for their invariably courteous and efficient assistance.

During my research work I came to the conclusion that, for practical purposes, the original scope should be expanded to embrace a survey of German-French relations since 1870, for they have once more acquired prime importance in European affairs. Consequently, I have collected material for two books, the present one being a precursor of the book originally planned. The second volume will treat German foreign policy under Hitler's chancellorship. Further material collected may be used for a third book dealing with foreign policy of Britain and the United States during World War II.

In addition to my old friend, others who also wish to remain unnamed, have actively assisted in the publication of the present book. One person, in particular, has made a generous contribution inspired by his desire to help in creating a better world by promoting sound international understanding. Professor Sidney B. Fay has kindly read the manuscript, and I have profited by various suggestions he, as well as other scholars, offered for improving it. My old friend, a skilled and veteran editor, has gone over my manuscript with great care and made changes and emendations in the interest of style and usage. I express my deep gratitude to all concerned.

Permission for lengthy quotations from certain publications has been given by the *Carnegie Endowment for International Peace;* by Alfred A. Knopf, Inc., New York; by Longmans, Green and Co., New York; and by The Macmillan Company, New York, as recorded in the text and in notes respectively.*

My sincere thanks are also due to the publisher who has ventured to bring out a book the theme of which, in large part at least, still appears to be rather unpopular with influential circles in the United States and elsewhere.

Finally, I wish to pay an especial tribute to my wife, Mrs. Marguerite Voorhees Lutz, who has acted as mediator between her home country and "better" Germany for almost half a century. Her general help, advice, criticism, patience, and faith have been most encouraging.

The Directors of the Foundation who enabled my extensive studies at the Hoover Institute and Library, expressed their belief that "independence of spirit" is "essential to creative research of any kind," and they expect that my writings will represent my "honest convictions." I have been guided by these principles. Thus, I am solely responsible for the contents of—or any omissions in—this book.

Visitors of the Hoover Institute and Library will find in the

---

* The books are: Dr. Alma Luckau, *The German Delegation at the Paris Peace Conference* (Columbia University Press, New York, 1941); William L. Langer, *European Alliances and Alignments, 1871-1890* (Alfred A. Knopf, New York, 1931); G. P. Gooch, *Recent Revelations of European Diplomacy,* 4th edition, revised and enlarged 1940 (Longmans, Green and Co., London and New York, 1940); Hugh R. Wilson, *Diplomat Between Wars* (Longmans, Green and Co., New York-Toronto, 1941); and Sidney Bradshaw Fay, *The Origins of the World War,* 2 vols. (The Macmillan Company, New York, 1928).

lobby the following dedication inscribed by its founder, the former President of the United States Mr. Herbert Hoover, dated June 20, 1941:

THE PURPOSE OF THIS INSTITUTION IS TO PROMOTE PEACE. ITS RECORDS STAND AS A CHALLENGE TO THOSE WHO PROMOTE WAR. THEY SHOULD ATTRACT THOSE WHO SEARCH FOR PEACE.

It is in this spirit that I have sought to carry out my historical studies ever since I first undertook them in Munich in 1919.

HERMANN LUTZ

Palo Alto, California
July, 1955

The above statements reflect accurately the situation at the time when research and exposition were to all intents and purposes complete, and early publication of my book was expected.

My work on the two other projected books is proceeding under the same favorable and pleasant conditions as before.

H. L.

February, 1957

Preface

The purpose of this book is made clear by its title and the dedication. On July 28, 1956, Foreign Minister H. von Brentano declared in the *Bundestag* that a lasting reconciliation of Germany and France and their partnership are the basis for a European community. Its attainment is primarily a *spiritual* process guided by a detached reconsideration of historical events which shaped the destiny of France and Germany in the last ninety years. Their unity is indispensable for the security of the West in the face of ever threatening dangers from the East.

In their political commentaries of November 16, and December 1, 1955, Joseph and Stewart Alsop stressed "the grand nightmare of Western diplomacy." They expressly endorsed the well-considered conclusion George F. Kennan had reached, namely, that the Germans may abandon their alliance with the West in order to buy re-unification of their country from the Soviets. Although the vast majority of the Germans are, and will no doubt remain, anti-Communist, it should be borne in mind that German-Russian friendship is a century-old tradition. Moreover, economic and technical cooperation between Germany and the Soviet Union, with its huge undeveloped "hinterland" Asia, offers alluring prospects to both. French statesmen are well aware of this. In July 1956, Premier Guy Mollet declared: "It is necessary to weave between the countries of Western Europe the bonds that will prevent Germany from turning to the East." And in January 1957, Foreign Minister Christian Pineau insisted, in view of the recent events in the Middle East, that it is now "more necessary than ever to realize the unification of Europe," adding, "For France it is perhaps a question of life or death" (*Time,* July 23, 1956, p. 28, and January 14, 1957, p. 24).

The unification of France with the virile German people, occupying the heart of Europe, will be a sure way of preventing "the grand nightmare of Western diplomacy" from becoming a disastrous reality.

In this effort the United States of America and Great Britain have, so it seems to me, the moral leadership. May this book facilitate their task, for the welfare of the Western world.

HERMANN LUTZ

Contents

Part One

Part One

Chapter One

Changing Opinions

In January, 1941, Sir Robert Vansittart, Chief Diplomatic Adviser to His Majesty's Government since 1938, opened a series of British broadcasts with an interesting reminiscence:

In 1907 I was crossing the Black Sea in a German ship. It was spring, and the rigging was full of bright-coloured birds. I noticed one among them in particular, strongly marked, heavier-beaked. And every now and then it would spring upon one of the smaller, unsuspecting birds, and kill it. It was a shrike or butcher-bird; and it was steadily destroying all its fellows. . . . I only had a revolver handy, and it took me the whole day to get that butcher-bird. And while I was doing it, a thought flew across my mind, and never again left it. That butcher-bird on that German ship behaved exactly like Germany behaves. I was twenty-six at the time, and life looked pretty good—or should have looked, for there were four hundred million happinesses of a sort in Europe. But already I could feel the shadow on them, for I had spent long enough in Germany to know that she would bring on her fourth war as soon as she thought the going good.

Sir Robert continued in subsequent broadcasts:

Well, by hook and by crook—especially crook—the butcher-bird got three wars before 1914 (in 1864, 1866 and 1870). Each of these wars was carefully planned and provoked by the butcher-bird. Then, in 1905 it nearly got another war. . . . There was another narrow squeak in 1911, but the butcher-bird landed its fourth war right enough in 1914. . . . And so Europe has had five wars in seventy-five years! . . . A German war every fifteen years on an average. . . . And there is nothing new in Hitler. . . . He is the natural and continuous product of a breed which from the dawn of history has been predatory and bellicose.

3

Concerning the German national character, Vansittart declared:

Force and fraud, fraud and force; that is the old German gospel. . . . Germans have pledged no word without breaking it, have made no treaty without dishonouring it, touched no international faith without soiling it. For generations they have been ruining all trust between men.

These broadcasts were given wide publicity in the British press and were later, "in response to very numerous requests," printed as a pamphlet of which 500,000 copies were sold within one year. On the back of the pamphlet the editors stated that Sir Robert's talks were designed to show that the German has always been the barbarian, the war-lover, the enemy of humanitarianism, liberalism and Christian civilization, and that the Hitler regime was only the logical fruit of German history, the German *in excelsis*. Sir Robert believed that this fact must be understood and faced, once and for all.

His indictment [the editors declared] is based upon wide scholarship, first-hand experience and the conviction of many years. No man living was better qualified to say these things. They needed saying. They cannot be ignored.[1]

Certainly, they cannot be ignored. Much of the indictment is true of Hitler's deeds. To a diplomatist of Vansittart's distinguished career the public attributes expert knowledge. Many millions in the Western world were, and still are, deeply influenced by his and similar views. Finally, the broadcasts and their distribution in print had official approval. According to a statement by a parliamentary group, Sir Robert was invited by the Minister of Information, Mr. Duff Cooper, to give these broadcasts on the history and the character of the Germans.[2] If the British Government or the leading men in the Cabinet had disapproved of their Chief Diplomatic Adviser's declarations, the broadcasts would have been promptly stopped and would not have been printed.[3]

When Sir Robert left public office as Lord Vansittart he continued his activity along these same lines. In 1943, he contended that 75 per cent of Germans have for 75 years "been eager for any assault on their neighbours." [4] And, in 1945, he issued an emphatic warning in both English and French:

The Germans are nationally false. . . . There is no moral health in them. Never forget, therefore, that no German bond or promise is of the slightest value; it is on the contrary a trap. . . . It is as a friend that I say to Europe: Do *not* forget. Remember what I have written.[5]

Lord Vansittart surely thought that he had the world's welfare at heart. His life-long sympathy for Austria, Germany's partner in the Triple Alliance, is well known. In the mid-thirties he urged, as Permanent Under-Secretary for Foreign Affairs, timely resistance to Hitler instead of the dangerous policy then pursued, viz., excessive appeasement. In those decisive years he should have been listened to. His descriptions of the German character have a vital bearing on present and future world policy. Therefore, they deserve to be carefully examined, for if they are only in the main true, the rearming of West Germany must be envisaged with the utmost caution, and must necessarily evoke wide-spread misgivings.

In October, 1953, and September, 1954, Lord Vansittart publicly treated this particular subject. "Nobody hates the rearmament of Germany more than I do," he stated; "it is the thing above all others that, during the war, I prayed we should never see again." But "the iniquities of Soviet policy have invalidated that prayer." So Lord Vansittart now advocated German rearmament, if strictly controlled, as a most unfortunate, though unavoidable "choice between two evils," the other—greater—evil being the rising Communist menace. In these recent public declarations Lord Vansittart has not retracted any of his former charges against the Germans. Indeed, he has rather confirmed them.[6]

As a correction of Lord Vansittart's sweeping indictment some historical facts may now be put forth.

The opening years of the twentieth century witnessed a revolutionary change in the attitude of Britain, France, Germany, and Russia towards each other. The change coincided with Britain's decision to abandon her position of "splendid isolation" in view of developments on the Continent which seemed to call for greater security.

For decades, France had been England's "hereditary enemy." The African Fashoda episode, in 1898, brought both countries to the brink of war. A leading authority on the subject, Professor William L. Langer, has stated that in most

British circles at the time a war against France would have been popular, and that "there was considerable sentiment in governing circles for a preventive war." [7] In those years, the frivolity and immorality of French life were accepted in England as an established dogma,[8] and the popular *Daily Mail*— later on bitterly hostile to Germany—urged that France should be fought and "rolled in the blood and mud where she belongs, her colonies taken from her and given to Germany." [9]

In France there was a similar feeling towards *Perfide Albion,* to which the publicist Paul de Cassagnac, a veteran of the Franco-Prussian War of 1870, gave forceful expression:

If Germany is an object of hatred it is for a definite past which can be effaced. But England's hatred against us is inextinguishable. England is the enemy of yesterday, tomorrow and forever.[10]

The Boer War intensified this anti-British sentiment. The author of this book spent the winter 1901-02 at the Universities of Grenoble and Montpellier and travelled extensively through the South of France from the Pyrenees to the Italian frontiers. When taken for an English youth, and that happened quite often, I regularly heard curses, the mildest being *À bas, les Anglais* (Down with the English), and good-sized stones were thrown at me. When recognized as a German, I was treated with friendly hospitality. Never during those six months did I encounter any anti-German feeling, and I have held the conviction ever since that a generous German policy towards France at the turn of the century could well have laid the basis for lasting conciliation between the two peoples. Imperial Germany then missed a great opportunity.

Next to France in those days, Britain's bitterest enemy was Russia, who at that time was steadily expanding in the Far East. In May, 1898, Joseph Chamberlain, the Colonial Secretary, publicly cited a very wise proverb, namely, "Who sups with the Devil must have a long spoon," thus alluding to Tsarist Russia.[11]

Joseph Chamberlain was the leader of an influential group in and outside the British Cabinet who looked eagerly for a suitable ally because the Boer War had aroused general hostility towards Britain. On November 30, 1899, he declared in a famous speech: "It must have appeared evident to everybody that the natural alliance is between ourselves and the great German Empire," adding that fundamentally the character of the Teutonic race differs very slightly indeed from the character of the Anglo-Saxon race.[12]

This was still the time in England when "it was not permitted to say a good word of France, or a bad one of Germany," as Norman Angell has recorded.[13] In accordance with this sentiment, the masses in Britain still adhered to the opinion that the Franco-Prussian War of 1870 had been provoked by the French. The English historian, J. Holland Rose, recalled in 1915 that very many British rejoiced at the unification of Germany and the downfall of Napoleon III, because no feeling of security was possible while he was in power.[14]

This attitude towards Germany gradually altered when Germany failed to respond with prompt appreciation to Chamberlain's overtures; when Britain concluded an Entente with France in 1904, and another with Russia in 1907; when Germany compelled France in 1905 to revise her arrangement with England over Morocco; when Germany followed Britain's lead in building Dreadnoughts; and when a series of crises led to the outbreak of hostilities in August, 1914.

Ever since World War I the charge has been inculcated into the Western mind that Germany has always been an unprovoked aggressor toward France, an allegation which was intensified throughout World War II. The statesman, Viscount Herbert Samuel, for instance, wrote of the curse Germany had been for Europe because of her five wars of aggression, in 1864, 1866, 1870, 1914, and 1939.[15] More picturesque, although less clear as to its meaning, was Winston S. Churchill's statement in 1948: "Five times in a hundred years, in 1814, 1815, 1870, 1914, and 1918, had the towers of Notre Dame seen the flash of Prussian guns and heard the thunder of her cannonade," followed, after a few intermediary sentences, by the definite assertion that the French also "remembered the preventive war which Bismarck had sought to wage in 1875."[16] There can be little doubt that the average Anglo-Saxon reader, whose mind has now for decades been trained to detect in Germany *the* aggressor, concludes that Britain's "Grand Old Man" fully shares the world's prevailing view of Germany's pernicious role throughout the 19th century and up to 1939.

As a matter of fact, the invasion of France in 1814 was carried out by a coalition of Austrian, German and Russian troops, allied with England, for the liberation of Europe from the curse of Napoleon I. And, in 1815, the Prussian Marshal

Bluecher helped the Duke of Wellington win the decisive battle at Waterloo in *La Belle Alliance,* an event then highly appreciated by the British. The war of 1864 was a joint war of Prussia and Austria against Denmark to secure the preponderately German Duchies of Schleswig and Holstein for Germany. The war of 1866 arose from this same issue, and was a fratricidal war between Germans in which the South German States, as well as Hanover, Hessen and Nassau, stood by Austria against Prussia. Both wars were fought for German unification, keenly desired by the people who had been stirred by the Napoleonic wars early in the century. True, Bismarck did his share in bringing about both wars, but in 1864 Denmark was largely to blame. In 1866, Bismarck's aim was to oust Austria from German affairs and to insure Prussian hegemony over the future united Germany he envisaged. Whatever responsibilities Bismarck incurred for the wars of 1864 and 1866, which King William of Prussia wished to avoid, they cannot in fairness be extended collectively to the "Germans" who were then ruled autocratically and had no part in German foreign policy.

It seems also appropriate to consider how small the losses of life were in both these wars. In 1864, the Prussians and Austrians together had only 889 dead, including the missing. The Danish losses were higher, but for both sides the total of killed and dead numbered probably less than 3,000. In 1866, the killed, the dead from wounds or illness, and the missing on all sides: that is of the Austro-Hungarians, their German Allies (seven states), of the Prussians and the Italians, totalled no more than 36,478. That corresponds roughly to the number of civilian people killed in Dresden through three Allied air bombardments on February 13 and 14, 1945, the official Dresden figure being over 35,000 dead; or to the people killed later in that year at Nagasaki by one atomic bomb.[17]

In the United States, there was also a reversal of opinion between 1870 and 1914 similar to that in Great Britain, towards France and Germany. In an introduction to a careful study, George H. Blakeslee wrote:

During the Franco-Prussian War of 1870-71, American sentiment was so strongly against the French that many an anti-French editorial of 1870 could easily pass for an anti-German editorial of 1914, if the name Napoleon the Third were changed to William the Second. . . . In 1870, to the majority of Americans, Germany was the land of universities and of religious freedom, fighting for national unity against an Imperial aggressor. Germany had been one of the few friends of the North during the Civil War; while Germans had formed a notably large proportion of the northern armies and had won for themselves in the nation a position of high regard. The German victories were regarded in the United States with as much enthusiasm in 1870 as they were with regret in 1914.[18]

Yet, in 1946, the former Under-Secretary of State Sumner Welles, evidently expressing the conviction of a majority in the Western world, declared that the French Republic had "suffered three German wars of aggression within the brief space of seventy years" [19]—virtually a confirmation of Lord Vansittart's opinion.

One of Europe's main problems after the war of 1870 was the tense relationship between France and Germany. This assumed even greater importance after the First World War.[20] It is now a central issue in European affairs. In September, 1954, the French Premier and the Chancellor of West Germany both emphasized the fact that the organization of Europe must be founded on Franco-German reconciliation. This can only be brought about by establishing the facts relative to the causes of, and responsibilities for, the Franco-Prussian War of 1870 and the two World Wars.

When, in 1898, Bismarck's manipulation of the famous Ems telegram became fully known, his "falsification" stimulated a reversal of opinion in favor of Imperial France. Subsequently, the episode was highly over-dramatized, as a number of other incidents have been, to the neglect of deeper, though less obvious, causes.

The origin of the Franco-Prussian War goes back to Austria's defeat at the battle of Sadowa in 1866 when Emperor Napoleon III failed to obtain "compensation" for Prussia's rise in the heart of Europe. The unification of Germany now loomed on the horizon threatening France's preponderance on the Continent. Many Frenchmen felt that this dreaded unification, which would create a powerful neighboring state with a larger population than that of France, categorically demanded for the latter substantial acquisitions of territory along the Rhine. The Germans, on the other hand, considered that their unifi-

cation was a domestic affair and that the French claims were
unjustified. "The situation was one from which it was difficult
to escape without a war," as Professor William L. Langer has
justly remarked.[21] He states that after 1867 both sides prepared for the conflict. Napoleon did his utmost to bring about
a coalition of France, Austria, and Italy. By the summer of
1870, no definite entente had been reached but among the
French statesmen the opinion prevailed that Austria and Italy
could be counted upon as allies if a crisis arose. Though
Bismarck did not know the details of these negotiations for a
hostile coalition against him he was aware of what was brew-
ing. In his searching study Professor Langer has come to the
following conclusion:

In his reminiscences Bismarck takes much credit (if one can call
it that) for precipitating the war with France in 1870. He certainly
encouraged the candidacy of the Hohenzollern for the throne of
Spain and did little enough during the crisis of July 1870 to prevent the outbreak of hostilities. But one should bear in mind that
the French government was hardly less culpable. It was no secret
in Europe that the statesmen in Paris meant to get revenge for
Sadowa as soon as they felt ready. The projected coalition against
Prussia could hardly be called a defensive arrangement. Bismarck
continually stressed the military importance of having a Hohenzollern on the Spanish throne. In other words, he regarded the
Hohenzollern candidacy as a necessary counterblast to the French
designs. With a friendly ruler beyond the Pyrenees, Prussia could
count on the French having to leave many thousand men on the
Spanish frontier in case of war on the Rhine. Viewed from this
angle, Bismarck's policy was more a defensive policy than was
that of the French.
Even in the crisis of July 1870 the German statesman left the
initiative to the French, and the French put themselves in the
wrong. Gramont, the French foreign minister, lived in the hope of
re-establishing the French position on the continent. He was determined not to accept another "humiliation." When news of the
Hohenzollern candidacy reached Paris, he immediately took a firm
stand. His declaration in the Chamber of Deputies on July 6 practically closed the door to compromise. Bismarck himself described
this action as an incredible blunder. Nevertheless, fortune was with
the French. The withdrawal of the Hohenzollern candidacy was a
great victory for French diplomacy, and one with which the French
statesmen might well have contented themselves. But they insisted
on more and demanded that King William of Prussia should write
Napoleon an apology as well as a promise that the candidacy

would never be renewed in the future. Even the most ardent defenders of the French position find it hard to say much in justification of these unreasonable demands. There was no hope whatever that the Prussians would agree to them. On the contrary these demands gave Bismarck exactly the opportunity he wanted to put the French in the wrong and practically force them into war.

Whatever opinion historians may now hold on the question of responsibility for the war, there was little difference of opinion on this point among contemporary neutrals. English statesmen, for example, had been on cordial terms with the French for some time, but the English public had come to distrust Napoleon and his advisers. When the war broke out, Englishmen were almost unanimous in believing that the conflict had been wantonly precipitated by the French Emperor, and that the fundamental cause for the war was the French desire to re-establish French hegemony on the continent by the defeat of Prussia and the acquisition of German territory.[22]

It is illuminating to note that even Pierre Larousse's celebrated *Grand Dictionnaire Universel* admits that, apart from Germany, "the Empire wanted the war," especially the Empress Eugénie; and that it describes the enthusiasm of the Parisians who, in the days before the outbreak of the war, sang *Le Rhin allemand* in the theaters and thronged the boulevards shouting *À Berlin! À Berlin!* [23]

The issue in 1870 was between Prussia and France. The Prussian people had no share in the Hohenzollern candidacy for the throne of Spain—the immediate cause of the war—or in Bismarck's editing of the Ems telegram calculated to react like a "red rag upon the Gallic bull." Therefore, Bismarck's share of responsibility cannot in fairness be extended to "Germany" which did not come into existence until January, 1871. What, above all, united the German states with Prussia was the people's vivid memory of the wars Napoleon I had fought on German soil, and of his oppressive encroachments. Indeed, the Germans of 1870 had many more reasons to recall Napoleon's aggressions from 1804 to 1813 than the French had to recall the thunder of Prussian guns in 1814 and 1815.

The actual fighting in 1870-71 lasted 6½ months. The losses of life of the war—killed, dead from wounds and illness, and missing—were on the German side 44,781, on the French side an estimated 140,000. It is instructive as to the horrifying and lethal effects of modern warfare to compare the losses of life in the wars of 1864, 1866 and 1870-71 with those caused by two atomic bombs in 1945. The official estimate is that the one bomb dropped on Hiroshima killed between 70,000 and 80,000 people and injured as many, whereas at Nagasaki over 35,000 people perished, as stated above.[24]

The war of 1870 was terminated by the Treaty of Frankfort in May, 1871. When Western public opinion was swung around against Imperial Germany early in our century, the peace settlement of 1871 was severely criticized as an abject example, particularly so during the First World War. Indeed, the forcible annexation of the provinces Alsace and Lorraine, without consulting the wishes of the local population, was a flat denial of the self-determination of the peoples concerned and became a major cause of the drift towards war.

In 1871, however, the reasons for the annexation were understood and appreciated abroad. In September of that year, Bismarck wrote to German diplomatists: "So long as France possesses Strassburg and Metz, her strategical position is stronger offensively than ours is defensively," and he recalled that, in more than twenty wars with France, the German States had never been the aggressors. Their demand was now for security. Quoting this, the historian, J. H. Rose, acknowledged in 1915 that, from the historical standpoint, Bismarck was right.[25] Similarly, Professor Langer stated in 1931, that in 1871 many less interested observers, even neutrals, recognized that Alsace and Lorraine had served the French as a base for attack upon Germany, and that, strategically speaking, the two provinces were the gateway to the South German districts beyond the Rhine.[26] Nevertheless, their outright annexation was the gravest political blunder which Bismarck committed in foreign affairs.

The other imposition wrung from France in 1871, which later became the subject of indignant reproach, was the indemnity of five milliards of francs. The French Republic was, however, able to pay off the whole in less than three years. Indeed, some years later the French Foreign Minister, Barthélemy Saint-Hilaire, told the American diplomat, Andrew Dickson White, that France would gladly have paid a much larger sum than five milliards if she could have retained Alsace and Lorraine.[27] As a compensation for their annexation, Bismarck encouraged France to acquire a large colonial empire in North Africa.

We have seen that Winston S. Churchill accused Bismarck of having sought to wage a preventive war against France in 1875. He echoes Lord Vansittart in this respect. Sumner Welles in his turn spoke in 1946 of Bismarck's decision "to conquer France only five years after the war he had forced upon her in 1870." [28]

This is a very serious charge, when pronounced from such high quarters. The episode has been carefully investigated by leading historians. It is true that, in 1875, some army chiefs in Germany advocated a preventive war because of France's rapid recovery, but there is no evidence to show that Bismarck was only restrained from war by Russian and British intervention. The French Foreign Minister, Duc Decazes, himself observed at the time: "Bismarck wants us to believe that he wishes for war, but he does not wish for it himself." [29] In 1951, a group of French and German historians met to discuss pre-war events, and they jointly agreed that Bismarck's aim after 1871 was to maintain for Germany the position she had attained, "and that he did not seek to provoke another conflict." [30] In fact, on the strength of a mass of revelations on the period after 1870 which poured out after the First World War, Dr. G. P. Gooch, the eminent British historian, found the belief "confirmed that from 1871 to his fall in 1890 Bismarck was the chief pillar of European peace." [31]

Now the vital question arises: Are the statesmen, such as Churchill and Welles, mentioned in the foregoing pages correct in their charges against Germany about the war of 1870 and the *Alerte*—as the French call it—of 1875? If so, it would mean a grave reflection on the judgment of those British Cabinet Ministers who, like Joseph Chamberlain and the Foreign Secretary, Marquess of Lansdowne, were ready in the years 1898 to 1901 to conclude with that "wanton aggressor," Germany, an Entente which would have been distinctly directed against France and Russia. If, however, the historians quoted and referred to are sound and accurate in their views, then those statesmen have deeply and unfortunately misled the minds of the masses, the more so as they naturally find an infinitely larger audience than scholars generally do. What such distortion means in world affairs in our day Sumner Welles illustrates when he writes that Bismarck's decision to conquer France only five years after the war he had forced upon her in 1870,

has shaped the history of Europe, and consequently the history of
the rest of the world, for seventy years. It has governed the thinking of the German people and has helped to make the German
nation the peril to humanity that it has since become.[32]

The lesson of this for all those who devote their efforts to
providing a sound historical basis for a constructive foreign
policy is obvious.

Under Bismarck's successors German leadership badly de-
teriorated. Nevertheless, early in our century the great American educator, Andrew Dickson White, who had spent some
eight years in Germany and was United States Ambassador to
Berlin from 1897 to 1902, wrote:

Germany, from a great confused mass of warriors and thinkers and
workers, militant at cross-purposes, wearing themselves out in vain
struggles, and preyed upon by malevolent neighbors, has become a
great power in arms, in art, in science, in literature; a fortress of
high thought; a guardian of civilization; the natural ally of every
nation which seeks the better development of humanity.[33]

Ten short years after the publication of this estimate in
1905 the Germans were being widely denounced as a "criminal
nation."

In the interval, Europe had passed through a series of crises.
The British Ententes with France in 1904 and with Russia in
1907, and the formation of the Balkan League in 1912, forged
under the auspices of Russia, spread a genuine fear in the
Central Powers that they were being encircled by a hostile
coalition. The outcome of the Balkan Wars in 1913 undermined the security of Austria-Hungary. For much of this unfortunate development the Central Powers were themselves to
blame. But France's conquest of Morocco, resulting from her
deal with Britain in 1904, was felt by Germany to be a provo-
cation which she, in her turn, opposed by provocative diplomacy. Moreover, her building of a large battle fleet was, for
England, a challenge to her sea power. On the other hand, it
is necessary to recall that the "Butcher-Bird" missed four
tempting opportunities to unleash a war under very favorable
conditions: in 1905 and 1911 over Morocco, in 1908 during
the Bosnian crisis, and in 1912-13 during the Balkan Wars,
all at times when Russia was still fatally weakened by her
defeat in the Far East and revolutionary disturbances at home.

The actual events in the decade before 1914 will, therefore, never provide a satisfactory explanation for the wholesale condemnation of Germany. The British historian, Edward Hallett Carr, has pointed out that the wicked nation thesis is a product of an emotional reaction, familiar in all periods of history, when enemies are branded as moral reprobates, particularly if a justification is desired for treating them as inferiors and outcasts. In other words, "it is propaganda for a certain policy." [34]

The present writer does not wish to give the impression that he would favor any counter-propaganda "for a certain policy." Far from it. Lord Vansittart is convinced that it will take fifty years to reform the fundamental German character. We have heard the opinions of other prominent statesmen which resemble those of Vansittart. We shall presently get acquainted with an official statement made in 1919 by representatives of twenty-seven Powers which condemns "Germany," collectively, as being outside the pale of civilized nations. In view of the tremendous issues at stake for Europe and the world, such indictments require the most careful consideration. At the same time it is a historian's duty to record divergent opinions, some of which we shall now list.

Sir Arthur Salter, after having acquired a fair knowledge of Germans through many years of personal contact, expressed the view in 1939, that the German people are among the greatest made by Western civilization; that they have certain national characteristics which are to their advantage and some which are not; and that the main differences between Germans and their Western neighbors are in large measure due to the difference in their national experience, "especially in the last two decades, for which we must share the responsibility." [35] Sir Nevile Henderson, the British Ambassador to Germany from 1937 to 1939, confessed that he liked and admired the German people, amongst whom he felt very much at home, and that he found them less strangers to him than almost any other foreign people.[36] Leonard Woolf ridiculed the wrangles in the last war about the number of "good" and "bad" Germans, and declared that the vast majority of Germans are ordinary people, not very different from the ordinary people of most European countries, and therefore capable, in certain circumstances, "of gross political stupidity and social barbarism," and in other circumstances capable "of becoming useful

members of human society." [37] Finally, an American lady,
even after having lived four years under the Nazi regime, came
to the conclusion, in 1938, that "Fundamentally, Germans are
good." [38]

These various evaluations are purposely selected as those
set forth during the later Nazi days when their brutalities were
well-known among foreigners.

For a clear conception of the German case the reader should
not concentrate his attention on the nauseating vision of the
inhuman atrocities perpetrated in World War II by a group
of perverted fiends, but should revert to the Imperial Germany
before the First World War when there was no Adolf Hitler
and no Fascism in sight, the Germany of 1913, as George F.
Kennan reflected in 1951, run by conservative but relatively
moderate people, a vigorous Germany, full of energy and confidence, and able to play a part in the balancing-off of Russian
power in Europe. The return of this old Germany, our American diplomat thought, would not make everybody happy, "but
in many ways it wouldn't sound so bad." [39]

By that year (1913), Germany's predominant position on
the continent had perceptibly weakened. What at that time impressed the Germans and Austrians most deeply was the ever-
growing Pan-Slavic menace on their Eastern borders. Later,
it turned out that, in the face of superior German military
leadership, this menace from Tsarist Russia was more apparent
than real. But in the Entente camp there was a comparable
over-estimation which found frequent expression in exultant
predictions that, in case of war, the "Russian steam-roller"
would, crushing all resistance, smash its way to Berlin in a
matter of weeks. The resulting German fear of Russia has not
been as fully appreciated by the West as has been the French
fear of Germany although the situation was very similar.
Europe's present plight in face of Soviet Russia should tend
to promote a better understanding of the German position
before 1914. An authority on the subject, as familiar with
Germany as with Russia, observed that even at times when
the best relationship prevailed between the two countries,
"Germany was never free from the dread of the colossus in
the East." [40] Norman Angell realized that the fear of Slav
domination "really did haunt Germany," adding that the very
power of Russia, semi-Asiatic, of enormous population and
terrifying fecundity, was in itself a menace.[41] Even in 1938,

after the incorporation of Austria and the Sudeten Germans, there were only 80 million inhabitants of Greater Germany, as against 226 million Slavic peoples, and the latter are increasing more rapidly than any other people in Europe.[42]

The American diplomat, Henry White, happened to be in Berlin at the outbreak of hostilities in August, 1914. There he gained the impression which became "firmly fixed in his mind," that it had been fear of Russia which was the immediate cause of Germany's entrance upon war, and not the desire to crush France.[43] It was the German plan of military operations through Belgium, calling for a quick victory over France before the Russians could gather their overwhelming strength in manpower, which distorted the real facts in the public mind in 1914.

It is of paramount importance to comprehend that the German people were convinced that they were waging a defensive war in 1914-18. There are numerous foreign witnesses for this fact.[44] A French authority may be quoted, Albert Rivaud, who acknowledged that "the good faith of the German masses cannot be doubted." [45] Indeed, they argued: Britain had not been threatened by the Central Powers, nor had Japan been threatened but obviously came in to grab for herself Germany's possessions in the Far East; later, the former allies of Germany came in to fight against her, Italy in 1915, and Rumania in 1916, both with the avowed intention of enlarging their territories at Austria-Hungary's expense. It was all so obvious to the German eye, and consequently the people clung to their original belief of 1914 throughout the war.

It was the same, of course, on the other side. All belligerents believed that they were on the defensive against aggression. Therefore, everywhere there was the same enthusiasm. Some American authors have well described how "for the men and the women who lived through the first week of August 1914," in the capitals of Europe—St. Petersburg, Berlin, Paris, London—"the outstanding impression was that of the cheering, singing, marching masses." [46] It was this universal conviction of their own government's clean cause which brought about the collapse of the Socialist *Internationale,* and of its boast that it would prevent war.[47]

Post-war publications have proved that none of the governments involved in the war told its people the whole unvarnished truth. Important details were kept from the Germans and

Austrians, whereas the peoples of the Triple Entente remained in ignorance of the facts about the Russian general mobilization in late July, 1914, which, for the Central Powers, was the determining factor that precipitated the outbreak of hostilities. Professor Raymond James Sontag explained the situation well:

With critical standards almost obliterated by passion, with opposing arguments either concealed by censorship or unheard in the tumult, with powerful engines of propaganda, official and unofficial, at its disposal, each government succeeded with ease in stamping its version of the facts indelibly on the public mind.[48]

The Allied version of war guilt found forcible expression at the Paris Peace Conference in a document of the highest importance, dated June 16, 1919, which will be discussed in the next chapter. It was a judgment by the victors—endorsed by "practically the whole of civilized mankind"—on German policy, and stated: The war was "the greatest crime against humanity" that "any nation, calling itself civilized, has ever consciously committed"; barbarities were practised "from which the most uncivilized peoples would have recoiled"; Germany's conduct "is almost unexampled in human history"; and her responsibility comprises seven million dead as well as more than twenty million wounded and other sufferers from the war—a responsibility shared by the German people.

This judgment may well be called an official precursor of Lord Vansittart's later pronouncements. But its significance is infinitely greater because the indictment was proclaimed in the name of all the twenty-seven Allied and Associated Powers, then assembled in Paris, which included Haiti and Liberia, The Hedjaz and Siam.[49]

Whoever is seriously concerned with a sound constructive policy for Europe must try to get an objective view of the causes that brought about the First World War, for—as an experienced American diplomatist has justly observed—all the lines of inquiry lead back to it.[50] The German masses were taught, and they still believe it, that their government was not responsible for the war. The masses in the opposite camp were taught the reverse and they believe it today more than ever as a result of the Second World War.[51] It is true that, in the later twenties and early thirties, the general public, especially in the Anglo-Saxon countries, had largely revised its former view of the "Hun." But it is noteworthy that, even as late as 1933, Winston S. Churchill replied to the question, if he thought that Germany was guilty of making the war in 1914, with a flat "Yes, of course." In later years, as Prime Minister, he repeatedly stated this.[52] On the American side, Under-Secretary of State, Sumner Welles, declared in 1944 that, when victory was won, Germany should be treated "in the light of the stark reality" that she "has twice within a quarter of a century brought war and devastation to mankind." [53]

It is obvious, therefore, that, in the pursuit of peacemaking, the question whether Germany was really *the* culprit in 1914, is of the utmost importance. It must be particularly so for the Anglo-Saxon peoples, especially for the American people, because they are the strongest moral force in the world today and because they wield an ever-increasing influence on foreign affairs. The Americans are, thanks to their geographical position, better fitted than the English to reach a detached view, free from self-interest; whereas both peoples are in equal measure champions in the practice of Fair Play. Their noble tradition, and the urgent necessity of laying a solid foundation for the creation of a harmonious world policy imposes upon the leading Anglo-American politicians a solemn obligation to obtain accurate information.[54] In this task they are, of course, dependent on experts, in our case on those historians who have made detailed and objective studies of the manifold causes of the First World War. It is clearly impossible for the average individual to sift for himself the huge mass of evidence contained in many thousands of documents.

The author has since 1919 investigated the matter.[55] Having recently gone over the whole field once more he may say that he finds himself in substantial agreement with the conclusions which have been reached by Professor Sidney Bradshaw Fay in America and by Dr. G. P. Gooch in England. Both are veteran and respected historians and have devoted a good many years to the study of this particular subject. The complicated question of the responsibilities for the war of 1914-18 requires lengthy quotations in order to present a comprehensive picture to the general reading public. The conclusions are reproduced with the permission of the authors who have both declared that they have not altered their position since they were written. Professor Fay stated in 1928:

None of the Powers wanted a European War. . . .

Serbia felt a natural and justifiable impulse to do what so many other countries had done in the nineteenth century—to bring under one national Government all the discontented Serb people. She had liberated those under Turkish rule; the next step was to liberate those under Hapsburg rule. She looked to Russia for assistance, and had been encouraged to expect that she would receive it. After the assassination [of the Archduke Franz Ferdinand, heir to the throne of Austria-Hungary], Mr. Pashitch [Prime Minister of Serbia] took no steps to discover and bring to justice Serbians in Belgrade who had been implicated in the plot. . . . That Mr. Pashitch was aware of the plot three weeks before it was executed, failed to take effective steps to prevent the assassins from crossing over from Serbia to Bosnia, and then failed to give Austria any warning or information which might have averted the fatal crime, were facts unknown to Austria in July, 1914; they cannot therefore be regarded as in any way justifying Austria's conduct; but they are part of Serbia's responsibility, and a very serious part.

Austria was more responsible for the immediate origin of the war than any other Power. Yet from her own point of view she was acting in self-defence . . . against the corroding Greater Serbia and Jugoslav agitation which her leaders believed threatened her very existence. . . . [The Austrian Foreign Minister Count] Berchtold gambled on a "local" war with Serbia only, believing that he could rattle the German sword; but rather than abandon his war with Serbia, he was ready to drag the rest of Europe into war. . . .

Germany did not plot a European War, did not want one, and made genuine, though too belated efforts, to avert one. She was the victim of her alliance with Austria and her own folly. Austria was her only dependable ally, Italy and Rumania having become nothing but allies in name. She could not throw her over, as otherwise she would stand isolated between Russia, where Panslavism and armaments were growing stronger every year, and France, where Alsace-Lorraine, [Foreign Minister] Delcassé's fall [1905], and Agadir [1911, both troubles over Morocco] were not forgotten. . . . Berchtold would hardly have embarked on his gambler's policy unless he had been assured that Germany would fulfil the obligations of the alliance, and to this extent Germany must share the great responsibility of Austria. . . .

Germany's geographical position between France and Russia, and her inferiority in number of troops, had made necessary the plan of crushing the French army quickly at first and then turning against Russia. This was only possible, in the opinion of her strategists, by marching through Belgium, as it was generally anticipated by military men that she would do in case of a European War. . . .

General mobilization of the continental armies took place in the following order: Serbia, Russia, Austria, France and Germany. General mobilization by a Great Power was commonly interpreted by military men in every country . . . as meaning that the country was on the point of making war. . . . It was the hasty Russian general mobilization . . . while Germany was still trying to bring Austria to accept mediation proposals, which finally rendered the European War inevitable.

Russia was partly responsible for the Austro-Serbian conflict because of the frequent encouragement which she had given at Belgrade. . . .

Russia's responsibility lay also in the secret preparatory measures which she was making at the same time that she was carrying on diplomatic negotiations. These alarmed Germany and Austria. But it was primarily Russia's general mobilization . . . which precipitated the final catastrophe, causing Germany to mobilize and declare war. . . .

In Professor Fay's estimate there follow observations on the attitude of the French and British Governments which may be left out because both had, comparatively, a lesser responsibility—the British Government ranking last—for the outbreak of hostilities in August, 1914. But it must be added that "Belgium was the innocent victim of German strategic necessity." [56]

Dr. G. P. Gooch who edited, jointly with Harold Temperley, the *British Documents on the Origins of the War, 1898-1914,* wrote his latest summary of the causes of, and responsibilities for, the First World War in 1940. The essential parts regarding the chief Powers involved read:

Fully to comprehend the World War and its causes we must stand above the battle and realize the truth of Hegel's aphorism, "Tragedy is the conflict not of right with wrong, but of right with right." Though the conduct of each of the belligerents appeared to its enemies to indicate a double dose of original sin, it was nevertheless in every case what might have been expected.

It was natural that Servia should aspire to unite under her sceptre the discontented Jugoslav subjects of her neighbour. . . . It was equally natural that Austria should resolve to defend herself against the openly proclaimed ambition to rob her of provinces which she had held for centuries. . . . The [Austrian] ultimatum was a gambler's throw; but it was envisaged as a strictly defensive action, offering the best chance of escape from a danger which was certain to increase and which threatened her existence as a Great Power.

The conduct of Germany was no less intelligible. Austria was the only Power on whom she could rely, since Italy and Roumania were allies in nothing but name. If Austria was broken up, Germany would stand alone in Europe, wedged in between a hostile Russia and a France bent on revenge. . . . Neither of them [Germany and Austria] desired a world war, but they were ready for all eventualities if Russia declined to permit the localization of the Austro-Serb conflict.

. . . The same instinctive pride of a Great Power which prompted Vienna to throw down the glove compelled St. Petersburg to pick it up. It is true that while Austria fought under the banner of self-preservation, Russia, whom nobody threatened to attack, marched to battle in the name of prestige; but in the accepted scale of national values safety, honour and prestige are motives of approximately the same weight. Moreover the support of Great Britain in the event of a general war was confidently expected.

For a quarter of a century the destinies of France had been linked with those of Russia, and when the long anticipated crisis arrived she took her place at the side of her partner with as little hesitation as Germany at the side of Austria. She had no desire for war, and took no step to precipitate it. Nor, on the other hand, did she seriously endeavour to keep the sword of her ally in its scabbard. She had never abandoned the hope of recovering the Rhine provinces, and for that reason could not be included among the satiated Powers who at any given moment are the most effective champions of peace. . . .

The course taken by Great Britain was marked out for her with equal clearness. . . . The violation of Belgian neutrality roused the country to righteous anger, but it was the occasion rather than the cause of our entry into the war. We fought for the Balance of Power. For better or worse we had departed from our traditional policy of "splendid isolation," and become entangled in the quarrels and ambitions of our friends. Had we stood aside at Armageddon the Central Powers would have won an easy victory, and we should have found ourselves alone in Europe. France and Russia would have scorned us as false friends who . . . deserted them in the crisis of their fate; and the German menace, intensified by the collapse of the Triple Entente, would have compelled us to arm to the teeth on sea and land. . . .

The war was the child of the European anarchy, of the outworn system of sovereign states. The Old World had degenerated into a powder-magazine, in which the dropping of a lighted match was almost certain to produce a gigantic conflagration. . . . Blind to danger and deaf to advice as were the rulers of the three despotic empires, not one of them desired to set the world alight. Yet, though they may be acquitted of the crime of deliberately starting the avalanche, they must jointly bear the reproach of having chosen the path which led to the abyss.[57]

The reader will notice the great similarity in the views of the American and the British scholar. Dr. Gooch lays the chief blame on the rulers of Austria-Hungary, Germany and Russia, to name them in alphabetical order. Professor Fay also places heavy responsibility on the Central Powers, but he stresses more than his English colleague does the responsibility of Russia and of Serbia. The present writer came in his studies to the conclusion that Russia and Serbia combined were more responsible than Austria-Hungary was. In regard to this another English scholar, G. Lowes Dickinson, raised the question: Which has the greater justification—a state that is defending itself against disruption, or one which desires to extend its power by the disruption of its neighbor? He thought that the whole controversy really turns on the point whether the Entente Powers are right in saying that the offence was Germany's backing of Austria, or the Germans in saying that the offence was Russia's backing of Serbia. To Dickinson's own mind the German position "is the more reasonable." [58]

There is also the question of how important one considers the general issue: Germandom versus Slavdom. Today, it is obvious that there should be a firm solidarity of Western Europe against an Eastern Power which derives so much of its tremendous strength and drive from Asia. This basic fact was not so clear in 1914. Yet, even then, there were statesmen who viewed with growing apprehension the rising, ever-rising tide of Slavic populations, and therefore felt that Austria-Hungary was worth supporting and preserving. In the interwar period of 1918-1939 many leading politicians deeply deplored the disappearance of the Dual Monarchy.

Whatever view is taken, there is no doubt in the writer's mind that for both the ulterior and the immediate causes of the First World War Austria-Hungary and her ally, Germany, incurred a heavy, in some respects a very heavy, responsibility, almost comparable to that of Tsarist Russia and her satellite Serbia. But for the purpose of practical policies there is no need of attempting to range the Great Powers according to the measure of their "guilt" in 1914. What matters above all in refuting the "Butcher-Bird" indictment is the fact that the rulers of Germany did not plot the war, and did not want it.[59]

As early as 1925, G. P. Gooch spoke of "the gradual recognition by informed opinion all over the world" that the responsibility for the war was divided.[60] In 1928 Sidney B. Fay observed that "the best historical scholars in all countries" generally recognized that the Versailles dictum of Germany's "guilt" was "no longer tenable or defensible." [61] Indeed, the number of historians and publicists who freely admitted this is so large that it is impossible to list even the more outstanding ones.[62]

Yet, when Hitler's terroristic regime became manifest, world public opinion moved rapidly back to the 1919 concept of the "criminal nation," although no new revelations had come to light which would have warranted a revision of the historical facts about 1914 as they had been firmly established by 1933. An American scientist told the present writer in 1934 that a few weeks of Nazi brutalities had practically wiped out in the people's minds the result of fifteen years' research work carried out by American historians.[63] With respect to this purely emotional reaction a very instructive case may be recorded to illustrate our specific topic, *Changing Opinions.* In 1947, a leading article in a prominent British paper asserted that Professor Fay "has recently, too late, regretted the conclusions to which he came." [64] This is not true. With Professor Fay's approval the following passage is quoted from a letter he wrote on May 7, 1947, to the present writer:

Though much new material has come out since I wrote in the twenties, it would only cause me to make a few minor changes in a new edition, but would not alter at all my essential position. There is hardly a word that I would change in the final chapter of "Conclusions." Though many people have said to me, "In view of what the Germans have done since 1919, I suppose you will rewrite your account of what happened before 1914." Such an *ex post facto* way of writing history seems to me to be most unhistorical—mere prejudiced nonsense.[65]

Indeed, it is astounding that an authority in the field should be expected to rewrite the history of past events because twenty years after they took place a man named Adolf Hitler—completely unknown to the world before 1919—assumed leadership over Germany. The rise of the Nazi regime and the emotional reaction to it led even to public attacks on the "Revisionists" amongst the historians for their efforts to enlighten the people about the background of the war.[66] Actually, these

historians deserve high credit for their work, for—as Professor
James T. Shotwell has pointed out in 1940—the controversy
around the question of responsibility for the war of 1914-18
is, by itself, "a great gain to the peace movement." [67]

In fact, an impartial investigation of the causes of the recent wars unquestionably serves the cause of peace—a truism
that cannot be too strongly emphasized. The author would,
however, prefer that the controversy be removed from the
opposing camps and be entrusted instead to competent *neutral*
authorities, as suggested in Part Two of this book.

In no country was the question of "war guilt" so passion-
ately discussed as in Germany where, soon after the conclusion of peace, a monthly magazine was entirely devoted to
that subject. And no wonder. As early as May 24, 1919, the
German delegation at Versailles declared in an official Note
to the Allies that Germany's alleged responsibility for the war
was "a question of life or death for the German nation." [68]
This feeling found ample justification in the Allied document
of June 16, 1919, referred to above. The notorious Article
231 of the Treaty of Versailles, the so-called "war guilt
clause," is by comparison a weak and misleading condensation of the terrible indictment hurled at the Germans generally in that document.

With a clear vision Mr. John Foster Dulles realized the
paramount significance of this question for the course of European events in the thirties. In 1919, as a member of the Reparation Commission in Paris, he deplored the inclusion of
Article 231 in the Treaty. In November, 1938, shortly after
a war over the Sudeten Germans issue had been avoided with
great difficulty, he made the following comment which is reproduced here with the kind permission of the present Secretary of State:

In the light of subsequent developments it may be that this article
was the most important single article in the Treaty. Thereby, in
German eyes, Germany was branded with moral guilt for the World
War, and the German people, under threat of wholesale starvation
and military devastation, were compelled to accept this verdict as
true. It was the revulsion of the German people from this article
of the Treaty which, above all else, laid the foundation for the
Germany which we see today. There was thus created a sense of
injustice and a reaction against the imputed moral inferiority which

was so intense as easily to lend itself to capitalization by leaders who were adept at arousing and directing human emotion.[69]

Perfectly true in 1938, and just as valid for today as it has ever been. Resistance to Germany's moral degradation came, as Frank H. Simonds has stated, "from the very soul of the German people"; it was instinctive, instant and unanimous.[70] In fact, the Germans would have been despicable as a nation if they had not unceasingly contested their defamation. Therefore, it aroused general satisfaction amongst them when, on January 30, 1937, Chancellor Hitler, in a solemn manifesto withdrew Germany's signature under the enforced declaration of 1919 that Germany was responsible for the war. Hitler's gesture was an arbitrary declaration, void of legality. It is noteworthy, however, that in 1937 none of the Powers protested against Hitler's action. Enlightened public opinion, particularly in the Anglo-Saxon countries, would at that time not have endorsed a protest. It was only after the outbreak of World War II, that the old accusations were illogically revived.

On June 10, 1945, Field Marshal Sir Bernard Montgomery broadcast an ominous message to the German population. *The London Times* of June 11 printed it under large headlines, "Why Germans Are Shunned. The Price of Guilt." The Field Marshal began with the war of 1914, "which was started by your leaders," and he stated that in the Treaty of Versailles "your leaders admitted that Germany was responsible for the war." The broadcast was officially given the widest possible publicity throughout Germany.[71] But the Germans commented on the assertions about World War I with bitter irony, with indignation, and with contempt, saying, "So they are dishing up again that old blasted lie!" Consequently, Montgomery's message had a most deplorable effect on the German masses.

On January 22, 1950, Dr. Thomas Dehler, at that time Minister of Justice in Adenauer's Cabinet, addressed a Rally of the Free Democratic Party. Rejecting the assertion of Germany's "aggressions during 200 years," he spoke particularly of the wars of 1864, 1866, 1870, 1914-18, and of Hitler's advent which was "largely a consequence of the Versailles Treaty." He declared that Napoleon III caused the Franco-Prussian War. The charge that Germany was primarily responsible for the First World War was "a fairy tale." He closed this part of his speech by stressing that these things "must be said in order to purify the political atmosphere in Germany" which "should not be poisoned by such historical lies," namely, Germany's alleged aggressions in a series of wars. Dr. Dehler's proclamation was repeatedly and loudly applauded. Abridged versions in the German Press somewhat accentuated Dehler's refutations. The French High Commissioner in Germany at once lodged an official protest in Bonn in which he characterized parts of the speech as "extremely shocking" and amounting to "flagrant distortions of history." The British Government expressed its serious displeasure with the speech, and the United States High Commissioner his regret, in view of the reaction abroad.[72]

Dr. Dehler, a leader of the Free Democrats, did not speak as a member of the Cabinet. Neutral historians would not accept all of his assertions without some qualifications. But the incident sharply illuminates the rather universal German feeling on the subject which persists in our day, burning under the surface, and likely to explode some time or other. And although Dehler referred to the situation "in Germany" his protest was also meant for foreign powers. We are thus once more back in the acrimonious dispute over the "War Guilt Lie" which had been throughout the inter-war period a festering sore in European policy.[73]

When, in the Anglo-Saxon countries, the passions aroused by the war of 1914-18 gradually cooled off there was a steadily growing recognition among all classes of citizens that the Treaty of Versailles contained some terms which were unwise and spelled evil for the future. Unfortunately, those terms were not revised during the existence of the Weimar Republic. Chancellor Hitler subsequently forced through revisions without serious interference from Britain and France. By the mid-thirties the Treaty was widely and vociferously condemned as a menace to the peace of Europe. When, however, Hitler rushed into war against Poland in September, 1939, many of those who had been loudest in decrying the Treaty as too harsh, now suddenly found that, on the contrary, it had been far too mild for the wicked Germans. The Versailles Treaty was no longer soberly judged on its own merits and defects but in relation to Hitlerism—which, in truth, was largely the product of the Versailles spirit.[74]

Very instructive for our topic is the extent to which in the course of seven years the opinion of Americans changed with regard to the question of whether they had made a mistake in entering the First World War. In 1937, 64 per cent answered Yes, and 28 per cent No; in 1944, only 18 per cent answered Yes, and as many as 61 per cent No. It was an almost complete reversal. Yet the essential facts of the situation in 1917 had not changed between 1937 and 1944.[75]

Even more curious is the fact that in the late twenties and early thirties hosts of Americans travelling in Germany observed, "I guess we fought on the wrong side." The main reason for this almost stereotype remark—frequently discussed in German political circles—was resentment that America's chief allies did not appreciate her decisive role in winning total victory in 1918, and that they had stopped paying their debts to her.

Between 1944, when all of Germany was to be "pastoralized" for the welfare and security of the rest of Europe, and the present day we have witnessed still another tremendous change of public opinion toward Germany, simply because the self-interest of the Democracies appears to demand that she should be incorporated into the North Atlantic bloc in order to serve as a military bastion in the dreaded event of a clash in arms between the Soviet Union and the West. The Germans know very well why they are being courted—that the chief reason for it is not a generous revision of the West's former opinion of them as a "criminal nation." [76] Moreover, the Germans naturally have no desire to be used merely as a strategic wall and as convenient cannon fodder.

A serious danger lurks in this situation, namely, that large numbers of Germans will accept the soldier role assigned to them with grave mental reservations. Indeed, how can anyone expect the Germans, after they have been branded as outcasts, to go heart and soul with the West if the official indictment of June 16, 1919, is left to stand, contradicted as it is by competent historians all over the world? That is an impossible psychological situation which must be cleared up, and urgently cleared up, if Europe desires to pursue a safe diplomatic and military course.

With judicious foresight Edward Hallett Carr wrote in 1942 that anyone who was to sway the destinies of Europe after the

Second World War must have the imagination to make a cogent appeal to the youth of Europe for service to a large cause.[77] That cause we now have—the creation of the United States of Europe in the Western sense. The cornerstone of this creation is, and always will be, a friendly understanding between the German and the French peoples. Without such a foundation politicians will be building as on shifting sand.

When General George C. Marshall received the Nobel Peace Prize he proposed in a lecture at Oslo on December 11, 1953, a well thought-out plan for World Peace. He advocated a careful study of the causes of war, and economic adjustments. But, he declared, in his opinion "the most important thing for the world today is a spiritual regeneration which would re-establish a feeling of good faith among men generally." [78]

These words evoked everywhere an appreciative, warm echo, and they aroused fervent hopes. Indeed, a spiritual regeneration is the prime necessity both for the present and for a happier future. It is badly needed amongst the vanquished in the last war, but it is also very much needed amongst the victors of the First World War. As a start, one should revert to a consideration of the 1919 Peace Conference and to the spirit it displayed, if we are to re-establish the indispensable feeling of good faith among men generally. Because it was at that Conference, when the peoples' minds were still inflamed by four years of a cruel war, and misled by artful propaganda, that so much good faith among men was destroyed.

For the promotion of the desired spiritual regeneration two factors are essential—a general acceptance of basic historical facts, and a fair degree of psychological understanding. This may not be easy with regard to Germany, as a collective unity, but the effort has to be made. Moreover, there exist excellent studies on the subject by a first-rate authority, the British psychologist, Dr. William Brown.[79]

The consensus of informed opinion is that—as a distinguished French scholar, Yves Simon, pointed out in 1942—the great mistake of the Versailles Treaty was to have created "an unbearable psychological situation" for the Germans.[80] The following chapter attempts to explain all this in some detail.

Chapter Two

The Peacemakers' Spirit, 1919

Under the auspices of the *Carnegie Endowment for International Peace,* Dr. Alma Luckau issued a voluminous book in 1941, entitled *The German Delegation at the Paris Peace Conference.* This contains twelve letters from Dr. Walter Simons, Commissioner General of the Delegation, written to his wife from Versailles, and seventy official documents. A lengthy introduction by Dr. Luckau outlines the essentials of the proceedings. In a Foreword dated August 7, 1941, Professor James T. Shotwell points out the importance of the publication for future peacemaking and declares:

No more challenging subject could be presented to the historian than . . . the effort of Germany to prepare and plead its case at Versailles in the summer of 1919. It is a story which has never been fully told.[1]

Due to the distraction produced by the Second World War and its aftermath this story did not receive the wide attention it deserved, especially by those who are concerned with the reconstruction of Europe, the central problem of which is the promotion of a genuine and enduring understanding between the German and the French peoples and their permanent reconciliation.

In 1927, Frank H. Simonds judiciously stressed the fact that it was the spirit of the Treaty of Versailles which made the settlement intolerable for all Germans.[2] And, in 1943, Herbert Hoover and Hugh Gibson stated: "The evil spirits of fear, hate, and revenge never did more destruction to civilization than at the Paris Conference." [3]

The writer will, therefore, reveal in this chapter the spirit that dominated the victorious nations in 1919, inflamed as they were by the passions and sufferings of a peoples' war lasting more than four terrible years, because this spirit explains to a very large extent why the infant Weimar Republic did not grow into maturity, and why Adolf Hitler succeeded in gaining a mass following in Germany.

The spirit of the Allied peacemakers, as well as that which animated the representatives of the New Germany, will emerge from the series of documents which are reproduced below in sections 1 and 2 of this chapter with the kind permission of the *Carnegie Endowment* and of Dr. Luckau, from their valuable publication. Some supplementary documents are reprinted in section 5.

This episode of the discussions between the Paris peacemakers and the German delegation is a tragic moment in history which covers no more than seven weeks, from May 7 to June 28, 1919. And it is a painful story. But for a full comprehension of European events in the twenty years that followed, a careful evaluation of the documentary evidence presented is indispensable.

Three vital questions have to be clarified and definitely answered: (1) Is it true, as Germany has contended, that the armistice terms of November, 1918, constituted a legally binding pledge to create a peace on President Wilson's basic program? (2) Is it true, as the Allied and Associated Powers at the Paris Conference have maintained, that the Treaty of Versailles was executed in conformity with their pledges, and was a just settlement? (3) Or is it true, as Germany—against twenty-seven governments—has asserted, that the Treaty was a flagrant breach of promise, and that the German people were betrayed?

It is obvious that clear and decisive answers to these questions are of paramount importance, not merely for settling old controversies, but even more for laying the foundation for a sound policy in the future. This is especially true today because, after Hitler broke the peace in 1939, public opinion in the Western world has tended to feel that the settlement of 1919 was, if anything, far too lenient towards Germany. [4]

1. The Proclaimed and Accepted Peace Terms

On various dates, in 1918, President Woodrow Wilson laid down a comprehensive peace program involving altogether twenty-three Points and four Principles (see Documents 1-4, section 5, below). On September 27, 1918, when victory was within the Allies' grasp, the President proclaimed as a fundamental rule that

the impartial justice meted out must involve no discrimination between those to whom we wish to be just and those to whom we do not wish to be just. It must be a justice that plays no favorites and knows no standard but the equal rights of the several peoples concerned.

The whole program, which included the creation of a League of Nations, was inspired by high statesmanship and lofty idealism. It voiced the desires of the masses all over the world. They saw in Wilson a messiah who would inaugurate an epoch of friendly cooperation between nations, an era of sublime justice in the relationship of the Powers, Great and Small, and, above all, a period of general freedom from the tortures of hatred and war.[5]

Some passages in the President's speeches played a prime role in influencing German opinion, and they must, therefore, be quoted. On April 2, 1917, four days before the United States Government declared war on Germany, he stated in Congress:

We have no quarrel with the German people. We have no feeling towards them but one of sympathy and friendship. It was not upon their impulse that their government acted in entering this war. It was not with their previous knowledge or approval.

In an address at Washington, D. C., on Flag Day, June 14, 1917, Wilson repeated, "We are not the enemies of the German people. . . . They did not originate or desire this hideous war," and he added significantly, "We are vaguely conscious that we are fighting their cause, as they will some day see it, as well as our own." This was generally understood as an allusion to the prospect that the Allies' victory would liberate the oppressed German masses for their good from arbitrary autocracy. The President certainly meant it in all earnestness. The allusion was widely discussed, and remembered, in progressive political circles throughout Germany.

On December 4, 1917, again in Congress, the President spoke of "the voices of humanity" that come from the hearts of men everywhere.

They insist [he declared] that the war shall not end in vindictive action of any kind; that no nation or people shall be robbed or punished because the irresponsible rulers of a single country have themselves done deep and abominable wrong

—meaning, of course, the rulers of Germany.

Finally, on April 6, 1918, Wilson proclaimed in an address at Baltimore:

We are ready, whenever the final reckoning is made, to be just to the German people. . . . There can be no difference between peoples in the final judgment, if it is indeed to be a righteous judgment. To propose anything but justice, even-handed and dispassionate justice, to Germany at any time, whatever the outcome of the war, would be to renounce and dishonor our own cause.

These pronouncements were carefully noted in Germany. They raised high hopes, and they were all recalled by the German delegates in their official correspondence with the Allies at Versailles in 1919.[6] It was with these pronouncements in mind that the German Chancellor, Prince Max of Baden, on October 6, 1918, asked President Wilson to take steps for the conclusion of a general armistice, accepting for the German Government his peace program as a basis for subsequent negotiations. Replying on the 8th, Secretary of State, Robert Lansing, inquired whether the German Government's object was only to agree upon the practical details of the President's program, and whether the Chancellor was speaking merely for the constituted authorities of the Empire who had so far conducted the war? The answers to these questions were "vital from every point of view." The reply on the 12th stated that the German Government accepted Wilson's terms "as the foundations of a permanent peace of justice"; the object of the discussions would be only to agree upon the practical details of their application; and the Chancellor spoke "in the name of the German Government and the German people."

Thereupon, Lansing, in a Note of the 14th, called attention very solemnly to the language and plain intent of one of the terms which the German Government had now accepted, namely, "The destruction of every arbitrary power anywhere that can separately, secretly, and of its single choice disturb the peace of the world." The Note added:

The power which has hitherto controlled the German Nation is of the sort here described. It is within the choice of the German Nation to alter it. The President's words just quoted naturally constitute a condition precedent to peace, if peace is to come by the action of the German people themselves. The President feels bound to say that the whole process of peace will, in his judgment, depend upon the definiteness and the satisfactory character of the guarantees which can be given in this fundamental matter. It is indispensable that the Governments associated against Germany should know beyond a peradventure with whom they are dealing.

The arbitrary power in question was Emperor William II, or, in a broader way, the Monarchy with its prerogatives, as established in 1871. The German Nation was thus invited to alter this situation as a preliminary condition for obtaining Wilson's peace terms—a fundamental matter for both parties.

The German Note of October 20 described the constitutional changes in progress and ended with the statement that "the offer of peace and an armistice has come from a Government, free from arbitrary and irresponsible influence," and supported by the approval of the overwhelming majority of the German people.

On the 23rd, the Secretary of State notified the German Government that the President has suggested to the Associated Governments—if they are "disposed to effect peace upon the terms and principles indicated"—that they submit armistice terms which could "enforce the details of the peace to which the German Government has agreed"; their acceptance by Germany would afford "the best concrete evidence of her unequivocal acceptance of the terms and principles of peace from which the whole action proceeds." But would the constitutional changes in Germany be permanent? Moreover, it did not appear that the heart of the present difficulty had been reached. "It may be," Lansing wrote, "that future wars have been brought under the control of the German people, but the present war has not been." The Note terminated with the following passage of the highest importance:

It is evident that the German people have no means of commanding the acquiescence of the military authorities of the Empire in the popular will; that the power of the King of Prussia to control the policy of the Empire is unimpaired; that the determining initiative still remains with those who have hitherto been the masters of Germany. Feeling that the whole peace of the world depends now on plain speaking and straightforward action, the President deems it his duty to say, without any attempt to soften what may seem harsh words, that the nations of the world do not and cannot trust the word of those who have hitherto been the masters of German policy, and to point out once more that in concluding peace and attempting to undo the infinite injuries and injustices of this war the Government of the United States cannot deal with any but veritable representatives of the German people who have been assured of a genuine constitutional standing as the real rulers of Germany. If it must deal with the military masters of the monarchical autocrats of Germany now, or if it is likely to have to deal with them later in regard to the international obligations of the German Empire, it must demand, not peace negotiations, but surrender. Nothing can be gained by leaving this essential thing unsaid.

The reader will do well to note once more the alternative: "surrender," if the military masters of the monarchical autocrats should remain in power, or else "peace negotiations" on the stated terms.

The German Note of October 27 affirmed that the peace negotiations were being conducted by a government of the people, having actual and constitutional authority to which also the military powers were subject. The German Government was now awaiting proposals for an armistice, "the first step toward a peace of justice, as described by the President in his pronouncements."

On November 5, Robert Lansing, in a concluding Note quoted from a memorandum of the Allied Governments:

Subject to the qualifications which follow they declare their willingness to make peace with the Government of Germany on the terms of peace laid down in the President's address to Congress of January 1918, and the principles of settlement enunciated in his subsequent addresses. They must point out, however, that clause 2, relating to what is usually described as the freedom of the seas, is open to various interpretations, some of which they could not accept. They must, therefore, reserve to themselves complete freedom on this subject when they enter the peace conference.

Further, in the conditions of peace laid down in his address to Congress of January 8, 1918, the President declared that invaded territories must be restored as well as evacuated and freed, the Allied Governments feel that no doubt ought to be allowed to exist as to what this provision implies. By it they understand that compensation will be made by Germany for all damage done to the civilian population of the Allies and their property by the aggression of Germany by land, by sea and from the air.

The Secretary of State added that the President was in agreement with the interpretation set forth in the last paragraph of the Allied memorandum as quoted above.

On November 11, 1918, the German Government accepted the armistice terms which rendered any further resistance by arms impossible.[7]

In the meantime, beginning on November 3, a revolutionary movement broke out in Germany and spread rapidly over the whole country. On the 8th, Chancellor Prince Max demanded the abdication of the Emperor. On the 9th, the Republic was proclaimed. By the 10th, all dynasties were overthrown. On that day, William II fled to Holland, followed by the Crown Prince on the 12th.

From the speeches and the official correspondence reproduced in the foregoing pages the following essential facts stand out in the Allied policy:

Repeated acknowledgment that the German people did not originate or desire the war;

Friendship for the German people, no enmity;

No punishment of the German people for the actions of their irresponsible rulers;

Surrender for the old masters of Germany; a negotiated peace on President Wilson's terms for a democratic Germany; the distinction between the two being maintained throughout;

Anything except justice would dishonor the American cause;

The Americans fought not only for their own cause, but also for the cause of the German people—liberation from autocracy.

Uttered by the President of the United States in good faith, these principles were accepted in equally good faith by the German masses who were deeply conscious that those pronouncements constituted a solemn pledge of the American Government and people toward the German people, and that they created a common bond of an exceptional order between them.

The peace terms, as laid down by President Wilson, were

explicitly accepted both by Germany and by the Allies in official Notes, with the two exceptions mentioned in Robert Lansing's Note of November 5th. The armistice terms did not in any way alter these fundamental facts. All the Governments concerned were thus legally bound to work out a peace of justice according to Wilson's program.[8]

The German people had completely fulfilled the preliminary conditions for such a peace. They came out of the revolution "in a great wave of democratic enthusiasm," their belief in a new social and political order taking on an almost religious fervor among the masses, as an American authority has truly stated.[9] They now confidently expected a just peace on the promised basis.

2. THE PARIS DRAMA

The Paris Peace Conference was attended by the representatives of twenty-seven states, the five Principal Powers being the United States of America, the British Empire, France, Italy, and Japan. It is important that the reader should know the list of the other twenty-two Allied and Associated Powers. They were, as given in the Preamble to the Treaty of Versailles:

Belgium	Liberia
Bolivia	Nicaragua
Brazil	Panama
China	Peru
Cuba	Poland
Ecuador	Portugal
Greece	Roumania
Guatemala	The Serb-Croat-Slovene State
Haiti	Siam
The Hedjaz	Czecho-Slovakia
Honduras	Uruguay [10]

Of these, Bolivia and Peru had broken off diplomatic relations with Germany, but they had not declared war on her; nor had The Hedjaz, which was not even yet recognized as an independent state.[11]

Among the initiated who were taking part in the Paris Conference, it became evident that the American peace program, as set forth by President Wilson, was in serious danger. On April 11, 1919, Mr. Herbert Hoover, member of a commission on economic questions, sent a memorandum to the President and his delegation, in which he stated that, if the Allies could not be brought to adopt peace on the basis of the Fourteen Points, "our national honor is at stake and we should have to make peace independently and retire," in order to lend American economic and moral strength to the whole world, or it "will swim in a sea of misery and disaster worse than the dark ages." [12] Unfortunately, Hoover's sound and timely advice was disregarded.

The Government of the Weimar Republic also became aware of the portentous atmosphere in Paris. Instructions to the designated plenipotentiaries, drawn up in the same month of April, opened with the sentence: "In all probability the Allies will submit a final draft of a treaty, with the explanation that it can only be accepted or rejected." The Government had received information that the Allies would justify the severity of the conditions by claiming that Germany was responsible for the war. [13]

Indeed, this was virtually a foregone conclusion. Ever since the outbreak of hostilities in August, 1914, the belligerents had reciprocally accused their enemies in the field of having provoked the war. It was quite natural that the responsibility for this unprecedented catastrophe would play a large role. Shortly after the armistice the German Government had proposed that the question of war guilt be investigated by a neutral commission, but the proposal was rejected on the plea that Germany's guilt was proven. [14] This was an ominous sign and made a deep impression all through the country as the author vividly remembers. The German Government opened its own archives. It initiated forthwith an internal investigation of the causes of the war, and it entrusted a commission of four distinguished and independent Germans, having expert knowledge, with the assignment to disprove, on the strength of the material collected, the Allied charge of sole German responsibility for the war. [15]

The German delegation, led by Foreign Minister Count Ulrich von Brockdorff-Rantzau, arrived in Versailles toward the end of April. They were kept isolated, and their quarters were surrounded with barriers in order to protect them from molestation and insults which were, however, unavoidable in the temper of the populace. Contrasting the negotiations of the peace treaty with Japan in 1951 with the handiwork of the so-called "realists" at Versailles, Secretary of State John Foster Dulles observed not long ago:

I remember vividly how, there, the members of the German peace delegation were put in a barbed-wire enclosure, exposed as animals in a zoo, denied any personal contact with Allied delegates. . . . We know the consequences of that realism.[16]

Early in May, French newspapers printed a plan for the seating of the plenipotentiaries in the Trianon Palace Hotel where the draft treaty of peace would be handed over to the Germans. On this plan the table for the Germans was marked as *Banc des Accusés,* that is, the Prisoner's Dock. Thereupon, Count Brockdorff-Rantzau told the Commissioner General of the German delegation, Walter Simons, that after receiving the draft treaty he would remain seated while making his reply; otherwise, he might appear like a criminal who was asked to stand in court before his judges.[17]

Before this happened on the afternoon of May 7—a crucial day of history—printed copies of the draft treaty were distributed during the early morning hours of the 7th to the prominent members of the Allied delegations. Herbert Hoover was awakened at four a.m. to receive his copy. He read it at once. Like most of the delegates he had known many details of the proposed treaty, but had never before envisaged it as a whole. He was greatly disturbed, for, as he wrote later, "hate and revenge" ran all through its political and economic passages. "Conditions were set up upon which Europe could never be rebuilt or peace come to mankind." It seemed to him that the economic consequences alone would pull down all Europe and thus injure the United States. He arose and went for a walk in the deserted streets at early daylight. And there he had a remarkable experience which is best recounted in his own description:

In a few blocks I met General Smuts [Delegate for the South-African Union] and John Maynard Keynes [British economic expert]. If ever there was something telepathic it was in that meeting. It flashed in all our minds why the others were walking about at that time of day. In comparing notes, I found Smuts and Keynes especially interested in the political pattern, while I had given more thought to the economic side. We agreed that it was terrible and

we would do what we could among our own nationals to make the
danger clear.[18]

All three did their honorable but futile share in a highly
adverse, frustrating atmosphere.

On the afternoon of that memorable day, May 7, 1919,
Georges Clemenceau, President of the Peace Conference, addressed the German delegates as follows:

This is neither the time nor the place for superfluous words. You
have before you the accredited plenipotentiaries of the great and
lesser Powers, both Allied and Associated, that for four years have
carried on without respite the merciless war which has been imposed upon them. The time has now come for a heavy reckoning
of accounts. You have asked for peace. We are prepared to offer
you peace. . . . There will be no verbal discussions, and observations must be submitted in writing.[19]

For two days the German delegation had known that negotiations would be refused. Now Clemenceau's short, staccato
sentences, with the ominous words *lourd règlement des
comptes,* shattered any illusions the one or other amongst
them may still have entertained. The charge that the four
years' merciless war had been imposed upon the Allies, placed
the Germans now literally in the prisoner's dock.

Knowing that the accusation was certainly not true for the
German people, Count Brockdorff-Rantzau, after Clemenceau's address had been translated, raised himself somewhat
from his seat, bowing slightly, and sat down again to read a
lengthy speech. By remaining seated he acquired unfortunate
notoriety.[20] The aged President had spoken standing, so the
Count's conduct was regarded as an insult to the Assembly,
and the Allied press cited it as a flagrant example of Hun
insolence.[21] President Wilson indignantly remarked to Prime
Minister Lloyd George, "Isn't it just like them!" [22]

The episode figures widely in world literature, much to the
detriment of Germans generally. The Count certainly committed a serious breach of public etiquette. The leaders of
New Germany had faith in him because of his past diplomatic
record, but he now did them a disservice by an arrogant and
defiant manner. The incident deserves to be fully explained
from a psychological point of view.

Discerning observers amongst the Allies have recorded the

Count's exceedingly broken, nervous physical condition. General Tasker H. Bliss, for example, did not believe he could have stood on his feet.[23] On the other hand, we know that the Count had previously decided to remain seated. Years later, he himself said to an English Lieutenant Colonel:

Do you remember that England and France accused me of deliberate insult because I remained seated when at Versailles? They couldn't see—those noble adversaries—they couldn't feel—those conquering heroes—that they had sapped my body of its strength just as they were sapping the lifeblood of my country. I could not stand, I could not move. They had paralysed me, had shocked the life from my body. Only my heart and my brain were alive. With the pistol at my head I regained control of my speech, and I delivered my country and my people into penal servitude rather than deliver them to death. And you—you could only see the insolent *boche* who remained seated while addressing the Conference. You —with your superior knowledge of human nature—with "your wonderful psychological insight," and—*those others!* My God! [24]

In this outburst Count Brockdorff-Rantzau stressed his physical incapacity at Versailles, but it also reveals the mental anguish of a super-sensitive patriot who probably realized after the event that his manner and speech on that May day in 1919 were not in the best interest of the German people he loved. As to *"those others"* he meant, no doubt, the representatives of some of the lesser Powers, whom he saw sitting there as judges over a great European nation. In fact, the Count never got over the humiliations suffered at that time. In 1928, a few hours before his death, he said to his twin brother: "Don't mourn. After all, I have been dead ever since Versailles." [25]

The foregoing may explain the spirit of defiance and revolt which runs through parts of the Count's speech. He opened it by saying:

Gentlemen, we are deeply impressed with the great mission that has brought us here to give to the world forthwith a lasting peace. We are under no illusions as to the extent of our defeat and the degree of our powerlessness. We know that the strength of the German arms is broken. We know the intensity of the hatred which meets us, and we have heard the victor's passionate demand that as the vanquished we shall be made to pay, and as the guilty we shall be punished.

The demand is made that we shall acknowledge that we alone

are guilty of having caused the war. Such a confession in my mouth would be a lie. We are far from seeking to escape from any responsibility for this World War, and for its having been waged as it has . . . but we with all emphasis deny that the people of Germany, who were convinced that they were waging a war of defense, should be burdened with the sole guilt of that war.

Continuing, he admitted that injustice had been done to Belgium, for which Germany would make reparations, and that during the war crimes had been committed—not solely, however, on the German side. He asked once more for an impartial inquiry in order to establish the measure of guilt of all participants in the war. He warmly welcomed the League of Nations which should be open to all men of good will. He emphasized that President Wilson's principles had become binding for both parties, and he warned against destroying the bases of peace which had been mutually agreed upon.[26]

Count Brockdorff-Rantzau's speech made a deplorable impression on the Assembly, and therefore further essential passages of it are reproduced below as Document 5, for closer study and evaluation. President Wilson understandably felt especially outraged by the repeated allusions in it to the pledge of a just peace. Leaving the Assembly he said to Lord Riddell, "This is the most tactless speech I have ever heard. It will set the whole world against them" [27]—a bitter criticism which was subsequently exploited by those in Paris who wished to uphold the terms of the draft treaty. On the other hand, Allan Nevins, commenting in later years on the speech, wrote that one of its chief statements, namely, the refutation of Germany's sole guilt for the war, was far truer than most of the spectators present then suspected.[28]

On May 8, two experienced American diplomatists in Paris recorded their views on the draft treaty. Henry White expressed the opinion that its "worst feature" was the abandonment of the Fourteen Points "in a number of cases." [29] More explicit was Robert Lansing. In virtue of the intimate knowledge he had gained of foreign affairs as Secretary of State since June, 1915, as having conducted the armistice negotiations in 1918, and as having taken part in the discussions at the Peace Conference, his evaluation of the proposed treaty is of capital importance. He embodied it in a memorandum which he published in 1921 and appears to be far too little known by the general public in the United States as well as abroad. It is, therefore, reprinted here for the careful study it deserves:

The terms of peace were yesterday delivered to the German plenipotentiaries, and for the first time in these days of feverish rush of preparation there is time to consider the Treaty as a complete document.

The impression made by it is one of disappointment, of regret, and of depression. The terms of peace appear immeasurably harsh and humiliating, while many of them seem to me impossible of per· formance.

The League of Nations created by the Treaty is relied upon to preserve the artificial structure which has been erected by compromise of the conflicting interests of the Great Powers and to prevent the germination of the seeds of war which are sown in so many articles and which under normal conditions would soon bear fruit. The League might as well attempt to prevent the growth of plant life in a tropical jungle. Wars will come sooner or later. It must be admitted in honesty that the League is an instrument of the mighty to check the normal growth of national power and national aspirations among those who have been rendered impotent by defeat. Examine the Treaty and you will find peoples delivered against their wills into the hands of those whom they hate, while their economic resources are torn from them and given to others. Resentment and bitterness, if not desperation, are bound to be the consequences of such provisions. It may be years before these oppressed peoples are able to throw off the yoke, but as sure as day follows night, the time will come when they will make the effort.

This war was fought by the United States to destroy forever the conditions which produced it. Those conditions have not been destroyed. They have been supplanted by other conditions equally productive of hatred, jealousy, and suspicion. In place of the Triple Alliance and the Entente has arisen the Quintuple Alliance which is to rule the world. The victors in this war intend to impose their combined will upon the vanquished and to subordinate all interests to their own.

It is true that to please the aroused public opinion of mankind and to respond to the idealism of the moralist they have surrounded this new alliance with a halo and called it "The League of Nations," but whatever it may be called or however it may be disguised it is an alliance of the Five Great Military Powers.

It is useless to close our eyes to the fact that the power to compel obedience by the exercise of the united strength of "The Five" is the fundamental principle of the League. Justice is secondary. Might is primary.

The League as now constituted will be the prey of greed and intrigue; and the law of unanimity in the Council, which may offer a restraint, will be broken or render the organization powerless. It is called upon to stamp as just what is unjust.

We have a treaty of peace, but it will not bring permanent peace because it is founded on the shifting sand of self-interest.[30]

When published in 1921, Robert Lansing's gloomy forecast, penned in May, 1919, may well have seemed much overdrawn. But now it is only too evident that he had the clear vision of a real statesman deeply concerned with the welfare of humanity. His luminous exposition needs little comment and history has vindicated his judgments and predictions.

The "Quintuple Alliance," as well as the "Five Great Military Powers" and "The Five" were, of course, the Five "Principal Powers" at the Conference, the United States of America, the British Empire, France, Italy, and Japan, two of which, Japan from 1931 on, and Italy from 1935 on, became "aggressor states," ultimately joining forces with Hitler-Germany, and all put in the prisoner's dock as the originators of the Second World War.

In his memorandum, Lansing, with good reason, dwelt upon the League of Nations. This was President Wilson's grand conception, his greatest merit which will secure him a lasting place of honor in history.[31] He had set all his hopes on the League as the agency to redress in due course the wrongs contained in the Versailles Treaty. Yet, he failed to realize the fatal defect in the Covenant, viz., the stipulation of unanimity in the Council which practically prevented peaceful revision of treaties and thus rendered the organization powerless, as the Secretary of State prophesied it would be.

A few days after Lansing wrote his memorandum he discussed the draft treaty in London with several of the leading British statesmen. The consensus, he noted, was that it was "unwise and unworkable, that it was conceived in intrigue and fashioned in cupidity, and that it would produce rather than prevent wars." [32]

When, on May 8, the German Government received a summary of the draft treaty, the general opinion was that such a document would make the Lansing Note of November 5, 1918, "a scrap of paper." The President of the Republic, Friedrich Ebert, and the Cabinet issued a statement to the German people, declaring the conditions to be unbearable, unrealizable, and contrary to the promises made in the armistice agreement. Premier Philipp Scheidemann, leader of the Social Democrats, requested the States of the Republic to demonstrate the "utter disillusionment and the inexpressible sorrow" over the treaty by suspending all public entertainments for a week.[33]

In the general discussion in the National Assembly on the 12th, Scheidemann declared that President Wilson, formerly acclaimed by all as an apostle of peace, had disillusioned the whole world and deprived the Germans of their faith in him. He ended his speech with the words: "Woe to those who caused this war, but thrice woe to those who now postpone a veritable peace!" Gustav Stresemann, leader of the People's Party, saw in the treaty the intent to destroy Germany politically and economically, and to dishonor her; the judgment of history, however, he believed, would be that the treaty was dishonorable to the victor, not to the vanquished. The Socialist, Mrs. Clara Bohm-Schuch, appealed ardently to the women of the world, for the sake of their own children, not to allow this treaty to be enforced because it would inevitably lead to new wars. The veteran Pacifist, Ludwig Quidde, speaking for the Democrats, pointed out that the treaty would destroy the basic principles of international reconciliation and could not be signed. Finally, the President of the Assembly, K. Fehrenbach, urged the Allies to think of their own children and grandchildren, for the concomitant hardships of the treaty would in Germany create a generation in whom the will to break the chains of slavery would be implanted from childhood onward.[34]

It should be noted that the most vehement protests came from the Left, from the representatives of the New Germany who felt instinctively the fatal consequences the treaty was bound to have for the infant Republic.

Expressing the general German impression, Foreign Minister Count Brockdorff-Rantzau declared in a Note to the Peace Conference on May 9, that the basis of the peace of justice mutually agreed upon had been abandoned; that the promises explicitly made to the German people, and to the whole of mankind, had been rendered illusory; that some demands were intolerable for any nation; and that many others could not be met. The delegation would establish their contention point by point.

The reply of the Allies on the 10th asserted that they had been constantly prompted by the principles on which the armistice and the peace negotiations had been based; that they could not permit any discussions of their right to uphold the fundamental conditions of the peace, such as they had agreed upon; and that they could only consider suggestions of a practical kind.[35]

At this point of dead-lock General Jan Christian Smuts intervened, true to the promise he had given to Mr. Hoover. In mid-May he wrote to Prime Minister Lloyd George and to President Wilson, stating that the more he studied the treaty as a whole, the more he disliked it. The combined effect of the territorial and reparation clauses would make it practically impossible for Germany to carry out the provisions. And he warned, "Under this treaty Europe will know no peace."

But President Wilson replied:

I feel the terrible responsibility of the whole business, but inevitably my thought goes back to the very great offence against civilization which the German State committed, and the necessity for making it evident once and for all that such things can lead only to the most severe punishment.

In these few lines the President's complete change of attitude since his pronouncements recorded above is painfully revealed. Having once vigorously repudiated any idea of vindictiveness, or even hostility, toward the German people, he now declared the most severe punishment to be necessary, punishment of "the German State," as a collective unity, which was now the Democratic Germany, the Republic, the creation of which he had himself desired and had actively promoted! Wilson's reply also makes it clear that the war guilt charge had come to hold the central position in the peacemakers' mind.

The statesman, Smuts, was not satisfied by Wilson's rejoinder. On the contrary, in another letter he spoke out more bluntly:

There will be terrible disillusionment if the peoples come to think we are not concluding a Wilson peace, that we are not keeping our promises to the world or faith with the public.

More emphatically than before he again warned that this treaty "may become an even greater disaster to the world than the war was." [36]

The same feelings which prompted General Smuts to write these letters, also moved a group of United States delegates at the Conference to action. Upon his return from London on May 17, Robert Lansing received letters from five of the principal American experts protesting against the terms of peace, for they considered them to be an abandonment of the principles for which their country had fought. They proposed to resign, but in the end they did not do so because they were told that it would seriously cripple the American Commission in the preparation of the Austrian treaty if they did not continue to serve. A sixth member of the group, however, the youngest, did not waver in his decision—William C. Bullitt.[37] He had been an assistant in the Department of State and an Attaché to the American Commission in Paris. Definitely resigning on May 17, he wrote a letter on that day to President Wilson, essential passages of which deserve to be recalled. They ran:

. . . I was one of the millions who trusted confidently and implicitly in your leadership and believed that you would take nothing less than "a permanent peace" based upon "unselfish and unbiased justice." But our Government has consented now to deliver the suffering peoples of the world to new oppressions, subjections, and dismemberments—a new century of war. . . .

. . . Unjust decisions of the conference in regard to Shantung, the Tyrol, Thrace, Hungary, East Prussia, Danzig, the Saar Valley, and the abandonment of the principle of the freedom of the seas make new international conflicts certain. It is my conviction that the present League of Nations will be powerless to prevent these wars. . . .

I am sorry that you did not fight our fight to the finish and that you had so little faith in the millions of men, like myself, in every nation who had faith in you.[38]

The similarity of the opinions and predictions of Lansing and Bullitt as to the consequences of the treaty and the powerlessness of the League is most striking. But even more noteworthy is the high spirit which inspired the writer. He expressed the idealism of his generation who had fought in the trenches, had suffered and had died for the creation of a better world where there would be dispassionate justice and permanent peace. He expressed the cruel disappointment that the immeasurable sacrifices during the four years' war should have been in vain. And he rightly deplored the President's lack of faith in the masses of every nation who had placed their faith in him. The letter reminds one of General Marshall's recent demand for a spiritual regeneration which would re-establish a feeling of good faith among men generally. That faith was being destroyed in the malignant atmosphere of 1919.

Reviewing the draft treaty, the Germans took vehement exception to the articles 227-230 under the heading "Penalties" for war crimes, and to article 231, introducing the section "Reparation," which appeared to place the sole guilt for the war on Germany and her Allies. German honor was deeply affected by these articles, and the protest against them was unanimous. They are printed below as Document 6.

On May 13, Brockdorff-Rantzau reminded President Clemenceau of the repeated Allied declarations that the German people should not be held responsible for the faults committed by their Government, adding that they did not will the war and remained convinced of having waged a defensive war. He rejected the allegation of Germany's sole responsibility and asked for the report of the Commission the Allied and Associated Governments had set up to establish this responsibility.

The request was denied on the ground that the report was of an internal character.[39]

This refusal aroused another protest from the German delegation. In a Note of May 24 it claimed the right to be informed as to what evidence supported basing the conditions of peace on Germany's alleged responsibility—"a question of life or death for the German nation," which must be discussed in all publicity.[40]

The Allied report on war responsibility was never communicated officially but parts of it were by now published in the press. It drew these conclusions:

The war was premeditated by the Central Powers together with their Allies, Turkey and Bulgaria, and was the result of acts deliberately committed in order to make it unavoidable.

Germany, in agreement with Austria-Hungary, deliberately worked to defeat all the many conciliatory proposals made by the Entente Powers and their repeated efforts to avoid war.

The neutrality of Belgium—and that of Luxemburg—were deliberately violated by Germany and Austria-Hungary.

The American representatives supplemented the report by a memorandum, dated April 4, 1919, in which they stressed the allegation that Germany, "flushed with the hope of certain victory and of the fruits of conquest, determined to force the war," a statement which singled out Germany and put her Allies into the background. Concurring with the conclusions, as quoted above, the Americans expressed the opinion that these acts should be condemned in no uncertain terms and that "their perpetrators should be held up to the execration of mankind." [41] This was subsequently done on June 16.

The good faith of the authors of the report and of the American representatives is not open to doubt. They expressed a general Allied conviction at the time, but it was based on incomplete, partly unsound evidence, and it was strongly influenced by the blinding passions which the war had aroused, as well as by propagandist misconceptions such as have been dealt with in the preceding chapter.[42]

In the meantime, the Commission of four independent Germans, mentioned above, had worked out observations on the published parts of the Allied report which Brockdorff-Rantzau submitted to Clemenceau on May 28. In an opening paragraph, the four experts expressed the opinion that the question of responsibility for the war could not be decided solely by one side which was itself a party to the war. Only a commission of inquiry, recognized by both sides as impartial, to which all records were accessible and before which both parties alike could state their case, could venture to pronounce judgment as to the extent to which each government was responsible for the catastrophe that had overtaken mankind.

This surely was a plain and obvious truth; moreover, it invoked a fundamental principle of justice, precious to all civilized communities—a neutral court in a disputed case.

In conclusion, the four experts underlined the Russian challenge in 1914 which, in the eyes of all German Social Democrats, had marked the war as one of defense against Tsarism.[43]

The next day, May 29, the German counterproposals for the treaty were presented, introduced by a covering letter. They are of capital importance for a proper evaluation of the spirit which guided the Government of the Weimar Republic. Some passages have, therefore, to be quoted here, while some

others are reproduced below as Document 7, because they are
far too little known outside of Germany. When perusing these
excerpts the reader should keep in mind that the German dela-
gation, although aware of some disillusionment and disagree-
ment amongst the Allied peacemakers, was in complete ignorance of the protests which Herbert Hoover, as early as April
11, Lansing on May 8, Smuts in mid-May, Bullitt on the 17th,
and others, had already made.

The Germans set forth in detail the legal basis for the peace
negotiations constituting a solemn agreement between the Contracting Parties. By abandoning the Wilson program, the Allies
would break that agreement. They recalled the declarations of
the Allies that they were not making war on the German
people, and that there was to be a peace of right, not a peace
of might, from which a new spirit would emanate to be embodied in a League of Nations. They pleaded for German admission to the League. And they warned emphatically against
the consequences of a peace of brute force:

In all nations the best spirits are longing for a peace of justice
after this terrible war. If this longing be betrayed, then the ideal
of justice will be annihilated for generations and an organization
of the world based upon morality will become utterly impossible.
A permanent peace can never be established upon the oppression
and the enslavement of a great nation. . . .

In the very moment of founding a new commonwealth, based
upon liberty and labor, the German people turns to those who have
hitherto been its enemies, and demands in the interests of all nations and of all human beings, a peace to which it may give its
assent in accordance with the dictates of its conscience.

This last sentence referred mainly to the German contention that the financial reparation demands were *positively impossible of execution*. For the settlement of this question 100,-
000,000,000 gold marks were offered.[44]

The Germans did not know that only the day before, on
May 28, a member of the British delegation, Harold Nicolson,
had characterized the reparation clauses as "the great crime"
in the treaty, which were quite impossible to execute, "sheer
lunacy." [45]

Now the Germans underscored the fact that, if the reparations conditions were actually imposed,

*then indeed is German democracy destroyed at the very moment
when the German people . . . were on the point of establishing it;*

destroyed by the very ones who during the whole war never grew
weary of insisting that they wanted to bring democracy to us! [46]

No less an authority than John Maynard Keynes has subsequently acknowledged that the arguments put forth by the
German Financial Commission at Versailles were "hardly an
exaggeration." [47] Yet they were of no avail.

The "great crime," to follow Harold Nicolson, was that
pensions costs had been included, contrary to the terms in
Lansing's Note of November 5, 1918.[48] This way the reparations bill, even when reduced, was swelled to a figure thirty
times as large as the indemnity which Bismarck had exacted
from France in 1871.[49]

Whoever takes the trouble to examine the bulk of the German counterproposals in the light of subsequent developments
may well agree to a considerable extent with the German Commissioner General at Versailles, Walter Simons, who stated on
May 30 his unshakable belief that the ideas for which the
Germans were fighting are those of the future, and that in the
conflict of ideas "the Germans and not the Allied delegates
will in the future be held to be the victors." [50] In fact, it was
a prominent American member of the Paris Conference, General Tasker Bliss, who voiced this very sentiment. Writing on
June 6 he predicted, "Five years from now the world will condemn the Conference if it does not listen" to the German counterproposals.[51]

Among the Big Five it was now, in June, 1919, Premier
Lloyd George who did listen. He was "fighting like a little
terrier" for modifications of the Eastern frontiers, in regard
to reparations, in the matter of the occupation army, and with
respect to Germany's admission to the League. In all this, he
roused the fury of the French.[52] General Smuts continued his
valiant efforts. He and some other British officials in Paris
communicated their views to the Cabinet in London. Leading
Cabinet officials came to Paris to discuss Lloyd George's handiwork in shocked terms.[53] The Empire delegation authorized
him to exert the strongest pressure on the French.[54] And, although the movement for revision was, as James T. Shotwell
has stated, most vociferous in the American delegation,[55] it got
scanty support from the President of the United States, to the
bewilderment of the British who had counted on him to stand
firmly by his principles.[56] Already, weeks before, he had in-

formed his staff that these endeavors had "left him tired." [57]
It was at this time, in early June, that J. M. Keynes coined his
famous witticism: "Lloyd George, having bamboozled Wilson,
could not de-bamboozle him." [58]

This is not the place to explain the tragic failure of Woodrow Wilson in Paris and, particularly, at this crucial point.
The President had put up a brave fight in an overwhelmingly
hostile atmosphere and was now worn out. His lofty program
was too idealistic for the warring nations to carry through after
total victory over the hated enemy had been achieved. His
final resignation to injustices in the face of seemingly unsur-
mountable odds may perhaps be best explained by two words:
"Punishment," and "League." We have seen that by mid-May
he had come around to the view, contrary to his former position, that the most severe punishment of the German State
was necessary as an unforgettable lesson for the future. On the
other hand, he placed his whole trust in the effectiveness of
his sublime creation, the League of Nations, which would, he
was confident, set things right under the decisive leadership of
the United States of America. [59]

On June 16, the Allies replied to the German counterproposals. For the topic of the present chapter, the covering letter
to their reply is the most important document in the exchange
of notes during the Paris Conference. It reveals with luminous
clarity the spirit which by then possessed the peacemakers in
their attitude toward Germany, the old and the new Germany,
and shaped the Treaty of Versailles. This covering letter received very wide publicity among the German masses but is
little known by the general public outside of Germany. It has
had a tremendous influence on the German mind and on the
shaping of post-war events. Hence, it is indispensable that it
should be closely studied by all those who are genuinely concerned with a constructive European policy. The most significant parts are reproduced below, together with some relevant
passages of the Allied reply itself. The covering letter states:

The protest of the German delegation shows that they utterly
fail to understand the position in which Germany stands today.
They seem to think that Germany has only to "make sacrifices in
order to attain peace," as if this were but the end of some mere
struggle for territory and power.
The Allied and Associated Powers therefore feel it necessary to

begin their reply by a clear statement of the judgment passed upon the war by practically the whole of civilized mankind.

In view of the Allied and Associated Powers the war which began on August 1, 1914, was the greatest crime against humanity and the freedom of the peoples that any nation, calling itself civilized, has ever consciously committed. For many years the rulers of Germany, true to the Prussian tradition, strove for a position of dominance in Europe. They were not satisfied with that growing prosperity and influence to which Germany was entitled, and which all other nations were willing to accord her, in the society of free and equal peoples. They required that they should be able to dictate and tyrannize over a subservient Europe, as they dictated to and tyrannized over a subservient Germany.

In order to attain their ends they used every channel in their power through which to educate their own subjects in the doctrine that might was right in international affairs. . . . They kept Europe in a ferment by threats of violence, and when they found that their neighbors were resolved to resist their arrogant will they determined to assist their predominance in Europe by force.

As soon as their preparations were complete, they encouraged a subservient ally to declare war against Serbia. . . . In order to make doubly sure, they refused every attempt at conciliation and conference until it was too late, and the world war was inevitable for which they had plotted, and for which alone among the nations they were fully equipped and prepared.

Germany's responsibility, however, is not confined to having planned and started the war. She is no less responsible for the savage and inhuman manner in which it was conducted.

Though Germany was herself a guarantor of Belgium, the rulers of Germany violated, after a solemn promise to respect it, the neutrality of this unoffending people. Not content with this, they deliberately carried out a series of promiscuous shootings and burnings with the sole object of terrifying the inhabitants into submission by the very frightfulness of their action. They were the first to use poisonous gas, notwithstanding the appalling suffering it entailed. They began the bombing and long distance shelling of towns for no military object, but solely for the purpose of reducing the morale of their opponents by striking at their women and children. They commenced the submarine campaign with its piratical challenge to international law, and its destruction of great numbers of innocent passengers and sailors, in mid-ocean, far from succour, at the mercy of the winds and the waves, and the yet more ruthless submarine crews. They drove thousands of men and women and children with brutal savagery into slavery in foreign lands. They allowed barbarities to be practised against their prisoners of war from which the most uncivilized peoples would have recoiled.

The conduct of Germany is almost unexampled in human history. The terrible responsibility which lies at her doors can be seen in the fact that no less than seven million dead lie buried in Europe, while more than twenty million others carry upon them the evidence of wounds and sufferings, because Germany saw fit to gratify her lust for tyranny by resort to war.

The Allied and Associated Powers believe that they will be false to those who have given their all to save the freedom of the world if they consent to treat this war on any other basis than as a crime against humanity and right.

. . . Justice, therefore, is the only possible basis for the settlement of the accounts of this terrible war. Justice is what the German Delegation ask for and say that Germany had been promised. Justice is what Germany shall have. But it must be justice for all. There must be justice for the dead and wounded and for those who have been orphaned and bereaved that Europe might be freed from Prussian despotism. There must be justice for the peoples who now stagger under war debts which exceed £30,000,000,000 that liberty might be saved. There must be justice for those millions whose homes and land, ships and property German savagery has spoliated and destroyed.

That is why the Allied and Associated Powers have insisted as a cardinal feature of the treaty that Germany must undertake to make reparations to the very uttermost of her power; for reparation for wrongs inflicted is of the essence of justice.

. . . It is said that the German Revolution ought to make a difference and that the German people are not responsible for the policy of the rulers whom they have thrown from power.

The Allied and Associated Powers recognize and welcome the change. It represents a great hope for peace, and for a new European order in the future. But it cannot affect the settlement of the war itself. The German Revolution was stayed until the German armies had been defeated in the field, and all hope of profiting by the war of conquest had vanished. Throughout the war, as before the war, the German people and their representatives supported the war, voted the credits, subscribed to the war loans, obeyed every order, however savage, of their government. They shared the responsibility for the policy of their government, for at any moment, had they willed it, they could have reversed it. Had that policy succeeded they would have acclaimed it with the same enthusiasm with which they welcomed the outbreak of the war. They cannot now pretend, having changed their rulers after the war was lost, that it is justice that they should escape the consequences of their deeds.

The Allied and Associated Powers therefore believe that the peace they have proposed is fundamentally a peace of justice. They

are no less certain that it is a peace of right fulfilling the terms
agreed upon at the time of the armistice. . . .

. . . The Allied and Associated Powers are satisfied that their
territorial proposals are in accord both with the agreed basis of
peace and are necessary to the future peace of Europe. . . .

In conclusion the Allied and Associated Powers must make it
clear that this letter and the memorandum attached constitute their
last word. . . .

They believe that it is not only a just settlement of the great
war, but that it provides the basis upon which the peoples of Europe can live together in friendship and equality. At the same
time it creates the machinery for the peaceful adjustment of all
international problems by discussion and consent, whereby the
settlement of 1919 itself can be modified from time to time to
suit new facts and new conditions as they arise.

It is frankly not based upon a general condonation of the events
of 1914-1918. It would not be a peace of justice if it were. But
it represents a sincere and deliberate attempt to establish "that
reign of law, based upon the consent of the governed, and sus-
tained by the organized opinion of mankind" which was the agreed
basis of the peace.

As such the treaty in its present form must be accepted or rejected.[60]

So much for the covering letter, ending with the threat
that, if the treaty as it stood was rejected, its terms would be
enforced.

The reader will do well to compare the opinions of Herbert
Hoover, Robert Lansing, General Smuts, J. M. Keynes, and
others, recorded above with the assertions in the covering letter
that the treaty was a just one enabling the peoples of Europe
to live together in friendship and equality.

The Allied reply of June 16 to the German counterproposals
dealt in Part VII with "The Responsibility of Germany for the
War" and with "Penalties." The conclusion on the question of
responsibility was:

Germany . . . has been the champion of force and violence,
deception, intrigue and cruelty in the conduct of international
affairs. Germany for decades has steadily pursued a policy of in-
spiring jealousies and hatred and of dividing nation from nation
in order that she might gratify her own selfish passion for power.
Germany has stood athwart the whole current of democratic progress and international friendship throughout the world. Germany
has been the principal mainstay of autocracy in Europe. And in

the end, seeing that she could attain her objects in no other way, she planned and started the war which caused the massacre and mutilation of millions and the ravaging of Europe from end to end.

The truth of the charges thus brought against them the German people have admitted by their own revolution. They have overturned their government because they have discovered that it is the enemy of freedom, justice and equality at home. That same government was no less the enemy of freedom, justice and equality abroad. It is useless to attempt to prove . . . that the responsibility for the terrible events of the last five years does not lie at its doors.

Under "Penalties," the Allied and Associated Powers repeated that

they regard this war as a crime deliberately plotted against the life and liberties of the peoples of Europe. It is a war which has brought death and mutilation to millions and has left all Europe in terrible suffering. Starvation, unemployment, disease stalk across the continent from end to end, and for decades its people will groan under the burden and disorganization the war has caused. They therefore regard the punishment of those responsible for bringing these calamities on the human race as essential on the score of justice.

They think it no less necessary as a deterrent to others who, at some later date, may be tempted to follow their example. The present treaty is intended to mark a departure from the traditions and practices of earlier settlements, which have been singularly inadequate in preventing the renewal of war. The Allied and Associated Powers indeed consider that the trial and punishment of those proved most responsible for the crimes and inhuman acts committed in connection with a war of aggression is inseparable from the establishment of that reign of law among nations which it was the agreed object of the peace to set up.

. . . Almost the whole world has banded itself together in order to bring to nought the German plan of conquest and domination. The tribunals they will establish will therefore represent the deliberate judgment of the greater part of the civilized world. They cannot entertain the proposal to admit to the tribunal the representatives of countries which have taken no part in the war. The Allied and Associated Powers are prepared to stand by the verdict of history as to the impartiality and justice with which the accused will be tried.[61]

The war-crimes trials did not take place as the Allies had decreed, because the Germans refused to extradite the accused, amongst whom figured Field Marshal von Hindenburg who became President of the Weimar Republic in 1925. A few Germans who had violated customs of warfare, were tried at the Supreme Court of Leipzig, in the presence of Allied observers, in the summer of 1921. In England, France and Belgium the sentences imposed were considered too mild.

The trial of the ex-Emperor, "The Mad Dog of Europe," was frustrated by the refusal of the Netherlands Government to extradite him although William II himself wrote to President Wilson on February 9, 1920: "If the Allied and Associated Governments want a victim let them take me instead of the nine hundred Germans who have committed no offence other than that of serving their country in the war." [62]

The last two paragraphs quoted above under "Penalties" make it quite clear that not only crimes committed during hostilities were to be judged by Allied tribunals but, and above all, the supreme crime in question, namely, the alleged German plan of conquest and European domination. The Allies rejected even the participation of representatives of neutral countries in the projected tribunals and were prepared to "stand by the verdict of history" as to their impartiality. Unfortunately, the matter was never tested before any tribunal, something which should have been done long ago. It is evident, however, that in 1919 the Allies were convinced of their ability to prove their contention to the satisfaction of the world at large.

When analyzing the excerpts from the covering letter and the reply of June 16, the reader must keep in mind that the Germany then at the bar was not the Hitler-Germany of the Second World War, but Imperial Germany the return of which, George F. Kennan thoughtfully reflected in 1951, would in many ways not sound so bad. [63]

The Allied report of April on responsibility, referred to earlier, had concluded that the war was premeditated by the Central Powers, *i.e.,* by Germany and Austria-Hungary, together with their Allies, Turkey and Bulgaria. Now, the whole responsibility was placed on Germany who—allegedly—encouraged a subservient ally, Austria-Hungary, to declare war against Serbia. This reminds one of the American supplement to the Allied report (cited earlier) and is in conformity with President Wilson's rejoinder to General Smuts' appeal in mid-

May in which the German State is singled out as the offender against civilization. There is no proof that this shifting of responsibility was due to American influence, although the documents quoted might suggest it. However that may be, the fact needs to be stressed that the covering letter and the reply of June 16 definitely altered the charge commonly attributed to Article 231 of the Treaty, in which "Germany and her Allies" were declared to have been the aggressors. Article 231 is not only of earlier date than the official document of June 16, but scholars have also demonstrated that, taken by itself, it does not necessarily accuse Germany and her Allies of having caused the war, although this interpretation has been accepted all over the world.[64] In reality, the disputed Article 231 was, so far as the war guilt is concerned, superseded by the document of June 16 which has remained unaltered ever since 1919 and is, in spiritual and moral respects, of infinitely greater importance than anything else in the framework of the Versailles Treaty. It is a document quite in the vein of Lord Vansittart's later writings.

The Allied covering letter asserts the German people's responsibility for the deeds of their government. In Part VII of the Allied reply it is contended that the German people, by their own revolution, have admitted their government's responsibility for the terrible events of the last five years. This assertion is not true. The German masses clung throughout to their original conviction that they were waging a defensive war, but they did realize the serious defects in their Constitution and their rulers' ill-considered conduct of the war. The Peace Resolution of the Reichstag on July 19, 1917, should here be recalled, when 212 members, against 126, voted for a peace of understanding and of permanent conciliation of the peoples.[65]

It was in response to Wilson's demands of October, 1918, that "a revulsion of popular feeling" set in "against generals, emperors, and kings." [66] This revulsion found clear expression in the elections for the National Assembly in January, 1919. Of 421 mandates the Social Democrats, with the Independent Socialists, obtained 185, the Democrats 75, the Centrists (Catholic parties) 71, the People's Party 19, and the Nationalists 44 mandates—a vast majority for New Germany. The election was, as Sydney L. W. Mellen stated, "an emphatic repudiation of militarism and reaction . . . an overwhelming demand for a peaceful and democratic government." [67]

The present writer may claim to be a witness to the fact that the dynasties in Germany were not overthrown because the people believed, or suspected, that their former masters were mainly responsible for the war. The popular revolt came because the President of the United States had made it perfectly clear that the autocratic rulers, above all the Emperor and the military leaders, were standing in the way of a peace on his generous terms. The passionate resistance of the New Germany to the Treaty of Versailles is ample proof of the plain truth that the German nation would not have laid down its arms in 1918 if it could have known in advance the outcome of the peace negotiations.[68] Moreover, the Allied contention that the German people could have at any moment, had they willed it, reversed the policy of their Government was, given the circumstances, a fallacious assumption.

All through the war, the Germans had been told "by all the resources of modern propaganda that the Allies were not fighting the German people, but only the Kaiser and the Junkers." [69] Most explicit, and wholly unequivocal, had been various pronouncements of President Wilson, who had even spoken of the Americans' feeling of "sympathy and friendship" towards them. Were there in the meantime any new revelations to show that the German people had been a party to the alleged plot of their masters? No, none whatever. Why then this extraordinary shift in Wilson's attitude? His declarations of the years 1917-18 sounded now, in June, 1919, like cruel mockery in German ears, like the cunning deception of an arch-hypocrite. This was a wrong impression. Wilson had meant what he had said about the German people in 1917-18. It was the spirit which permeated the Peace Conference that had caused his change. There he gradually convinced himself that the German people must fully share the responsibility of their former autocratic rulers, that it was a collective responsibility extending to all Germans.

There was, of course, another, a vital explanation, namely, the necessity of justifying the harshness of the peace terms, the numerous deviations from the accepted program.[70] Therefore the repeated assertions in the covering note that the terms were entirely just. Should there be anything wrong in them, then the League would fulfill the task assigned to it for peaceful adjustments and for eventual modifications—an illusion which the Secretary of State Robert Lansing and William C. Bullitt had clearly foreseen.

The covering letter conveyed an ultimatum to the Germans. It was the last word of the Allies. It was drawn up by politicians, not by historians. It expressed a majority opinion of the masses in the Allied countries at that time.[71] Yet it clearly reveals what Herbert Hoover had seen running through the treaty itself: hate and revenge.

The letter was issued in the name of all the Allied and Associated Powers. They comprised twenty-seven states from all over the world, the British Empire counting as one. The fourth of the Principal Powers was Italy who had joined the war in 1915 against her former Allies, not because she was threatened in any way but because the Democracies offered her more booty than Austria could honorably cede, including the South Tyrol, a century-old German territory. The fifth of the Principal Powers was Japan who, also, had not been threatened in any way but was welcomed into the war by the British Government with the prospect of acquiring German overseas possessions. Among the minor Powers was Rumania, in 1914 an Ally of Germany, also in no way threatened, but who, too, chose, as Italy had done, to join the opposing camp for the sake of territorial acquisitions from the Dual Monarchy.

Never in history had such a terrible indictment been passed on a European nation as a whole.[72] In 1919 and the following years millions of Germans read this indictment, or were lectured on it by word and in the press; and the masses were at least vividly conscious of its meaning. It was a humiliation without example. It deeply affected the heart and mind of a great number of Germans.

If that indictment had been written about the Second World War it would have been in large part valid for Adolf Hitler, for numbers of Nazi leaders, and for a section of the German people who followed submissively in their wake and actually placed themselves outside of the pale of European civilization. But the indictment of 1919 was against Imperial Germany before and during the First World War, when Hitler was a struggling would-be artist in Vienna, or an unknown corporal in a German unit, and long before Nazism had come into existence. It was also levelled against the Germany of 1919, the revolutionary republican Germany that was in this way branded as an outcast, as the most barbarous nation that the world had so far known, as the enemy of civilization—in short, as a criminal nation, and as the pariah of Europe.[73]

None of the twenty-seven states which, in June, 1919, passed this judgment, claiming that it was the judgment of "practically the whole of civilized mankind," has since modified, much less withdrawn this indictment. Though the Treaty of Versailles is dead, the covering letter and the reply of June 16, 1919, stand unaltered to this day as an *official* statement made deliberately by those governments. World War II has revived its spirit, its assertions. But the judgment has always lacked the sanction of impartial, of neutral authority.

If it was, and is, a well-founded judgment, then obviously Lord Vansittart, Under-Secretary of State Sumner Welles, and the other statesmen whose verdict is recorded in the preceding chapter, are perfectly right. In this case it must appear most hazardous to permit West Germany to rearm up to 500,000 men. Will the proposed safeguards prevent any future misuse of such a formidable army? To this query United States General A. M. Gruenther has given the right answer: "The only real safeguards you are going to get are those that come from the heart." [74]

It is quite natural that the opponents of German rearmament today point to past official verdicts. The Soviet Union is now leading this campaign. On September 10, 1954, its Foreign Ministry issued a declaration in which it stated:

The regeneration of German militarism . . . would immeasurably increase the danger of a new war in Europe and thus also the danger of a new world war. One only needs to recall the last fifty years of European history in order to establish the fact that during that time militarist Germany has twice unleashed a war which has brought untold misery to the peoples of Europe.[75]

Similar statements were made by the Kremlin in two Notes to the Western Powers, dated October 23, and November 13, 1954. In the latter, German militarism was denounced as "that deadly enemy of the nations of Europe." Again, at the "Conference for European Security" held at Moscow from November 29 to December 2, 1954, Foreign Minister Molotov urged that under no circumstances should the regeneration of

German militarism be permitted "which has unchained the
First and the Second World War." [76]

These declarations are, of course, in flat contradiction to
former Soviet findings that the past wars were essentially the
product of imperialism and capitalism. But now it suits the
Kremlin to use the Western Powers' former charges against
Germany for its own purpose, namely, to frustrate the implementation of a program vital to the Democracies. We have to
expect that the Soviet Union will continue to make the most
of its new war guilt argument. This development disproves all
those who maintain that the war guilt question has, at most,
only an "academic" interest today. On the contrary, it is coming again to the forefront of practical politics.

It should therefore be ascertained whether the Versailles
judgment was just. Was it not, perchance, based on one-sided,
unsound evidence, influenced by preconceived notions, by the
passions of war, by propagandist misconceptions? Suppose the
findings of such authorities as Sidney B. Fay and G. P. Gooch,
recorded in the preceding chapter, and of their large following
in all countries, are substantially true?

As far back as 1925, Gooch drew attention to the gradual
recognition by informed opinion "all over the world" that the
responsibility for the war was divided.[77] As far back as 1928,
Professor Fay stated that the verdict of the Versailles Treaty
should be revised.[78] Yet nothing has been done by any of the
Governments involved.

In 1919, the war guilt indictment, combined with the repeated refusal of the Western Powers to submit the matter to
neutral arbitration, shattered German faith in the honor of
the Democracies, in their fair dealing, in their integrity of purpose. Much has been forgotten since—but will old memories
not be revived? The numerous opponents of Germany's align-
ment with the West today continually operate, under Soviet
leadership, with the argument that the Western Powers will
never be true, disinterested friends of the Germans. Moreover,
it cannot be emphasized strongly enough that the arbitrary
Versailles verdict was *the spiritual core of the European drama
in the inter-war period*—the "twenty-years armistice."

The Allied covering letter was drafted chiefly by Lloyd
George's secretary, Philip Kerr, who later, as Marquess of
Lothian, was the British Ambassador to Washington at the

outbreak of World War II. His draft was, according to André Tardieu, in every essential point the eloquent expression of the ideals which France had upheld in Paris for five months.[79] Indeed, the letter, though composed by an Englishman, breathes vigorously the French spirit that permeated the Peace Conference and inevitably affected also some American representatives.

A few years later, Mr. Kerr began to regret his handiwork. In 1925, the present writer was in England on a good-will mission dealing with the subject of that very document of June 16, 1919, when he met Philip Kerr and others interested in the matter. Friends of Kerr made no secret of his sincere repentance. He became actually conscience stricken, and subsequently he did his best to redress what he now considered to have been a grievous wrong. In April, 1936, while defending the German reoccupation of the Rhineland, he told a meeting at the Royal Institute of International Affairs:

I do not think that anybody can read the documents relating to the origins of the War without recognizing that the view that any of the nations was solely responsible is untenable.[80]

The Allied reply of June 16 being really an ultimatum, the German delegation went back to Weimar and submitted a report to their government on the 18th. They stated that the peace terms were modified only in points of secondary importance; that they remained unbearable and impossible of fulfillment; that the foundation upon which the whole treaty was based, namely, the assertion of Germany's sole guilt for the war, had been intensified in a hateful manner; and that under that treaty Germany could not continue to live honorably as a nation. Honesty being the best policy, they advised against signing this treaty of might and accepting obligations that could not be met.[81]

In the National Assembly heated debates ensued after a new government was formed by the Social Democrat Gustav Bauer as Premier. On the 22nd, he declared in the Assembly:

At this hour of life and death under the threat of invasion, I for the last time raise in free Germany protest against this treaty of violence and destruction, protest against the mockery of the right of self-determination, against this enslavement of the German people, against this new menace to the peace of the world under the mask of a treaty of peace.[82]

The Assembly finally resolved to accept the treaty, but with
significant reservations. In view of the fact that, later on, German governments were loudly accused of bad faith, the essential parts of the German Note of June 22 to the Allies
must be quoted as showing the spirit which animated the representatives of the German people. The Note stated:

. . . the Government in harmony with the whole German people
must regard these conditions as being in sharp contradiction with
the principle which was accepted by the Allied and Associated
Powers . . . as being binding in accordance with the law of nations. . . .

Relying upon this principle of justice which was agreed upon
between the parties to the negotiations . . . the Government has
left no stone unturned in order . . . to obtain some mitigation of
the unbearably harsh conditions which might render it possible for
the Government of the German Republic to sign the Treaty of
Peace without reservations, and to guarantee its execution.

These endeavors . . . undertaken in the interest of the peace
of the world, and the reconciliation of peoples, have failed. . . .

. . . No people, including those of the Allied and Associated
Powers, could expect the German people to agree with thorough
conviction to an instrument of peace, whereby the living members
of the very body of the German people are to be cut off without
consultation of the population concerned, whereby the dignity of
the German State is to be permanently impaired, and whereby un-
endurable economic and financial burdens are to be laid upon the
German people.

. . . The Government of the German Republic solemnly declares . . . that it yields to force, being resolved to spare the
German people, whose sufferings are unspeakable, a new war, the
shattering of its national unity by further occupation of German
territories, terrible famine for women and children, and mercilessly
prolonged retention of the prisoners of war. . . .

The Government . . . engages to fulfill the conditions of Peace
imposed upon Germany. It desires, however, in this solemn moment to express itself with unreserved clearness, in order to meet
in advance any accusation of untruthfulness that may now or later
be made against Germany. The conditions imposed exceed the
measure of that which Germany can in fact perform. The Government of the German Republic therefore . . . makes all reservations and declines all responsibility as regards the consequences
which may be threatened against Germany, when, as is bound to
happen, the impossibility of carrying out the conditions comes to
light even though German capacity to fulfill is stretched to the utmost.

Germany further lays the greatest emphasis on the declaration that she cannot accept Article 231 of the Treaty of Peace which requires Germany to admit herself to be the sole and only author of the war, and does not cover this article by her signature. . . .

Likewise, it is equally impossible for a German to reconcile it with his dignity and honor to accept and execute Articles 227 to 230, by which Germany is required to give up to the Allied and Associated Powers for trial individuals among the German people who are accused by the Allied and Associated Powers of a breach of international law and of having committed acts contrary to the customs of war.

Further, the Government of the German Republic makes a distinct protest against the seizure of all the colonial possessions of Germany, and against the reasons given therefor, which permanently deny to Germany fitness for colonial activity, although the contrary is clearly established and irrefutable evidence to this effect is contained in the observations of the German Peace Delegation on the Conditions of Peace.

Closing its Note, the German Government added:

. . . in view of the condition of constraint into which the German people are forced by the requirements of the Allies, a condition of constraint such as has never been inflicted on any people in a manner more crushing and more disastrous in its consequences . . . the German Government believes itself to be entitled to address the following modest request to the Allied and Associated Governments in the expectation that the Allied and Associated Governments will consider the following declaration as an integral portion of the Treaty:

"Within two years counting from the day when the Treaty is signed, the Allied and Associated Governments will submit the present Treaty to the High Council of the Powers, as constituted by the League of Nations according to Article 4, for the purpose of subsequent examination. Before this High Council the German plenipotentiaries are to enjoy the same rights and privileges as the representatives of the other contracting Powers of the present Treaty. This Council shall decide in regard to those conditions of the present Treaty which impair the rights of self-determination of the German people, and also in regard to the stipulation whereby the free economic development of Germany on a footing of equal rights is impeded." [83]

The German "modest request" was rebuffed. Yet not many years passed before it was recognized that it had been a statesmanlike proposal.[84] While World War II was raging, Sir Nevile

Henderson wrote that there was one major, even vital, *lacuna* in the Versailles Treaty: "It contained no clause prescribing that after a fixed period (say two or three or five years) it would come up for revision where necessary by negotiation."

He added that it would be utter folly if the next peace treaty did not contain such a clause.[85] The same conviction was expressed in August, 1941, by James T. Shotwell to whom it seemed clear that the Versailles Treaty "offers one outstanding lesson to the world today," namely, that there must be adequate provision in any peace settlement for adjustment in the light of changing circumstances.[86] Indeed, the necessity for such a provision can today be regarded as a vital principle which all leading statesmen have accepted. In June, 1919, however, the victorious Powers were too eager to reap their harvest; for later readjustments they believed that they had the League of Nations, and they felt too superior to their beaten enemy to consider his circumspect counsel.

Instead, they replied to the German appeal on the very same 22nd of June that the time for discussion had passed; no qualifications or reservations could be accepted or acknowledged; the Treaty as finally formulated had either to be accepted as a whole, or not accepted at all. If it was signed, the Allied and Associated Powers must hold Germany responsible for the execution of every stipulation of the Treaty.

Thereupon the Weimar Republic transmitted the following Note on June 23:

The Government of the German Republic is overwhelmed to learn . . . that the Allies are resolved to enforce, with all the power at their command, the acceptance even of those provisions . . . which, without having any material significance, are designed to deprive the German people of their honor. . . . The German people . . . are wholly without the means of defending their honor against the outside world. Yielding to overpowering might, the Government of the German Republic declares itself ready to accept and to sign the treaty imposed by the Allied and Associated Governments. But in so doing, the Government of the German Republic in no wise abandons its conviction that these conditions of peace represent unparalleled injustice.[87]

At that time Germany was torn by Communist uprisings. To the 237 members of the National Assembly—against 138 —who voted for surrender there appeared to be no choice left but to sign. It was a fatal mistake for the reasons the German delegation gave in their report of June 18, as recorded above.[88]

The Treaty was to be signed at Versailles on June 28. Versailles had been the Headquarters of the German armies in 1870-71; there, on January 18, 1871, King William of Prussia was proclaimed Emperor of a unified Germany; and there, on February 26, 1871, the preliminary peace was signed. Since 1870, Versailles had been the symbol of French defeat. It was natural that it should now become the symbol of French victory, marking the long-desired *revanche,* very dearly bought at the cost of frightfully devastated territories and with streams of precious French blood.

But the date of the signature? June 28, was the fifth anniversary of the assassination of Archduke Franz Ferdinand and his Consort, heir to the throne of Austria-Hungary. The plot, carried out by Austrian Serbs, had been hatched and prepared with the active assistance of some Serb officials, and the shots that killed the Imperial couple were the first shots fired in the ensuing World War. The choice of June 28 thus acquired an especial significance. It implied for many—though this was not the official intent—the condoning of political murder in the supposed interest of one's country.

The ceremony staged for the signing of the Treaty is a glaring illustration of the spirit that prevailed at the Paris Conference. We have some graphic descriptions of this weighty page of history, for instance the following from the pen of Walter Millis. When the representatives of the Allied and Associated Powers were assembled in the Hall of Mirrors, President Georges Clemenceau said with a snap, "Bring in the Germans!" The two delegates were brought in through a small side entrance "as if they had been criminals." They were seated at the lower end of the table between the Japanese and the Brazilians, and opposite the delegates of Peru, Ecuador and Liberia. After signing the Treaty, the Germans were hurried away through the same side door.[89]

The English historian, E. H. Carr, corroborates this fact that the German signatories were escorted in and out of the hall "in the manner of criminals conducted to and from the dock." [90] And Colonel House recorded in his diary that the affair was made "as humiliating to the enemy as it well could be." [91]

Yet, among the Allied representatives, there was some consciousness of shame. Two of the principal signatories told Herbert Adams Gibbons on the eve of the ceremony that they felt they were going to do something dishonorable. To Gibbons himself the ceremony was "like a funeral." [92]

Two representatives of the British Empire, both from the South African Union, signed under protest—General Jan Christian Smuts and General Louis Botha. They will forever be honored for their conscientiousness, their courage, their wisdom. Many British and foreign papers published Smuts' protest. It contained the sentence: "The real peace of the peoples ought to follow, complete, and amend the peace of the Statesmen." [93]

The French were jubilant and highly satisfied. Upon being congratulated after the signature, President Clemenceau, "tears in his bleary eyes," acknowledged, "Yes, it is a fine day." Harold Nicolson, recording this scene, went to bed that evening "sick of life." [94] There were thoughtful Britons who were deeply troubled in their minds, and so were not a few of prominent Americans. General Tasker Bliss wisely predicted: "We are in for a low period, then a high period, then the devil will be to pay all over the world." [95]

On the other hand, President Wilson declared in a message to the American people that the Treaty was "severe only because great wrongs done by Germany are to be righted and repaired," and he announced that there was ground "for deep satisfaction, universal reassurance and confident hope." [96]

Deep down in his heart, however, Woodrow Wilson did not seem to be entirely easy. In his final week in France he was invited by the President of the Republic, Raymond Poincaré, to dine at the Elysée Palace, but he had to be persuaded to accept. He was full of resentment against Poincaré for the part he had played during the Conference. He believed, not without evidence, that the French President and Marshal Foch had tried at every step to balk his plans and "to convert a peace of justice into a peace of injustice." [97]

3. POINTS OF COMPARISON

The territorial settlements made in 1919 and 1920, particularly those relating to Austria, the Sudeten Germans in Bohemia, to Danzig and generally to the new Eastern frontiers will be treated in a later book, dealing with Chancellor Hitler and European policy. For the present chapter, however, some other topics have still to be discussed before definite conclusions concerning the Paris Peace Conference and its outcome can be reached.

In 1914, the German case was at the outset fatally disgraced in the public eye by the violation of Belgian neutrality. The plea of strategic necessity was understood by professional soldiers, a small group of men, whereas world opinion was painfully impressed by the ravages of war devastating an innocent country. Some deplorable acts were committed by the invading armies but it was erroneously believed by vast masses abroad that the "Hun" systematically bayonetted babies, chopped off childrens' hands, raped nuns, crucified prisoners of war, and manufactured soap from their boiled corpses. An astute and not too scrupulous propaganda seized upon the exaggerated or faked war crimes as a formidable weapon to influence public opinion all over the world. In this respect, British propaganda proved highly effective, particularly in the United States, where the bulk of the people soon looked upon the struggle of 1914-18 as a conflict between the forces of good and the forces of evil, a mental attitude which inevitably had a large influence on the peacemakers in 1919.[98]

After the war, the facts about the actual, the imagined, and the invented atrocities were disclosed by a number of investigators.[99] Writing in 1947, W. L. White rightly thought one might say that in the Second World War the Nazis methodically and on a mass scale perpetrated every atrocity of which the German people were unjustly accused in the former war.[100] In respect to atrocities during the First World War, however, the reader should again, for a fair evaluation, concentrate his mind on the Germans of 1914-18, when there was no Nazism even dreamed of.

During the armistice negotiations, on October 14, 1918, Secretary of State Lansing demanded that the acts of inhumanity, spoliation, and desolation by the German Armed Forces must cease.[101] This referred to the unrestricted submarine warfare and to the devastations carried out by the retreating armies. The German reply of the 20th protested against the reproach of illegal and inhuman actions made against the

German land and sea forces, and thereby against the German people, and the Government proposed that the facts about all such charges be cleared up by neutral commissions.[102] In his speech on May 7, 1919, Count Brockdorff-Rantzau repeated the request for an impartial inquiry.[103] And, finally, in their Notes of May 24 and May 29 the German delegation urged that the controversial subject of the breaches of international law committed on both sides be submitted to an impartial international court of arbitration.[104]

The Allied and Associated Powers rejected the German demand on June 16, refusing even the admission of neutral representatives to the projected Allied tribunals.[105] Their negative attitude toward this basic principle of justice made a deep and most unfavorable impression on the German mind. Indeed, it is highly regrettable that the violations of international law which each side charged against the other, were not submitted to neutral investigation. The verdict of a neutral court would have contributed greatly to a better understanding between the peoples affected, and it might well have had a beneficial influence on the conduct of the Second World War.

At the Paris Conference, the German Government freely admitted the grave injustice done to Belgium by having been "aggressed with the terrors of war through an act contrary to the Law of Nations." [106] Other German acts in violation of the customs of warfare were also freely admitted, but countercharges were put forth. In fact, as Dr. Gooch has stated, the fighting was disgraced by atrocities on both sides.[107]

From the German point of view, the British starvation blockade was, in its effects, worse than any other atrocity committed in the war, especially as it was denounced as an illegal measure.[108] That there was some truth in this contention is evident from a passage in the covering letter of June 16, which declared:

If the Allied and Associated Powers have imposed upon Germany a blockade of exceptional severity, which throughout they have consistently sought to conform to the principles of international law, it is because of the criminal character of the war initiated by Germany and of its barbarous methods adopted by her in prosecuting it.[109]

According to this explanation, the blockade was a retaliatory measure.

After the war, many Westerners were genuinely appalled when they realized what havoc the food blockade had wrought on the German civilian population. A British authority, Arthur Bryant, states:

In the last two years of the war, nearly 800,000 non-combatants died in Germany from starvation or diseases attributed to under-nourishment—about fifty times more than were drowned by sub-marine attacks on British shipping. The biggest mortality was among children between the ages of 5 and 15, where the death rate increased by 55 per cent. . . . A whole generation grew up in an epoch of undernourishment and misery such as we have never in this country experienced.[110]

This horrible situation remained almost unknown to the outside world. As Professor Thomas A. Bailey has pointed out, the Allied slow starvation of Germany's civilian population was quiet, unspectacular, and censored.[111]

Though the armistice in November, 1918, had rendered the German people helpless, the blockade was continued—and even aggravated by Allied prevention of German fishing, in order to make doubly sure that the Germans would accept the victors' terms. In fact, the country was actually starved into submission, "a blacker crime," an Englishman thought, "than the whole of the submarine campaign." [112]

It is much to the credit of Britons that some of their promi-nent men have vigorously condemned the maintenance of the blockade after November, 1918, as an act of unpardonable cruelty. Gilbert Murray, writing in 1933, considered it prob-able that a future historian will regard the establishment and the continuance of the blockade as "one of those many acts of almost incredible inhumanity" which made the war conspicu-ous in the annals of mankind and have shaken thoughtful men's faith in the reality of modern civilization.[113]

The food blockade had far-reaching psychological and mental effects on the German masses which facilitated Hitler's advent. The millions of families who were afflicted by daily suffering through undernourishment extending over years never forgot their excruciating experience, because its marks on the growing generation remained visible. The American diplomat, Hugh R. Wilson, witnessed it. He records that, in 1920, the traces of undernourishment and of children's diseases, espe-cially rickets, "were found on every hand." [114]

One of the most humiliating demands made by the Allied and Associated Powers was that Germany should renounce all her rights and titles over her colonial possessions. On May 29, 1919, the German Government set forth that this demand was in flat contradiction to Point 5 of President Wilson's address to Congress of January 8, 1918. It admitted that blunders and mistakes had been made such as happened in the colonial history of other nations, but gave an account of the successful work Germany had accomplished in her colonies.[115] However, the Allies replied on June 16:

Germany's dereliction in the sphere of colonial civilization has been revealed too completely to admit of the Allied and Associated Powers consenting to make a second experiment and of their assuming the responsibility of again abandoning thirteen to fourteen million of natives to a fate from which the war has delivered them.[116]

The German protest of June 22, reprinted above was in vain.

Germany had acquired her overseas colonies in the eighties and nineties. There had been mismanagement in some. But, learning by experience, her administration improved steadily. Great Britain acknowledged this implicitly in 1898 by concluding a treaty with Germany which provided for the eventual partition of certain Portuguese African possessions between them in case Portugal should be forced by financial difficulties to dispose of them. It should be noted that Portugal was an old-time Ally of Britain.[117]

In the years before the war of 1914-18 it was generally admitted in well-informed colonial circles abroad that in most of Germany's overseas possessions her administration was good and efficient. After the war, the validity of this estimate was amply confirmed by American and British authorities. One of them, Colonel E. Alexander Powell, who was personally well acquainted with every German colony in Africa, declared that the rule in them, although stern, was in general just; and he added that the German colonies certainly enjoyed better administration than the French possessions in Equatorial Africa.[118] A British expert, William Harbutt Dawson, states that since the beginning of our century the administration of the German colonies had been "at least as clement and humane as in any of the other overseas empires, and far more efficient than in most." [119]

In order to soften or obscure the harshness of the Allied demand, it has been contended that, after all, the colonies had no great value and that Germany did not need them for her normal economic development.[120] That is, of course, wholly beside the point, because, as a distinguished English author observed, it would plainly inflict grave dishonor on Germany if an impartial investigation showed her unworthy to own colonies.[121]

Part of the German colonial territory was given to Belgium. Such a transfer seemed justified as a compensation for Belgian losses and misery during more than four years of war. In Germany, however, the notorious "Congo atrocities," committed during the reign of the avaricious King Leopold II, were widely known. They had horrified millions in the Western countries.[122] Therefore, the transfer of territory bordering on the Congo to Belgium, ostensibly for reasons of humanity, was in German eyes sheer hypocritical mockery.[123] Besides, there was the fact that Japan, who had entered the war upon Britain's invitation for the sake of booty, was considered worthy to take over the administration of valuable colonies in the Pacific.

W. H. Dawson recalled that Germany had been accused of having "militarized" the native population in her colonies. That was not true, he declared. The only country which had done this was France, and France is still doing it today, Dawson wrote in 1933, "even in Germany's colonies, by the express permission of the other Allied Powers." [124] Incidentally, France is reaping now—and will probably reap at an increasing rate—what she herself has sown during past decades in her African and Far Eastern possessions.

By the mid-thirties, the grave injustice done to Germany by depriving her of all of her colonies was so evident that leading British statesmen, with the reluctant approval of some French politicians, were willing to admit even Hitler-Germany into the privileged group of colonial Powers. It was at that time that R. W. Seton-Watson, who had ties with British governing circles, drew up a program of adjustments, in which the fourth point read: "The convenient thesis of Germany's unfitness to administer colonies is as untrue as it is insulting, and should be recanted." [125]

Hitler spoiled the projected recantation. But for our present study the crucial point still needs to be set forth. And that is that Germany's alleged unfitness for colonial administration was proclaimed on June 16, 1919, by twenty-seven states scattered all over the world, of which only seven had any experience in colonization at all. Amongst these seven were two, Belgium and Portugal, whose record was none too good. Portugal did not have the financial resources with which to develop her vast overseas empire to the extent desirable for the prosperity of both herself and her neighbors, and therefore, Great Britain, in 1898, conceded the eventual purchase by Germany of large parts of Portuguese African possessions. As regards Belgium, maladministration in the Congo during the nineties and the first decade of our century caused the death of hundreds of thousands, and the misery of many more hundreds of thousands of negroes for the sake of huge European profits in rubber, so that *Red Rubber* became a symbol of ruthless exploitation of native populations.

It would be a grave fallacy to argue that, since the old-style colonization by the White Man is obviously drawing to its close, there is no longer any point in reviving the question whether the Allied verdict of 1919 concerning German colonial methods was justified or not. Such convenient evasion would miss entirely the vital psychological factor involved. The bulk of Germans took pride in their overseas possessions with which hundreds of thousands were personally linked.[126]

Very judiciously, Professor Bailey observed that even partially to justify the seizure of the German colonies on the pretext that the Germans were brutes, "was to turn the knife in the wound." [127] It is still an open wound with a considerable section of Germans.

President Wilson's idea of a League of Nations was warmly welcomed in Germany. A German Foreign Office memorandum, drafted in March or April, 1919, declared: "Germany emphatically lends her support to the establishment of a permanent League of Nations, based on equality for all great and small nations." This was also contained in the instructions to the German plenipotentiaries. On May 7, 1919, Count Brockdorff-Rantzau praised "the sublime idea of deriving from the most terrible catastrophe in history the greatest of forward movements in the development of mankind, by means of the League of Nations." It was taken so seriously that on May 9 the German delegation submitted to the Peace Conference their own proposals for the establishment of a League. Subsequently, Germany, advancing sound reasons, appealed again and again for immediate admission to the League, invoking the solidarity of human interests. She argued that membership in the League would constitute the most inviolable guarantee of the good faith of every German Government.

We have seen that Premier Lloyd George finally favored compliance with the German request, but he was overruled. In their covering letter of June 16, the Allied and Associated Powers stated:

In the present temper of international feeling, it is impossible to expect the free nations of the world to sit down immediately in equal association with those by whom they have been so grievously wronged.[128]

Germany, the New Germany, had first to prove her worthiness to be a member. The refusal was the more galling as from the start Asiatic and African peoples were admitted.[129] Not many years passed before it was generally recognized that German membership from the beginning would have benefited the European community.

At the Paris Conference, two peace treaties which Germany had exacted before, were held up to condemn her. The first one was the Treaty of Frankfort in 1871. This has been discussed in the preceding chapter. The German delegation at Versailles admitted the injustice done to France by the annexation of Alsace-Lorraine.[130]

A detailed comparison of the Treaty of Frankfort with the Treaty of Versailles still needs to be done. G. P. Gooch has declared, however, that the peacemakers of 1919 have no title to cast stones at the peacemakers of 1871.[131] Above all, the spirit of the victor toward the vanquished in 1871 and in 1919 was totally different. In 1871, there was no moral castigation, no dishonoring humiliation, no degradation of a brave opponent. From this point of view, the Italian statesman Francesco S. Nitti has truly asserted that the Treaty of Frankfort was "a humanitarian act" compared with that of Versailles.[132]

The other treaty invoked against Germany at the Paris Conference was the Treaty of Brest-Litovsk which was forced on
the Bolsheviks in March, 1918. This was a victor's peace imposed upon the vanquished and correctly denounced as such
by the Allies. The German delegation admitted the validity of
their criticism.[133]

Allied apologists have tried to show, as sort of an excuse,
that the Treaty of Versailles was less harsh and brutal than
that of Brest-Litovsk. This is, however, beside the point. The
Allies had proclaimed that they would not take such a peace
as a model, and two wrongs do not make a right.[134] Indeed,
how can any fairminded person, having condemned a certain
action, excuse a similar action of his own by the action he
has formerly condemned?

Moreover, those who uphold the Treaty of Versailles against
that of Brest-Litovsk should first of all make themselves fully
acquainted with the latter. The main conditions imposed on
the Bolsheviks in March, 1918, and supplemented by further
stipulations in August, 1918, were: renunciation of Russian
sovereignty over Finland, the Baltic States, Poland, and the
Ukraine; recognition of an independent Georgia; return to
Turkey of some territories in the Caucasus region which she
had lost to Russia in the war of 1877-78; and payment of six
milliards of gold marks.

It is on record that V. I. Lenin, in the course of a speech
on the Russo-Polish War of 1920, declared:

You know that the Allied imperialists—France, England, America and Japan—concluded the Versailles Treaty after the destruction of Germany, which, at any rate, is incomparably more brutal
than the notorious Treaty of Brest which caused such an uproar.

This statement from the head of the country that was most
deeply affected by the Treaty of Brest-Litovsk, should be con-
vincing.[135]

The Treaty was not made in breach of a promise, and the
frontiers drafted in March, 1918, along the Baltic coast remained as part of the map of Europe. Of course, the Germans desired to establish their hegemony over the Baltic
States, over Poland and the Ukraine. But is there any doubt
in the reader's mind that in 1918 the vast majority of the
populations concerned did genuinely prefer—and would prefer now—German hegemony to that of the Soviets? Finally,

it must be said that at Brest-Litovsk, too, there were no dishonoring humiliations or degradations imposed on the vanquished. It was this favorable psychological factor that contributed in no small degree to the early collaboration between the Weimar Republic and the Soviet Union. This fact provides both a lesson, and a warning.

After a first perusal of the draft treaty the German delegation, as we have noted above, declared on May 9 that many demands could not be met. This was the unanimous opinion of the National Assembly. The German Government persistently maintained that certain terms—above all the financial terms—were impossible of fulfillment. They made, therefore, explicit reservations in their Note of June 22.[136] Prominent Allied experts, as has been shown in this chapter, fully confirmed the German contention. Yet, the Allied and Associated Powers insisted in their reply of June 22, that they must hold Germany responsible for the execution of every detail in the Treaty.[137] This insistence created in Germany the impression that unrealizable demands were purposely made in order to accuse her, at the proper time, of bad faith, and to apply sanctions, as actually happened before long. Apprehending such an unfortunate development, the German delegation urged their Government not to sign that treaty of might based on the assertion of Germany's sole guilt for the war, and containing obligations that could not be met. Under that treaty, the delegation rightly contended, Germany could not continue to live honorably as a nation.[138]

Subsequently, there were evasions on the German side, financial evasions, and evasions in military matters, quite deliberate evasions. The conclusions to be drawn from the Peace Conference, and its outcome, should enable the reader to pass a fair judgment on these evasions, and to ask himself what, under the circumstances, Americans, and Britons, and Frenchmen would have done.

4. Summary and Outlook

The preceding analysis established as facts: (1) President Wilson's program was the legal basis for a peace of justice; and (2) the German people were not to be punished for the actions of their rulers.

With regard to the first fact, it is evident from the fully recorded steps taken by American and British members of the Peace Conference before the Treaty was signed that vital features of Wilson's program were not carried out. John Maynard Keynes, one year after the Conference he attended, wrote as follows:

There are few episodes in history which posterity will have less reason to condone—a war ostensibly waged in the defense of the sanctity of international engagements ending in a definite breach of one of the most sacred possible of such engagements on the part of the victorious champions of these ideals.

In a footnote to this plain statement Keynes added: "Only after the most painful consideration have I written these words." [139] His moral courage deserves ever to be remembered.

A junior English member of the Peace Conference, Harold Nicolson, was equally frank. Having analyzed Wilson's Fourteen Points, Four Principles and Five Particulars, he came to the conclusion that nineteen of these were "flagrantly violated" in the final terms. [140] Less drastic is Herbert Hoover's estimate that, in general, twenty out of twenty-five points were "variously violated or distorted." [141] The Italian statesman, Francesco S. Nitti, saw in the peace treaties of 1919 a "fundamental negation of President Wilson's Fourteen Points which constituted a solemn obligation." [142] Fact one is thus abundantly proved beyond any possibility of dispute.

As to the second fact it is also evident that the assurances which had been profusely given to the German people were not kept. Numerous non-German authors admit this only half-heartedly, for they content themselves with saying that the Germans *felt* they had been cheated, or had been betrayed. That is an evasion of a vital issue. A people may well feel they were cheated, but actually were not cheated. Some authors have plainly stated the hard fact. Vincent C. Sheean declared in 1944 that the Versailles *Diktat* was "a swindle," departing so widely, in so many notable respects from the agreed basis that Germans were able to say for twenty years that they had been cheated. [143] Professor Charles Callan Tansill wrote that the Treaty of Versailles had been "built upon the dubious sands of betrayal" which began on October 5, 1918. [144] And Professor Thomas A. Bailey, commenting on the familiar assertion made by Germans that Germany was not beaten but betrayed, stated: "The truth is that in a very real sense she was beaten and then betrayed." [145]

It seems high time that this double truth be generally accepted in both camps—by Germans that they were beaten in 1918, unable to continue the war for longer than some months; and by the peoples of the Allied and Associated Powers that in 1919 the German people were betrayed.

This truth, uncomfortable as it may be, has special relevance for the American people. Did not their President declare in April, 1917, that "we" have no feeling towards the German people "but one of sympathy and friendship"? And on Flag Day, 1917, that "we are not the enemies of the German people"? Did President Wilson not then continue, "we are vaguely conscious that we are fighting their cause, as they will some day see it, as well as our own"? In June, 1919, these solemn pronouncements from the mouth of the one man in whom the bulk of the Germans had cherished a reverent faith, were recalled by them with bitter comments. Naturally, the experience made a deep impression on the Germans.

The Allied Powers did not directly dispute the fact that Wilson's program was binding. In their covering letter of June 16, they stated they were certain that the proposed peace "is a peace of right fulfilling the terms agreed upon at the time of the armistice." Implicitly, however, even they admitted that there were deviations from the agreed basis; for they declared that the treaty is "frankly not based upon a general condonation of the events of 1914-18. It would not be a peace of justice if it were." And they vindicated the peace terms with the charges: (1) that, in 1914, the German Government consciously committed the greatest crime against humanity, that it waged a war for the domination of Europe in a most savage way, and that seven million dead, and more than twenty million wounded and sufferers were the victims of its lust for tyranny; and (2) that the subservient German people must share their autocratic masters' responsibility.[146]

This second charge was a direct contradiction of Allied proclamations during the war, and especially of President Wilson's assurances.

As regards the first charge, the Allies believed in 1919 that they had ample evidence on hand to prove it. But its validity was subsequently disproved, amongst many others by such

recognized authorities as G. P. Gooch and Sidney B. Fay.
Hundreds of historians and publicists confirmed their findings.
From a large choice the following may be quoted as representing a conviction of well informed scholars throughout the
world.

W. Arnold-Foster wrote in 1933: "It is impossible to defend the lie of Germany's sole war guilt." In the same year,
Sherwood Eddy recorded that of sixty-seven historians from
eleven countries only one maintained the Versailles imputation. Dwight E. Lee declared in 1942, that in the light of history all Great Powers must share the moral guilt pinned upon
Germany in 1919. Walter Millis stated in 1940 that few
thoughtful men even in the Allied countries really believed
that Germany had been solely guilty of starting the war. Gilbert Murray, a leading British scholar, thought in 1933 that
the terms of the Allied Note of June 16 were "indefensible,"
and that on the subject of war guilt "in strict fairness some
public and official statement might well be made by the Principal Allied and Associated Powers." Finally, R. W. Seton-
Watson, a prominent British historian whom nobody would
consider to have been pro-German, declared in 1938 that
the charge of exclusive war guilt was "absurd and untenable,"
and that this should be publicly admitted.[147]

This was not done. On the contrary, the charge has since,
and *because of,* the Second World War been revived by leading British and American statesmen, with the result that it is
once again almost an article of faith with the masses among
the Western Powers.

There are three aspects in the case, a legal aspect, a practical aspect, and a moral aspect.

The legal aspect is this:

In 1919 the Allied and Associated Powers passed a judgment—in a matter of life or death for Germany, as she contended—which subsequent revelations proved to have been
flagrantly misleading. They rendered that verdict acting as sole
judges in their own cause. They thereby openly flouted a
basic principle of justice. Yet, thus far, none of the twenty-
seven states in question has done anything officially to set the
record right.

The honor and integrity of the Allied and Associated
Powers of 1919 are seriously involved in this matter. They
will be perpetually open to the grave charge that they, who

claimed to speak for "practically the whole of civilized mankind," have, themselves, for their own sake, consciously violated a sacred law of civilized mankind—the law of impartiality.

The practical aspect is this:

The German people, a virile nation living in the heart of Europe, were deeply conscious of having been wronged in a threefold way—by the denial of solemn pledges given in 1918; by an unjust verdict pronounced in 1919; and by the repeated rejection of their government's pleas for neutral arbitration.[148] The treatment meted out to the German people in 1919 thus undermined their faith in the integrity and righteousness of the Allies. This has not been forgotten in present-day Germany.

Most important of all, the Versailles verdict prevents any sincere understanding between the Germans and the French, without which no solid foundation for a stable Western Europe can be provided.[149]

Harold Nicolson has judiciously observed that, given the atmosphere of the time, given the passions aroused in all democracies by four years of war, it would have been impossible even for supermen to have devised a peace of moderation and righteousness.[150] This is, indeed, a fact which should be recognized by Germans more than they have done or are doing. The Treaty of Versailles had good features, and it *is* remarkable that, under all the circumstances, it was not more imperfect.[151] Moreover, the writer holds strongly the view that the worst feature was not the Treaty as it emerged in 1919. Far more disastrous for Europe and the world in general was the failure of the victors to revise the Treaty in the early years of the Weimar Republic at a Good Will Conference, as the German Government had requested in 1919. In 1933, Sir Norman Angell recorded, it was "now almost everywhere admitted" that the Treaty was so unjust "that there can be no peace until it is revised." [152] Too late—a terrible word in history, for by that time Adolf Hitler was already in power to carry out revision by force. This tragic failure justifies the statement that the Treaty was not worthy of the men who died to win it; [153] that it rendered the military victory futile; [154] that it was, and remained, a potential declaration of war.[155]

Yet, we have seen that, early in 1919, some statesmen in Paris clearly foresaw the fatal consequences inherent in the draft treaty. To them should be added Philander C. Knox, the former Secretary of State, who declared in the autumn of 1919: "The Treaty indicts those who drew it up. It is a crime against civilization." [156]

This was not, however, solely the fault of the peacemakers. They worked under almost irresistible popular pressure which had a pernicious effect on the shaping of the Treaty and tended to make it essentially the kind of Treaty which the masses in Britain, and especially in France, wished it to be at the time.[157]

This fact does not by any means absolve those at the Peace Conference of their responsibility, but it does raise the pertinent question whether the peoples of the Western Powers have ever been conscious of having, according to the principles of democracy, a well measured co-responsibility for the Versailles Treaty? Germans, in particular, may pose that question, inasmuch as, in 1919, they were made *fully* co-responsible for the deeds of their autocratic rulers.

The writer is of the opinion that in no country responsibility for the conduct of foreign policy extends beyond its statesmen, its politicians, its leading men in public life, and its *intelligentsia*. In that very complicated, obscure and difficult game of foreign affairs, the masses are quite obviously unable to arrive at sound judgments; they are necessarily dependent upon their leaders and advisers.

The peacemakers of 1919 had to grapple with another embarrassing factor, in addition to the feelings of their peoples, namely, with the secret treaties which had been concluded during the war, mainly for territorial acquisitions which were in part incompatible with both Allied pretences and President Wilson's program. They were, thus, in a sore dilemma. But there was a convenient way out of all such troubles, viz., to throw the whole blame for the war, for its millions of victims, for its frightful general destruction, on the German nation, rulers and people. This was a simple device. It was carried out to such an extreme extent that Germany, the new Democratic Germany, was forced at the point of the bayonet to admit her guilt. This extorted admission was, as an outspoken Englishman put it, "intended to exhibit her to the world as a justly punished criminal" in order "to remain pilloried to eternity as the one great and horrible example." [158]

In this way, the unprecedented vindictiveness of the Treaty was made to appear as mere atonement.[159] But from that simple device there emanated a special spirit of pernicious virulence. Harold Nicolson has described it. Years after the event he wrote: "Seldom in the history of man has such vindictiveness cloaked itself in such unctuous sophistry." And he had the feeling that the judgment of posterity will concentrate not upon the errors of the Conference so much "as upon its appalling hypocrisy." [160]

This leads us to the moral aspect of the case which has been much ignored and neglected. Yet it must be elaborated for the sake of achieving that spiritual regeneration which is indispensable for our future welfare.

Before the First World War, there had been a good deal of immorality in international relationship. Imperial Germany had exhibited her measured share of it, as had other European and non-European Powers. Diplomacy cannot do entirely without it. But the "appalling hypocrisy" surrounding the peacemaking in 1919 swept a wave of immorality into the European body politic which has produced a terrifying harvest.[161] The Social Democratic leader, Philipp Scheidemann, felt that this would inevitably be the case. As Prime Minister he said in the National Assembly on May 12, 1919, that the proposed treaty would bring about "an unparalleled deterioration of the concepts of ethics and morals." [162] Among other things it taught the Germans one great lesson: that MIGHT is the only factor that really counts in foreign relations [163]—one of the main charges brought against the Germans in Allied propaganda throughout the war.

The weighty moral issues involved were, of course, felt by many observers. Monsignor Cerretti, the Papal Nuncio in Paris, gave vigorous expression to the grave apprehensions in high ecclesiastical circles. He bemoaned that "the devil at his worst could hardly have conceived so thorough a destruction of the soul of mankind." [164]

Enlightened opinion has generally recognized that the confession extorted from Germany of her sole guilt for the war was a crowning humiliation. It aroused the passionate indignation of all Germans from left to right.[165] Not only were they honestly convinced of having waged a defensive war, they saw in the Allied insistence on the war guilt avowal a ruse to cover up Allied guilt. The palpable exaggerations and the evident bias in the Note of June 16 led to the assertion by Germans that they were not guilty in the sense of the Versailles accusations. That was certainly true. But, stretching the argument, many Germans later asserted that their country was quite innocent, implying that the war guilt lay wholly on the other side. As a corrective of this perversion of historical truth it should be noted that, in 1919, the German delegation at the Paris Conference freely admitted Imperial Germany's share of responsibility.[166]

It is an undeniable fact that the French spirit dominated the scene at the Peace Conference. This is understandable enough when one considers the terrible losses of France's youth and manhood, the vast destruction of her goods and territory, the misery of her people in the occupied regions, the torturing anxieties of over four years of war. Paris was, therefore, an unfortunate choice for the negotiation of a durable peace. We have seen that President Wilson bitterly resented the French frustration of his idealistic aims, and that Premier Lloyd George was unable to give effect to his belated better judgment because of French opposition. Alfred Fabre-Luce, one of the best spirits of present-day France, has frankly acknowledged that on his country rests the main responsibility for the Versailles Treaty.[167]

A noteworthy reaction occurred even in Georges Clemenceau's mind. After the signing of the Treaty, on June 28, 1919, he called that day "a fine day." Yet, a few months later, he warned Herbert Hoover: "There will be another world war in your time and you will be needed back in Europe." [168] Clemenceau had himself been a determined champion of the idea of *revanche* for France's defeat and spoliation in 1870-71. Reflecting on the Versailles Treaty, he evidently felt that the enemy of 1919—infinitely more humiliated and despoiled than France had been—would inevitably strive to settle accounts.

There would be no point in measuring out the share each of the Five Principal Powers had in the shaping of the Treaty of Versailles. One important fact, however, needs to be plainly stated, namely, that the victorious Powers have the exclusive responsibility for the Treaty, and that Germany has none. On the contrary, she strove to have some of its worst features modified, and she sought to have a crucial clause inserted to provide for peaceful adjustments and revisions which, if adopted, would have given history another and happier turn of events.

Americans may contend that, since their government repudiated the Treaty in 1920 and concluded a separate peace with Germany in 1921, they have no more share in the matter. Such an argument would, however, be a fallacy. The United States of America was the leading Power at the Peace Conference. Congress rejected the Versailles Treaty chiefly on account of the obligations imposed by the Covenant of the League of Nations, as an integral part of the Treaty, and not because of the harsh terms imposed on Germany.[169] Moreover, in March, 1921, there were two official confirmations of the war guilt charge involving the United States. When, early in that year, Foreign Minister Walter Simons raised the question of responsibility for the war, Premier Lloyd George, addressing a Reparations Conference in London, declared on March 3:

For the Allies German responsibility for the war is fundamental. It is the basis upon which the structure of the Treaty has been erected, and if the acknowledgement is repudiated and abandoned, the Treaty is destroyed. . . . We wish therefore once and for all to make it quite clear that German responsibility for the war must be treated by the Allies as a *chose jugée*.[170]

At that time, the United States was still one of the Allies in whose name Lloyd George spoke because her separate peace with Germany was not concluded until later in the year in August, and ratified in November, 1921. Moreover, the United States Government itself reiterated the charge against Germany immediately following the British Premier's declaration. In reply to a memorandum on reparations which the German Government presented to the American Commissioner at Berlin on March 21, 1921, Secretary of State Charles E. Hughes stated on the 29th in a telegram to the Commissioner, for transmission to the German Government: "This Government stands with the Governments of the Allies in holding Germany responsible for the war. . . ." [171]

America's separate peace with Germany did not remove the charge made against the latter. Above all, the United States Government has never withdrawn its signature under the Allied Note of June 16, 1919. It is true, however, that the Governments of Great Britain and France are more deeply involved in the matter than the United States Government is, as will be shown in the next chapter dealing with tribulations of the Weimar Republic.

In the years following 1918, only one of the Allied belligerent Powers of 1914-18 did not join in the defamation of Germany: the Soviet Union. On the contrary, the Bolsheviks demonstrated in official manifestations and publications the heavy responsibility of the Tsarist Government—and of other Western Governments—for the war. This active assistance was much appreciated by Germans of all political creeds. It created a certain bond between the two countries, and smoothed the way for the negotiations of the Treaty of Rapallo in 1922 and for the subsequent intimate collaboration of the *Reichswehr* and the Red Army, to the advantage of both sides—a fact which deserves to be kept in mind in view of future potentialities.

Of President Wilson's pronouncements during the war there was one upon which leading German politicians relied most. It was his address at Baltimore on April 6, 1918, in which he said: "To propose anything but justice, even-handed and dispassionate justice, to Germany at any time . . . would be to renounce and dishonor our own cause." The Germans saw in this proclamation the strongest possible guarantee of a just peace. They argued that no Government, least of all the leading Allied Government, could afford to expose itself to the grave accusation that it had, after all, dishonored its own cause, an accusation which would be voiced not only by Germans but by neutral opinion. The German delegation at Versailles drew explicit attention to Wilson's Baltimore address.[172] Did America's rejection of the Treaty definitely eliminate from the realm of political agitation all that the address implied?

One thing is certain, namely, that the United States Government and the American people today have assumed the moral leadership of the world. They had this leadership in 1918 and 1919, but they chose to withdraw from Europe. People over there have strongly maintained that in those years America had a special duty to perform in virtue of her dominant position in the world. It was American military intervention that decided the war in favor of the Allies, and it was an American program, accepted by all, that was to bring permanent peace to the suffering peoples. It was generally felt by the best European spirits that America was in duty bound to see to it that the failures at the Paris Conference would later be amended and adjusted.

No less an authority than Henry L. Stimson, one-time Secretary of State and Secretary of War, keenly felt the American neglect in this respect. He wrote in 1947:

For more than a generation the increasing interrelation of American life with the life of the world has out-paced our thinking and our policy; our refusal to catch up with reality during these years was the major source of our considerable share of responsibility for the catastrophe of World War II.[173]

This points straight back to the events from 1917 to 1919.

When the Weimar Republic was courted into entering the League of Nations, the German Government, on August 28, 1924, issued a solemn public protest against the imposed confession of war guilt. Its proclamation closed with the words: "So long as a member of the community of nations is branded as a criminal to humanity, a real understanding and reconciliation between the peoples is impossible of realization." [174]

This was a valid argument but the plea was turned down by Britain and France. The argument applies in a striking way, however, to the present situation in the summer of 1955, when West Germany is being courted as a powerful partner of the Western European Union. Germany still officially remains the "criminal nation" of 1919, and the "criminal nation" of 1945. For the necessary harmonious relationship between the Union Powers and their new Ally it is obviously indispensable to reconsider past verdicts.

Two thirds of the present German population have, at a mature age, lived through the humiliations and miseries comprised in the term "Versailles," and the younger generation was, until 1945, amply taught about it, not impartially, but very impressively. So the bulk of the Germans have a vivid memory of those times and allegations.

It was under American and British-French leadership that
the Allied and Associated Powers emphasized in their Note
of June 16, 1919, that "reparation for wrongs inflicted is of
the essence of justice." [175] It is expedient in the present situation to apply this principle without delay to the case of Germany. If she was wronged in 1919, reparation involves a
moral rehabilitation within the strict limits of a verdict by
neutral arbitration. Such a course would bring about that
"spiritual regeneration" for which General Marshall pleaded
"in order to re-establish a feeling of good faith among men
generally."

The spirit of the Peace Conference in 1919 offers a fertile
field for such a regeneration.

5. DOCUMENTS

Document 1. President Wilson's Fourteen Points, January
8, 1918:

I. Open covenants of peace, openly arrived at. . . .

II. Absolute freedom of navigation upon the seas. . . .

III. The removal, so far as possible, of all economic barriers
and the establishment of an equality of trade conditions among all
the nations consenting to the peace. . . .

IV. Adequate guarantees given and taken that national armaments will be reduced to the lowest point consistent with domestic
safety.

V. A free, open-minded, and absolutely impartial adjustment of
all colonial claims, based upon a strict observance of the principle
that in determining all such questions of sovereignty the interests
of the populations concerned must have equal weight with the
equitable claims of the government whose title is to be determined.

VI. The evacuation of all Russian territory. . . .

VII. Belgium, the whole world will agree, must be evacuated
and restored, without any attempt to limit the sovereignty which
she enjoys in common with all other free nations. No other single
act will serve as this will serve to restore confidence among the
nations in the laws which they have themselves set and determined
for the government of their relations with one another. Without
this healing act the whole structure and validity of international
law is forever impaired.

VIII. All French territory should be freed and the invaded portions restored, and the wrong done to France by Prussia in 1871
in the matter of Alsace-Lorraine, which has unsettled the peace of

the world for nearly fifty years, should be righted, in order that peace may once more be made secure in the interests of all.

IX. A readjustment of the frontiers of Italy should be effected along clearly recognizable lines of nationality.

X. The peoples of Austria-Hungary . . . should be accorded the freest opportunity of autonomous development.

XI. Rumania, Serbia, and Montenegro should be evacuated. . . .

XII. The Turkish portions of the present Ottoman Empire should be assured a secure sovereignty. . . .

XIII. An independent Polish state should be erected which should include the territories inhabited by indisputably Polish populations, which should be assured a free and secure access to the sea, and whose political and economic independence and territorial integrity should be guaranteed by international covenant.

XIV. A general association of nations must be formed under specific covenants for the purpose of affording mutual guarantees of political independence and territorial integrity to great and small states alike.

Document 2. President Wilson's Four Principles, February 11, 1918:

The principles to be applied are these:

First, that each part of the final settlement must be based upon the essential justice of that particular case and upon such adjustments as are most likely to bring a peace that will be permanent;

Second, that peoples and provinces are not to be bartered about from sovereignty to sovereignty as if they were mere chattels and pawns in a game, even the great game, now forever discredited, of the balance of power; but that

Third, every territorial settlement involved in this war must be made in the interest and for the benefit of the populations concerned, and not as a part of any mere adjustment or compromise of claims amongst rival states; and

Fourth, that all well defined national aspirations shall be accorded the utmost satisfaction that can be accorded them without introducing new or perpetuating old elements of discord and antagonism that would be likely in time to break the peace of Europe and consequently of the world.

Document 3. President Wilson's Four Points, July 4, 1918:

1. The destruction of every arbitrary power anywhere that can separately, secretly, and of its single choice disturb the peace of the world; or, if it cannot be presently destroyed, at least its reduction to virtual impotence.

2. The settlement of every question, whether of territory, or sovereignty, of economic arrangement, or of political relationship,

upon the basis of the free acceptance of that settlement by the
people immediately concerned, and not upon the basis of the material interest or advantage of any other nation or people which may
desire a different settlement for the sake of its own exterior influence or mastery.

3. The consent of all nations to be governed in their conduct
towards each other by the same principles of honor and of respect
for the common law of civilized society that govern the individual
citizens of all modern states in their relations with one another; to
the end that all promises and covenants may be sacredly observed,
no private plots or conspiracies hatched, no selfish injuries wrought
with impunity, and a mutual trust established upon the handsome
foundation of a mutual respect for right.

4. The establishment of an organization of peace which shall
make certain that the combined power of free nations will check
every invasion of right and serve to make peace and justice the
more secure by affording a definite tribunal of opinion to which
all must submit and by which every international readjustment
that cannot be amicably agreed upon by the peoples directly concerned shall be sanctioned.

Document 4. President Wilson's Five Points, September
27, 1918:

First, the impartial justice meted out must involve no discrimination between those to whom we wish to be just and those to whom
we do not wish to be just. It must be a justice that plays no favorites
and knows no standard but the equal rights of the several peoples
concerned;

Second, no special or separate interest of any single nation or
any group of nations can be made the basis of any part of the
settlement which is not consistent with the common interest of all;

Third, there can be no leagues or alliances or special covenants
and understandings within the general and common family of the
League of Nations.

Fourth, and more specifically, there can be no special, selfish
economic combinations within the League and no employment of
any form of economic boycott or exclusion except as the power
of economic penalty by exclusion from the markets of the world
may be vested in the League of Nations itself as a means of dis-
cipline and control.

Fifth, all international agreements and treaties of every kind
must be made known in their entirety to the rest of the world.

Document 5. Essential parts of Count Brockdorff-Rantzau's
speech on May 7, 1919, except the two passages previously
quoted:

Nobody would wish to contend that the catastrophe goes back merely to the fateful moment when the successor to the throne of Austria-Hungary fell a victim to murderous hands. In the past fifty years the imperialism of all European states has constantly poisoned the international situation. The policy of retaliation, the policy of expansion, and a disregard of the right of national self-determination have played their part in that illness of Europe which came to its crisis in the World War. The Russian mobilization made it impossible for statesmen to find a remedy, and threw the final decision into the hands of military power.

Public opinion in every enemy country is echoing the crimes Germany is said to have committed in the war. Here, too, we are ready to admit that unjust things have been done. We have not come here to diminish the responsibility of the men who have waged the war politically and economically, and to deny that breaches of the law of nations have been committed. We repeat the declaration which was made in the German *Reichstag* at the beginning of the war: injustice has been done to Belgium and we shall make reparations.*

But in the manner of waging war, Germany was not the only one that erred. Every European nation knows of deeds and of individuals which the best of their people remember only with regret. I do not want to reply to reproaches with reproaches, but, if we alone are asked to do penance, one should remember the Armistice. Six weeks went by before we obtained an armistice, and six months before we came to know your conditions of peace. Crimes in war may not be excusable, but they are committed in the struggle for victory, when we think only of maintaining our national existence, and are in such passion as makes the conscience of peoples blunt. The hundreds of thousands of non-combatants who have perished since November 11, because of the blockade, were destroyed coolly and deliberately after our opponents had won a certain and assured victory. Remember that, when you speak of guilt and atonement.

The measure of guilt of all those who have taken part can be established only by an impartial inquiry, a neutral commission before which all the principals in the tragedy are allowed to speak,

* The reference is to the speech of Chancellor von Bethmann-Hollweg on August 4, 1914, when he declared: "Our troops have occupied Luxemburg and have possibly already entered on Belgian soil. Gentlemen, that is a breach of international law. . . . We were forced to ignore the rightful protests of Luxemburg and Belgium. The injustice—I speak openly—the injustice we thereby commit we will try to make good as soon as our military aims have been attained." Quoting this passage in *The Great Globe Itself* (New York, 1946), p. 162, William C. Bullitt points out the difference of moral standards in 1914 and in the Fascist epoch.

and to which all archives are open. We have asked for such an inquiry and we ask for it once more.

At this conference, where we alone and without our allies are facing our many opponents, we are not without protection. You yourself have brought us an ally: that justice which was guaranteed us in the agreement as to what should be the principles governing the treaty of peace. In the days between October 5 and November 5, 1918, the Allied and Associated Governments swore that there would be no peace of violence, and inscribed on their knightly banners a peace of justice. . . . The principles of President Wilson thus became binding for both parties to the war, for you as well as for us, and also for our former allies.

Certain of the foregoing principles call upon us to make heavy national and economic sacrifices. But by such a treaty, the sacred and fundamental rights of all peoples would be protected. The conscience of the world would be behind it, and no nation that violated it would go unpunished.

Upon that basis you will find us ready to examine the preliminary peace . . . with the firm intention of joining with you in rebuilding that which has been destroyed, in making good whatever wrong has been committed, above all the injustice to Belgium, and in showing mankind new goals of political and social progress. . . . Our principal problem will be to restore the broken strength of all the nations which took part in the war, and do it by providing international protection for the welfare, health, and freedom of the working classes.

I believe we should then proceed to restore those parts of Belgium and Northern France which have been occupied by us and which have been destroyed by the war. We have taken upon ourselves the solemn obligation to do so, and we are resolved to execute it to the extent which has been agreed upon between us. . . . To continue to have this done by German prisoners of war would be the worst of methods. Unquestionably such work can be done cheaply. But it would cost the world dear if hatred and despair should overcome the German people, forced to think of their sons, brothers, and fathers still held prisoners, and languishing as if in penal servitude. We cannot arrive at a lasting peace without an immediate solution of this problem, a problem which has already been postponed too long.

Experts on both sides will have to give thought as to how the German people can best meet the financial obligations called for by such reparations, without collapsing under the weight of their burden. A financial breakdown would take from those who have a right to reparations the advantages which are theirs by right, and would throw into irreparable disorder the whole European economic system. The victors as well as the vanquished must guard themselves against this menacing danger and its incalculable consequences. There is only one means of removing it: belief without reservation in the economic and social solidarity of all nations, and in a free and all-comprising League of Nations.

Gentlemen, the sublime idea of deriving from the most terrible catastrophe in history the greatest of forward movements in the development of mankind, by means of the League of Nations, has been put forth and will make its way. But only by opening the gates of the League of Nations to all who are of good will can the goal be attained, and only by doing so will it be that those who have died in this war shall not have died in vain.

In their hearts, the German people will resign themselves to their hard lot if the bases of the peace, as mutually agreed upon, are not destroyed. A peace which cannot be defended before the world as a peace of justice would always evoke new resistance. No one could sign it with a clear conscience, for it could not be carried out. No one could venture to guarantee its execution, though this obligation is implied in the signing of the treaty.

We shall, with every good intention, study the document submitted to us, in the hope that our meeting may finally result in something that can be signed by all of us.

Document 6. Articles 227 to 231 of the Treaty of Versailles:

Article 227

The Allied and Associated Powers publicly arraign William II of Hohenzollern, formerly German Emperor, for a supreme offence against international morality and the sanctity of treaties.

A special tribunal will be constituted to try the accused, thereby assuring him the guarantees essential to the right of defence. It will be composed of five judges, one appointed by each of the following Powers: namely, the United States of America, Great Britain, France, Italy and Japan.

In its decision the tribunal will be guided by the highest motives of international policy, with a view to vindicating the solemn obligations of international undertakings and the validity of international morality. It will be its duty to fix the punishment which it considers should be imposed.

The Allied and Associated Powers will address a request to the Government of the Netherlands for the surrender to them of the ex-Emperor in order that he may be put on trial.

Article 228

The German Government recognises the right of the Allied and Associated Powers to bring before military tribunals persons ac-

cused of having committed acts in violation of the laws and customs
of war. Such persons shall, if found guilty, be sentenced to punish-
ments laid down by law. This provision will apply notwithstanding
any proceedings or prosecution before a tribunal in Germany or in
the territory of her allies.

The German Government shall hand over to the Allied and Associated Powers, or to such one of them as shall so request, all persons accused of having committed an act in violation of the laws
and customs of war, who are specified either by name or by the
rank, office or employment which they held under the German
authorities.

Article 229

Persons guilty of criminal acts against the nationals of one of the
Allied and Associated Powers will be brought before the military
tribunals of that Power.

Persons guilty of criminal acts against the nationals of more than
one of the Allied and Associated Powers will be brought before
military tribunals composed of members of the military tribunals
of the Powers concerned.

In every case the accused will be entitled to name his own counsel.

Article 230

The German Government undertakes to furnish all documents
and information of every kind, the production of which may be
considered necessary to ensure the full knowledge of the incriminat-
ing acts, the discovery of offenders and the just appreciation of
responsibility.

Article 231

The Allied and Associated Powers affirm and Germany accepts
the responsibility of Germany and her allies for causing all the
loss and damage to which the Allied and Associated Governments
and their nationals have been subjected as a consequence of the
war imposed upon them by the aggression of Germany and her
allies.

Document 7. Essential passages from the covering letter of
the German delegates and from their counterproposals, May
29, 1919:

. . . We expected the Peace of Right which had been promised
to us. We were grieved when we read this document to see what
conditions victorious Might demanded of us. The more we entered
the spirit of that Treaty, the more we were convinced of the im-

possibility of carrying it out. The demands of that Treaty are beyond the strength of the German people.

. . . Germany has expressly accepted nothing but President Wilson's Fourteen Points and his subsequent proclamations. No other bases have been demanded either by President Wilson, or after him, by any of the Allied Governments.

A solemn agreement as to the basis of peace therefore exists between the two Contracting Parties. Germany has a right to this basis of peace. By abandoning it the Allies would break an international legal agreement.

. . . Our enemies have repeated again and again that this war without parallel should be followed by a new kind of peace, a peace of right and not a peace of might. A new spirit should emanate from this peace and should be embodied in a League of Nations, of which Germany should also be a member.

. . . We appeal to the innate sense of right of men and nations, under whose token the English State developed, the Dutch people freed itself, the North American nation established its independence, France shook off absolutism. The bearers of such hallowed traditions cannot deny this right to the German people, that now for the first time has acquired in its internal politics the possibility of living in harmony with its free will based on law. A treaty such as has been proposed to Germany is incompatible with the respect for this innate right.

. . . Every nation requires the trusting support of its neighbors if it is to become an efficient and reliable member of the family of nations. The new Germany is convinced that it deserves this confidence, and it may therefore demand its place in the League of Nations. Germany's membership in the League of Nations would in itself alone constitute the most inviolable guarantee for the good faith of every German Government.

. . . The new peace must revert to the solemn agreement entered upon by both parties. . . .

Justice and the free agreement of all parties to the treaty will prove to be the strongest, in course of time the only guarantees of the pact to be concluded. In the very moment of founding a new commonwealth, based upon liberty and labor, the German people turns to those who have hitherto been its enemies and demands in the interests of all nations and all human beings, a peace to which it may give its assent in accordance with the dictates of its conscience.

Chapter Three

Tribulations of the Weimar Republic

The political leaders of the first German Republic have been severely criticized for their failure to preserve democracy. This is not the place to discuss in detail the history of the Weimar period from 1919 to January, 1933. A rapid survey of the main factors that eventually destroyed the Republic will fulfill the purpose of this book.

The transformation of Germany's social structure from autocratic monarchy to republicanism was not in reality a natural evolution produced by internal forces in a crisis of the nation. It was much more the direct consequence of President Wilson's clear announcements that the complete elimination of autocracy was indispensable to obtain a peace on his terms.[1] Recognizing this vital necessity, the German people in January, 1919, elected to the National Assembly 350 members of the Socialist, Democratic and Centrist parties, as against 64 conservative members, thereby endorsing by an impressive majority the establishment of the Republic. In a special study, S. William Halperin states that there were nowhere stauncher believers in Wilsonian idealism than the men and women who composed the parties of the Weimar coalition in 1919.[2] Of course, there were considerable sections amongst the Germans whose conversion to democracy was not genuine but was rather a tactical move in the effort to attain a bearable peace. Nevertheless, the potentialities for a firm establishment of the

96

new regime were clearly manifest. The general consensus among Allied observers at the time was, as Sumner Welles has recorded, that the moral conversion of the German people could have been successfully undertaken in 1919 within a brief period.[3] The present writer, who was then active in German public life, is able to confirm the accuracy of this estimate.

The spirit of the peacemakers, as revealed in the foregoing chapter, frustrated the achievement of all such possibilities. The Treaty of Versailles dealt the German Republic a staggering blow at the outset; it almost suffocated it at its birth. Moreover, Versailles and its aftermath thoroughly discredited with the German masses those of their leaders who had pleaded for surrender in 1918 while placing their faith in the Allied assurances given to the German people.[4] Soon these men, mostly Social Democrats, saw themselves betrayed by the victors. Before long they were to be branded by chauvinists and Nazi agitators as despicable traitors to their country, as "The November Criminals" who dealt the undefeated German armies a dastardly "stab in the back" and who cowardly accepted "The Treaty of Shame."

It was a fatal mistake of the Allies at the Peace Conference not to have made a proper distinction between the old Imperial Germany and the new forces in the country that had surged forth chiefly under the impetus given to them by the Western Powers who had so ardently propagated the slogan that they were out to make the world safe for democracy. In reality, they were now, victory won, destroying the fair prospects of democracy which the new Germany offered, as her delegates at Versailles had emphatically warned them they would do if they insisted on their intolerable demands.[5]

A grave mistake was also made by those members of the Weimar coalition who voted for signing the Treaty, although their decision is understandable enough under the harrowing circumstances of the time. They should have heeded the cogent reasons for rejecting the Treaty which the German delegation to Paris stated in their report of June 18, 1919 (see above, p. 63).

It is noteworthy that the veteran leader of German pacifism, Ludwig Quidde, an old-time democrat, beseeched the National Assembly, on historical as well as on moral grounds, not to sign. He foresaw the disastrous consequences for the

New Germany if she put her signature under a Treaty which
contained impossible and dishonoring conditions. Professor
Quidde subsequently hoped in vain for an early change in the
victors' attitude. In the twenties, he repeatedly said, in distress, to the author that the Allies' policy was steadily ruining
German democracy.[6] Indeed, the Democratic Party which, in
January, 1919, polled 74 seats for the Assembly, gradually
lost all influence. In the next elections, June, 1920, it obtained
45 seats out of 466; in May, 1924, only 28 out of 472. And,
in the last free elections, November, 1932, the party, rebap-
tized *Deutsche Staatspartei,* returned only two solitary members to the *Reichstag.*

It indicates a grievous lack of psychological insight that, in
1919, the Allies were blind to the fact that the infant German
Republic, born of defeat and desperately struggling against
internal disruption, needed above all moral encouragement
and sympathetic assistance. Instead, the reverse policy was
applied. This Allied policy in the end proved fatal to the survival of the Republic.[7]

America's repudiation of the Treaty of Versailles in 1920
raised optimistic expectations in Germany that the United
States would use its powerful influence to secure just modifications of the peace terms. Americans rapidly grew popular.
Hugh R. Wilson, who represented the United States in Berlin
as Counsellor of Embassy in the years 1920 and 1921, was
deeply impressed. He wrote:

I have never seen a people of a great nation who so ardently and
vociferously desired peace, friendship and affection. . . . [T]here
was wide-spread and almost pathetic belief that somehow or other
a better international order had been created, that the rest of the
states would disarm, that as soon as Germany's pacific spirit was
recognized the economic bonds of the Treaty would be lifted. . . .
The Germans, then, in 1920, wanted to be friends with the world,
but particularly they wanted to make friends with the Americans.[8]

It caused bitter disappointment throughout Germany when,
in March, 1921, as recorded in the foregoing chapter, the
United States Government expressly reiterated the war guilt
charge, linked as it was with the burden of reparations. In
1919, under the leadership of the Social Democrats, the Germans had protested most vehemently against this charge, as

well as against the indemnity provisions which, in the view of some leading American authorities, rendered inevitable the death of German democracy.[9] It is certainly true that the Weimar Republic never fully recovered from the Versailles Treaty and its admitted basis,[10] and that no item in it was more useful to those who were hostile to the Republic and to the policy of fulfillment than Article 231.[11]

The reparations provisions in 1919 had doleful consequences for both the vanquished and the victors, as Allied experts had foreseen. When Germany became in arrear with some deliveries, Premier Raymond Poincaré seized the opportunity to invade the Ruhr in January, 1923, an action which was severely condemned by British and American opinion.[12] French efforts at that time to set up a separatist "Autonomous Republic" in the Rhineland was, also in English eyes, felt to be treachery to the Weimar Republic.[13]

The Ruhr occupation and German passive resistance to French exploitation of the country's industrial heart had disastrous political and economic results. Ever since the Armistice of November, 1918, German currency had depreciated in value. The normal pre-war rate of exchange for one dollar was 4.20 marks. At the end of 1920 it was 73.37 marks; one year later 184 marks; and at the end of 1922 it had risen to 7,350 marks. Then, in 1923, paper money was printed on a vast scale in a desperate effort to finance the passive resistance. The value of the mark dropped rapidly from day to day until it reached its lowest level in November, 1923, when one dollar was worth more than four billion marks.

For people who have never lived through such an economic and financial catastrophe it is well-nigh impossible to grasp fully all the misery and daily despair that the wild inflation involved. Americans are prone to speak with horror of their "economic blizzard" in the early thirties, but the German inflation of 1923 was infinitely more devastating. Hugh R. Wilson may be cited as a competent witness. He states:

The effects of devaluation are appalling. If I were given the right to condemn to punishment the most iniquitous of peoples, I would never condemn them to devaluation, the results are too barbarous. It meant the destruction of the result of all thrift, the impoverishment of the most stable and bourgeois elements of society. . . . It is the last crucifixion that a people can suffer.[14]

Indeed, the inflation of 1923 was a veritable inferno for Germany's great middle class which was financially ruined within the space of a few months. The British historian, E. H. Carr, has with sound reason expressed the view that the inflation was a greater disaster for Germany than the Versailles Treaty itself.[15] And not only for Germany, because the recollection of this unparalleled economic disaster continually haunted the minds of the German masses so that some years later, during the Great Depression, they flocked to Hitler as their apparent savior from a repetition of their unforgettable experience in 1923.

Poincaré's Ruhr adventure failed in its ultimate aim. It brought about a marked change in French policy under the leadership of Aristide Briand, a European-minded statesman. On the German side, the era of Gustav Stresemann ensued. In September, 1926, Germany was admitted to—or rather welcomed into—the League of Nations, particularly by Great Britain. For Germany it meant a kind of moral satisfaction and it offered her, besides, some political advantages. But the German people were far from enthusiastic about their tardy membership in a League which had been so vigorously condemned by the former Secretary of State, Robert Lansing, whose book was widely read in a German translation.[16] The fact that the League of Nations was the creation of the President of the United States but was promptly rejected by his people as being part and parcel of the Treaty of Versailles made the Germans very sceptical about its usefulness. They had witnessed the fact that the League was unable to prevent aggressions and that it had sanctioned some solutions which appeared to be unjust.[17] But, above all, the League was manifestly an organization managed by the victors for the preservation of the *status quo,* and the German people could entertain but little faith that Article XIX of the League, calling for treaty adjustments, would ever play the healing role which had been assigned to it.[18] Yet, there was a faint hope in Germany that, some day, the Covenant might be altered through American influence in order to make it effective in producing the peaceful adjustments which President Wilson had envisaged. Germans felt, in fact, that there was a clear moral duty of the Americans to strive actively toward this end.

The withdrawal of the United States in 1920 was certainly

a heavy blow to the League. Britons have made much of it. Some of their authors have termed it "a very great disaster," and "as great a tragedy for peace as the failure of German liberals to unify Germany in 1848." [19] They thereby place by implication, or even openly, a grave responsibility upon the United States which the present writer would emphatically reject as highly exaggerated. The leading Western Powers knew perfectly well from the outset the most fatal weakness in the structure and operation of the League, namely, the unanimity principle of Article XIX; and they were from the mid-twenties on well aware of the necessity for revision of some of their peace settlements. They had between them sufficient competence and power to take the required action if there had been sound statesmanship and a determined will, mainly in Great Britain and France, to lay a safer foundation for a durable peace than the architects of the imposed treaties had done in 1919 and 1920. David Lloyd George felt this very keenly. In his *apologia* he reproached the successors of the peacemakers bitterly for their failure to use the League as a revisionary agency. Speaking of Poincaré he stated:

Under his influence . . . the League became not an instrument of peace and goodwill amongst all men, including Germans; it was converted into an organization for establishing on a permanent footing the military and thereby the diplomatic supremacy of France.[20]

In the Briand-Stresemann phase of European history, Germany enjoyed a period of economic prosperity, nursed by voluntary and excessively large loans from abroad, parts of which were spent lavishly for embellishments rather than necessities. Fundamentally, it was more a sham prosperity than a real one, but it brought enormous relief to the country, revived confidence in the Republic, and brightened up Europe's political horizon. After a scrutiny of German elections, Sidney L. W. Mellen drew the conclusion that, in the first election in 1919, before Versailles, "the German people strongly repudiated militarism and aggressive nationalism, and showed their overwhelming preference for a liberal or progressive democratic republic"; that, by May, 1924, after Versailles, the Ruhr struggle, and the inflation, "the German people had made a violent swing toward the militaristic and reactionary Right"; but that, by May, 1928, after four years of slow reconstruction and economic recovery, "they had reversed the previous trend and made unmistakable progress back toward the democratic and non-militaristic line-up of 1919." [21] This hopeful development was cut short by the ravages of the Great Depression, and by two political events in 1931-32, viz., the projected German-Austrian Customs Union, and the stagnating disarmament problem. Both assumed singular importance for the Weimar Republic.

The economic crisis started in the United States in the autumn of 1929. In the opinion of Secretary of State Cordell Hull, it was largely caused, and certainly accentuated, by America's high tariffs.[22] The "economic blizzard" hit Germany with special ferocity. Foreign loans, which had been so generously offered during the prosperity period, were now called in. The number of unemployed soared. To mitigate the fatal impact of the crisis, Germany and Austria negotiated a Customs Union early in 1931. France immediately protested, followed by Czechoslovakia and Italy. France withdrew considerable sums from Germany as a means of applying political pressure. Her opposition was the decisive factor in wrecking the project. This precipitated the final collapse of the Weimar Republic.[23]

In the question of disarmament Germany had an undisputed case embodied in the Versailles Treaty itself; for the limitation of her army to 100,000 men was to be the first step towards general disarmament. Great Britain made strenuous efforts in this direction but the continental Powers held back. Germany was especially anxious about the security of East Prussia, severed from the Reich by the Polish "Corridor" and claimed by many Poles as theirs by right. The province would be an easy prey. With a frontier open for long stretches to invasion, Germany's position in the heart of Europe was practically defenseless, and therefore "unspeakably humiliating," as British and American authorities admitted.[24] The whole country was roused to indignation over this intolerable situation. Lloyd George severely criticized the post-war statesmen of Britain's Allies because they refused to carry out the solemn undertaking they gave to Germany in 1919 that, once she were disarmed, they would follow her example.[25] Finally, in December, 1932, a Conference at Geneva granted Germany, in principle, equality of rights in armaments, within a system that would give security to all nations concerned, a justified provision but one which held out little prospect for early achievement.

A shrewd observer at the Disarmament Conference, Hugh R. Wilson, gained there the conviction that practically no French Government had the faintest intention of surrendering or impairing its power to dictate to Germany.[26] This was, in fact, a general impression and it bears out a blunt statement Lord Londonderry, Secretary of State for Air at that time, made in a letter to Sir Henry Page Croft, namely, that "the French deliberately wrecked every possible chance of accommodation at Geneva." [27]

The Government of Dr. Heinrich Brüning, who became Chancellor of the Reich in March, 1930, was thought by many foreign diplomatists in 1932 to be the last stronghold of the Republic.[28] Numerous authorities believe that Brüning could have been kept in power if only a fraction of the concessions which Hitler extorted from the Western Powers a few years later had been granted to him. A comparatively small concession in the question of armaments, vital for Germany's security and national honor, might well have been decisive.[29] It is in this connection noteworthy that, in the presidential elections in April, 1932, some weeks before Brüning's fall, Hindenburg obtained nearly six million more votes than Hitler could poll, despite a lavish Nazi campaign—a clear popular demonstration in favor of the maintenance of the Republic.

It is true that there were concessions in 1932. At the Lausanne Conference, in the summer of that year, the reparations calamity was definitely ended, however not through any good-will action of the Allies. It was an enforced result of the depression. Therefore, the effect on the German people was much impaired, the more so as the economic crisis was then at its peak, reviving the terrifying spectre of a new inflation inferno.

Incidentally, Brüning's successor, Franz von Papen, endeavored at the Lausanne Conference to have the war guilt clause of the Versailles Treaty cancelled on the ground that it was directly linked with the indemnity provision. Prime Minister Ramsay MacDonald was sympathetic, but Premier Edouard Herriot declined. Compliance with the German request would have buttressed the Republic.[30]

Born of defeat and crushingly humbled at Versailles, the Weimar Republic was never popular with the German masses. Hostility from the Nationalists, the Communists, and from the National Socialists grew steadily with the years as they went by without resounding successes in foreign affairs. The "economic blizzard" shook the Republic to its very foundations. Its internal difficulties are well summarized by C. W. Guillebaud, who saw in it a state "sorely tried from within and without, lacking above all in internal unity of purpose, and finally brought to ruin by the greatest economic depression of modern times," a state in which, during seven out of its fourteen years of rule—the liquidation of the war until the end of inflation, 1919 to 1923, and the depression, 1930 to 1932—its normal administration was "virtually paralyzed." [31]

Stressing the impact of external forces on the Republic, William Harbutt Dawson found that, in 1933, there was a Germany quite other than its enemies had designed, largely because the Allies had

done the utmost to weaken and destroy Germany—in body by annexations, in pocket by the reparations, in reputation by misrepresentation and calumny, in spirit by an accumulation of affronts and humiliations of every imaginable kind.[32]

Considering the tribulations the Weimar Republic had to endure from 1919 to 1932, scholars have, therefore, come to the conclusion that its survival "during these years of suffering and shame" was "a wonder." [33]

British diplomatists have laid the chief blame for the Republic's short-lived existence at France's door. Lord Tyrrell, Ambassador to Paris, on March 20, 1933, wrote that the fatal mistakes of French post-war diplomacy led to the discrediting of the Weimar Republic "and to the very reaction which we are witnessing," namely Hitler's election success on March 5.[34] More objective was Lord Tyrrell's colleague in Berlin, Sir Horace Rumbold, who declared that "our" post-war policy toward Germany was deplorable, adding: "The French are principally to blame for this but we must share the blame owing to the subservience of our policy to that of the French." [35]

Chapter Four

Why Hitler Rose to Power

INTRODUCTION

In preceding chapters there have been repeated references to the fact that one of the most notable results of the Treaty of Versailles and the fall of the Weimar Republic was the rise of Adolf Hitler and the establishment of National Socialism in Germany. In this chapter, we shall examine the more important causes of Hitler's advent to power. The material is divided into two sections. The first deals with "Hidden and Indirect Factors" accounting for Hitler's rise, chiefly moral and material support from abroad. It throws light on a field which has so far been inadequately explored. It presents unusual difficulties and challenges further research. The second section sets forth the "Obvious and Direct Factors," mostly acknowledged as such, that explain Hitler's triumph. The chapter ends with the conclusions to be drawn from the material presented in the preceding two sections, and the various factors are ranged according to their relative importance for Hitler's rise.

An Appendix, printed at the end of this book, exposes the untruths and falsifications contained in an English, a Dutch, and five Swiss publications of the years 1933, 1936, 1948, 1949, and 1952, regarding the alleged financing of Hitler and the Nazi movement before 1933 by American corporations to the amount of more than $32 million. The documentary evidence exposing the untruths and falsifications involving the Guaranty Trust Co., General Motors, J. P. Morgan & Co.,

105

Standard Oil Co., Henry Ford, and others, is published in this Appendix to the book.

1. HIDDEN AND INDIRECT FACTORS

In the vast literature on Hitler's rise to power, the factor of moral and material support given to him from abroad has been rather scantily treated. Such aid was given to him chiefly for his campaign against Moscow and Communism.

An outstanding example of moral support was an article which Viscount Rothermere, after a lengthy interview with Hitler, published in his *Daily Mail* on September 24, 1930. Impressed by the rapidly growing Nazi movement, he wrote:

I believe it would be a blunder for the British people to take up an attitude of hostility towards it. . . . If we examine this transfer of political influence in Germany to the National Socialists we shall find that it has many advantages for the rest of Europe. It sets up an additional rampart against Bolshevism. It eliminates the grave danger that the Soviet campaign against civilization might penetrate to Germany thus winning an impregnable position in the strategical center of Europe. . . . For the welfare of Western civilization it would be of the best possible augury that a Government should come to power in Germany inspired with the same sound principles as those by which Signor Mussolini in the past eight years has regenerated Italy.

Hitler's paper, the *Völkischer Beobachter,* was given the privilege of printing the entire article in German on the 25th, with glaring headlines splashed over the front-page: "HITLER'S VICTORY—REGENERATION OF THE GERMAN NATION. A NEW ERA IN WORLD POLITICS, by Viscount Rothermere." The next day, the editor, Alfred Rosenberg, commented at length on the Englishman's enthusiastic effusion with glowing satisfaction. His London correspondent telegraphed on the 25th that Lord Rothermere's sensational article on Germany was attracting much attention in London's diplomatic and political circles.[1]

Nazi propaganda made the utmost of this praise. It had a very powerful psychological effect on German sceptics and waverers. They naturally concluded: "If a British politician of Rothermere's calibre sees so much good for Europe in National Socialism, then we may safely join the Party." In the press, over the radio, and in meetings the Germans were continually reminded of such foreign admirers of Nazism.

Viscount Rothermere continued to support Hitler, personally, and through his representative in Germany, G. Ward Price. The books which both published bear witness to this fact.[2] There were, of course, other foreign moral and political supporters in the early thirties, but, because of the wide circulation of Rothermere's newspapers, he and Price were the most influential of all.

The general financing of the *Nationalsozialistische Deutsche Arbeiterpartei* (abbreviated NSDAP) and its various organizations has puzzled many economists, and has given rise to much speculation. In 1938, R. W. Seton-Watson thought that it would probably never be known what practical forms the assistance from German industrialists assumed and how far it contributed to the Nazi triumph. He added:

Still less likely is it that the persistent allegations of foreign financial help will ever be clearly established. If, however, all these varied threads be woven together, it might doubtless be argued that they form a vast pattern in the web of fate and are far from being merely accidental.[3]

The difficulties foreseen by the British historian before the war have since multiplied. If Hitler had turned out to be a benefactor of mankind, his financial backers would hardly object to revealing their credit for Hitler's rise. But, since he ultimately brought disaster to Europe, all those who, erring in judgment, assisted him would now prefer to keep their contributions to the Nazi movement secret.

The question of non-German financial aid given to the NSDAP has been casually discussed in a number of books and in articles in the press, but thus far no comprehensive study has been published. In the following pages an attempt is made to throw some light on the subject. The falsifications treated in the Appendix are an emphatic warning to proceed with due caution in such a delicate and obscure matter. On the other hand, it is imperative to present all the available material in order to facilitate further research. The hope may also be expressed that persons who know positive facts, one way or the other, will be encouraged to disclose them in the service of history.

At the outset, the writer wishes to underscore his conviction that the bulk of the Party's huge outlays was provided by *German* transactions. Yet, there is sufficient evidence to show that foreign financial contributions were a factor of no mean importance for Hitler's advent to power.

In a letter which was widely read, ex-Chancellor Dr. Heinrich Brüning stated in 1947:

One of the main factors in Hitler's rise . . . was the fact that he received large sums of money from foreign countries in 1923 and later, and was well paid for sabotaging the passive resistance in the Ruhr district. In later years he was paid to foment disorder and to encourage revolutionary tendencies in Germany by men who imagined that this might weaken Germany permanently and make the survival of any constitutional, central government impossible.[4]

This statement, coming as it does from a generally highly esteemed statesman with wide experience, deserves the closest attention.

We have to separate Hitler's early period, up to the time of his famous beer-hall *Putsch* on November 8/9, 1923, from his later years because of the inflation which has been described in the foregoing chapter.

From about the middle of 1922 onward Hitler's still very modest movement was chiefly supported by foreign exchange. Dr. Gansser collected money in Switzerland (330,000 francs), Baron von Bissing in Holland; Czech crowns came from Sudeten Germans, other contributions from Sweden and from Germans with American connections.[5]

A witness of dubious integrity, Werner Abel, alleged that an Italian, Migliorati, evidently acting for Mussolini, gave Hitler a considerable sum in 1923 for a pledge that he would never claim the South Tyrol. The truth of this has been denied. On the other hand, Frenchmen of repute assert that Mussolini supported Hitler financially, and with arms, from 1930 to 1932.[6] This does not seem to have been definitely cleared up.

But it appears to be an established fact that, in 1922-23, French money flowed into Hitler's coffer. It sounds incredible and requires a plausible explanation.

At the end of the First World War influential French elements had fostered separatist movements in the Rhineland and the Palatinate. As mentioned above, they were revived when French and Belgian troops occupied the Ruhr in January, 1923. In June of that year, there was a trial for high treason in Munich. It was ascertained that the two chief accused, Professor Georg Fuchs and Hugo Machhaus, had worked for the return of the Bavarian Kings, that an agent of the French Secret Service, Lieutenant Colonel Augustin-Xavier Richert, had supplied them with "more than a hundred million marks," and that part of this money was passed on to the Swastika movement. Machhaus, who committed suicide in prison, had earlier been an editor of Hitler's *Völkischer Beobachter*.[7]

A French publicist, Paul Allard, has furnished further remarkable details. According to him, Fuchs and Machhaus were reported to have received 560,000 French francs from Colonel Richert. And Allard states:

It is certain that amongst Hitler's friends and confederates were several separatists who were incontestably subventioned by the Quai d'Orsay. On the other hand it cannot be denied that the French diplomatic and military occupation authorities had been kept informed, beforehand and from day to day, of the preparations for the *Putsch* Hitler-Ludendorff, and that they had encouraged it.

In addition, Allard reproduces a letter written to him by "an eminent diplomatic official" who had served for twenty-five years in Germany. This Frenchman wrote:

In 1932, at a time when it became evident that Hitler would come into power, urgent steps were taken in order to have published in all German papers a receipt signed by Hitler which proved irrefutably that he had been subventioned from the Secret Funds. At that time the German press was still independent, and the German people would have been able to judge by which means Hitler had been helped on in his ascendancy. But those steps met with a formal *veto*. The objection was that such a revelation would have aggravated the dissatisfaction which England and America had already manifested toward France on account of the Rhenish separatist movement.[8]

The urgent steps were, in all probability, taken by German politicians who had obtained inside knowledge of the 1923 affair. And it was, of course, the French Foreign Office, or its Secret Service, which refused to hand over the receipt.

The writer of the letter wished to remain anonymous, but Allard considered his information authentic. Could his correspondent have invented the story? Not very likely.

It is quite plausible that Hitler and Ludendorff would seek
to make sure that, if they launched their projected *Putsch,* the
French, being already in the Ruhr, would not seize the opportunity provided by the ensuing turmoil in Germany for a
further advance into German territory. It was plainly in the
interest of the French to encourage a restoration in Bavaria.
Hitler, himself, may well have pretended that he favored a
return of the Wittelsbachers. He used the same trick in 1932
and in January, 1933, when he made vague promises for an
eventual restoration of the Hohenzollerns.

Allard declares that Hitler, in 1923, "manifestly courted"
the French; that his battle-cry then was not "Down with the
French!" but "Down with the November Criminals!" [9] In fact,
while virtually all Germany was united in passive resistance
to Poincaré's Ruhr adventure, Hitler rather welcomed it as
an opportunity for him to seize power in Munich, from which
he would march on Berlin—not against the French (for the
time being). This led to the charge that Hitler had been in
"French pay." This was not true in the sense of the usual
interpretation of the term. As for the seemingly impressive sum
of "more than a hundred million marks," it amounted actually
to only about $25,000 because of the inflation.

Fortuitously, the present writer became involved in this
money affair. Early in October, 1923, E. D. Morel, Labour
Party member of Parliament, told us, when our guest in
Munich, that Hitler was being supplied with money by the
French, probably without suspecting its origin. Morel had
learned this from a former French Cabinet Minister who was
in close touch with the Quai d'Orsay and whose written information he regarded as reliable. Morel did not know of Machhaus' trial. For a week I acted as interpreter for my English
friend at interviews with Bavarian statesmen and politicians,
and each time the French money was discussed. Morel intended to enlighten Hitler himself who, however, did not respond to an invitation for a meeting.

The evidence here presented from German, French and
British sources strongly supports Dr. Brüning's statement for
the year 1923. It was a unique episode in Hitler's career
which he never forgot. In the mid-twenties some of his adversaries used Morel's revelations effectively as a political weapon
in order to discredit the Nazi movement. Subsequently, Hitler
declared repeatedly that in those years nothing had done so

much harm to his cause as "that malicious, damned lie" invented by "that international pig of a dog" (*Schweinehund*) Morel. The episode rankled so deeply in his mind that, even ten years later, as Chancellor, in an interview with Mr. St. John Gaffney, formerly American Consul General in Munich, he gave vent to his resentment in such violent terms that this gentleman warned us immediately of Hitler's vindictive feelings.[10]

The fact is that, whenever foreign financial support for the Party was mentioned, Hitler flew into a rage. For instance, at a lawsuit against Werner Abel in 1932, when directly questioned about his foreign monetary sources, Hitler foamed at the mouth and was fined RM 1,000 for contempt of court and for refusal to answer.[11]

An early member of the NSDAP who assisted it during the inflation period with foreign exchange, was Kurt G. W. Ludecke. He was familiar with conditions in the United States. When, after the abortive *Putsch* of November, 1923, Hitler planned the reconstruction of his Party, he gave Ludecke a written authorization, dated January 4, 1924, to collect funds in America. Reproducing a photostat of this document in 1937, because he had fallen out with the Nazis when they came into power, Ludecke commented: "In court and out, Hitler has repeatedly and emphatically denied ever having solicited—let alone accepted—money from abroad. His own letter gives him the lie." [12]

The truth is that Hitler, as a former Prussian Minister has asserted, systematically collected funds all over the world.[13]

On this subject the writer had the privilege of a correspondence with an Anglo-Saxon ex-diplomat of high standing who did excellent service in Berlin during Hitler's rise to power, subsequently in a country neighboring on Germany, and later on in the Western Hemisphere. He wrote, in summary:

I had to inform myself as much as I could on the financing of the Party, especially before it came into power. . . . That the Party did solicit funds and commissioned persons to do so, from non-Germans, there is no doubt, and there is also no doubt that they did receive considerable moral and financial support from non-Germans. These men made those contributions not because they thought they were contributing to a cause which was fighting Communism, but because they thought the Party was going to control Germany and eventually Europe and would be a tremendous force,

and they wanted to be in the favor of the Party in their respective
countries when all this came about. There are those who could
mention names of such persons who out of personal ambition made
these financial contributions and/or because they thought their
business would be favoured by the Party if they contributed considerable sums. . . . There were some of us, of wide experience
in many countries, who had a pretty good idea of who was contributing, and I would not like the impression that most of these
were in England or the U.S.A., as you might gather from a remark
made previously in this letter. There were a good many of these
in the Scandinavian countries, in Holland and in other European
countries.[14]

This was written for guidance in research work, and sincere
gratitude is due for the privilege of being able to profit by
this distinguished diplomat's expert knowledge.

In May, 1928, during the elections for the *Reichstag,* the
NSDAP polled roughly 800,000 votes, obtaining 12 seats out
of a total of 491. But, after the Great Depression set in, late
in 1929, the Party grew rapidly in proportion to the increasing
intensity of the social misery. In the elections of September,
1930, its votes soared to nearly 6,500,000, and it won 107
seats out of 577. This was the time when Viscount Rothermere
proclaimed his enthusiasm all over Great Britain for the Party
and its leader. The Nazi movement now became a serious
factor in relation to both foreign policies and international
trade. The "economic blizzard" ravaged most of Europe, even
most of the industrial world, and big business in and outside of
Germany turned its attention more and more to the man who
lavishly assured the suffering masses that, when once in power,
he would be their savior from both economic distress and the
growing Bolshevist threat. In the elections of July, 1932, the
votes for the NSDAP reached a peak of nearly 13,750,000,
and they returned 230 members to the *Reichstag* out of 608.
Hitler's final triumph appeared to be certain. The years 1931
and 1932 were the time when business people in countries
surrounding Germany considered it politic to ingratiate themselves with the prospective master of Germany and eventually
—they believed—of Europe.

It is a matter for speculation, until further research has been
carried on, which branches or types of foreign industry de-

termined to support Hitler by financial contributions. For one branch we have some clues, namely, the armaments industry.

It was unfortunate that the Disarmament Conference at Geneva tackled its extremely difficult task at a time when a large percentage of Europe's heavy industry was idle. For these business interests, general disarmament, as decreed by the Peace Treaty in 1919, meant now, in the world-wide depression, a grave menace which must, they thought, be combated.[15] Indeed, some authorities contend that the Geneva Conference was more or less sabotaged by agents of the munitions makers.[16]

In February, 1932, Paul Faure, a specialist on the French armaments industry and Secretary General of the Socialist Party, asserted in the *Chambre des Députés* that two directors of the famous Skoda factory in Czechoslovakia had helped to finance the Nazi elections in Germany, namely, Herr von Duschnitz and Herr von Arthaber. M. Faure pointed out that Skoda was then controlled by Schneider-Creusot, the chief French armaments manufacturers, and that the German-Czech directors would not have acted contrary to French wishes. Faure's charges were never disputed.[17]

It is noteworthy for our topic that William E. Dodd, American Ambassador to Germany from 1933 to 1937, learned soon after his arrival in Berlin that the French munitions makers had helped Hitler to power.[18] That does not necessarily mean financial assistance. The explanation may be found in activities of the *Comité des Forges* which are discussed below.

More illuminating than Dodd's entry in his diary is an entry in a German diary, according to which General von Schleicher, while Chancellor, said early in January, 1933:

Hitler must be arrested, his Party dissolved and outlawed, the whole scandal of the Nazis' revenues brought to light, their connection with the armaments industry abroad, with Deterding, with Ivar Kreuger made public.[19]

The diarist is believed to have been General Kurt von Bredow, an intimate friend of General von Schleicher. Both were murdered in the massacre of June 30, 1934. It may be taken for granted that they knew the contents of a file of papers in the possession of the Prussian police which proved that foreign financial support was being given to the Hitler movement.[20] Apparently, the file disappeared after the Nazis came into power.

It is striking that General von Schleicher put in first place the Party's connection with the foreign armaments industry about which more will be said presently. With regard to Ivar Kreuger, the Match King, it is on record that he told an American banker his business interests would profit greatly by Hitler's election to the Presidency (1932).[21] Some authors assert that, after Kreuger's suicide, a receipt for 100,000 marks, signed by Hitler, was found among his papers, and that he had repeatedly given large sums to the Nazis as the natural enemies of the Soviet Union from which Kreuger obtained aspen wood for his matches.[22] A far more important person for the NSDAP, however, was the Oil King, Sir Henri Deterding of the Royal Dutch and Shell Combine.

Deterding's power behind the scenes has been compared to that of the mysterious Sir Basil Zaharoff, the Armaments King. Before World War I, Deterding had acquired large oil interests in the Caucasus region which he wished to regain from the Russians. He became a passionate anti-Bolshevik and collaborated with Russian émigrés, with Ukrainian and Georgian nationalists, and with General Hoffmann, Ludendorff's former Chief-of-Staff, in laying out grand schemes for wresting the oilfields from Moscow's grip. Hoffmann, an expert in warfare against Russians, was to lead the military operations.[23] In the early thirties, Deterding regarded the struggle against the Communists as "the only task left for him to accomplish." [24] He was, thus, a natural ally of Adolf Hitler.

In 1932, the Netherlands' press reported that the Dutch-born Sir Henri had subsidized the NSDAP with 4,000,000 gulden, a statement which was allegedly never denied.[25] To avoid publicity, Deterding used as an intermediary Dr. Georg Bell, a Bavarian of Scotch parentage. Bell was a political adventurer, connected with various intelligence services, and had for years been intimate with the Nazi publicist Alfred Rosenberg—hanged in 1946—and also with the leader of the SA, the Storm Troopers, Captain Ernst Roehm—killed in the "purge" of 1934. But, around 1932, Bell—for reasons not yet clearly established—began to furnish Dr. Fritz Gerlich, an ardent anti-Nazi in Munich, with material about the underworld activities of the Party for his weekly *Der Gerade Weg* (The Straight Path). Immediately after the *Reichstag* fire, February 27, 1933, Bell brought Dr. Gerlich several important documents, one of which was a contract of the NSDAP, represented by Chief-of-Staff Roehm, with the English-Dutch petroleum King Deterding, concerning the financing of the SA in the years before the seizure of power, against the assurance to favor his oil interests after the seizure of power.[26]

Gerlich took this contract to the State President of Wuerttemberg, Herr Eugen Bolz, and to Prince Erich von Waldburg-Zeil. They were all deeply impressed by the document and highly indignant that the German campaign against Hitler was thus seriously undermined by assistance to the Nazis from abroad.[27] The Prince arranged to have the paper smuggled into Switzerland.

Early in March, 1933, before Gerlich could make public use of the documentary material provided by Bell, the office of *Der Gerade Weg* was stormed by SA men. Bell was at the moment with Gerlich and managed to escape over the roofs, while Gerlich was beaten and arrested. Bell fled to Austria, but a month later he was murdered there near the German border by some of Roehm's thugs, because of his suspected disaffection, and because he knew too much about the *Reichstag* fire, about Roehm's private life, and "about the subventions going into the millions which Deterding put at the disposal of the Hitler Party for its fight against Bolshevism." [28]

Fritz Gerlich was shot in Dachau on June 30, 1934; Bolz was hanged by the Nazis in 1945; and Prince Erich von Waldburg-Zeil died in May, 1953. So there seems to be no witness living who has seen the contract of Deterding with Roehm. In view of Bell's career and reputation, the existence of that document, therefore, needs corroboration. The following arguments may be advanced.

The higher Nazi circles were familiar with Hitler's plan eventually to induce Poland to join in a crusade against the Soviet Union for the "liberation" of the Ukraine and the Caucasian populations. This plan—which will be discussed in another book—evidently offered much brighter prospects for the realization of Sir Henri Deterding's ambitions than the insurrection projects he had sponsored in the early twenties. Marshal Pilsudski, the ruler of Poland, was known to cherish the idea of forming, under Polish leadership, a federation of states which would comprise the Baltic countries, White Russia, and the Ukraine.

Deterding had worked his way up from a modest bank clerk

to a dominant figure in the world's oil industry. As a shrewd calculator, he would naturally think of making certain that he would get adequate compensation for his outlay. It is recorded that, at Christmas 1936, he presented Hitler with a hundredweight of platinum, well worth 300,000 marks, which the *Fuehrer* graciously accepted with the significant remark that he would use the platinum for the manufacture of medical instruments.[29] Deterding had also been a good friend of Hermann Göring ever since the latter's early days.[30] Why, then, did he not make a contract with one of these men who stood higher in the Party's hierarchy than Roehm who, besides, had an unsavory personal reputation? The explanation may well be his knowledge, through Bell, of Roehm's vast, ambitious program, namely, the incorporation of the SA, numbering by 1934—after the inclusion of the *Stahlhelm,* the *Kyffhäuserbund* and other nationalistic organizations—4,500,000 men, into the *Reichswehr,* with himself as the supreme Commander-in-Chief of a huge People's Army. In former years, Sir Henri had been in contact with General Hoffmann as the prospective head of military operations against Soviet Russia. It would be in keeping with this precedent that he would subsidize, from about 1930 onward, not so much the NSDAP as the future German Army that was to carry out the dream of his life.

Thus far, there is no absolute proof of the existence of the alleged contract. Is it likely that Bell would have dared to invent the story and to fake a document of such importance at a time when his employer, Sir Henri, could have exposed him as a forger? Fritz Gerlich found that Bell's information as given to him always proved reliable.[31] All circumstances considered, it is certainly plausible that such a contract was at least seriously discussed between the two partners, if not actually concluded.

It is noteworthy that E. A. Mowrer heard "unfriendly Germans" accuse Deterding of having put up a considerable sum for the 1932 presidential campaign in the hope ("or on the promise?" Mowrer inserted) "of being granted an oil monopoly in the Third Empire." [32] When Sir Henri Deterding died in February, 1939, the German press was instructed not to mention that he had been a sincere friend of Nazi Germany.[33]

The total amount of his subventions must remain uncertain. One rumor mentioned £55,000,000,[34] a figure so fantastically high that it does not deserve credence. But a conversation which Ambassador Dodd had with the Dutch Minister in Berlin on November 8, 1934, is revealing. Dodd told him that Sir Henri Deterding was supposed to be coming to see Hitler soon, and asked: "Does Sir Henri support Sir Oswald Mosley, England's Fascist Fuehrer?" The Dutch Minister replied: "I know him well and I am sure he would give Mosley £100,000 to help him win." [35] If Sir Henri was thought liberal enough to give the weak British Fascist leader two million marks, it may be safely concluded that his contributions over the years to the Hitler movement, infinitely more important to him, comprised a good many millions of marks. He may surely be considered the largest single foreign financial backer of the NSDAP.[36]

For a true perspective in the matter of foreign monetary contributions we have to review the budget of the NSDAP and its organizations. The largest of these was the SA, which had its own fiscal administration. Alan Bullock estimated that the maintenance of the SA around 1933-34 must have involved an expenditure of something like 2,800,000 marks a week.[37] When Roehm's dreams were wrecked in the "purge" of 1934, the debts of his SA are said to have amounted to from sixty to one hundred million marks.[38]

It is generally accepted that, in January, 1933, when Hitler was put into power, the debt of the Party proper ranged from ten to twelve million marks. But Professor Edgar Prochnik, formerly in the Austrian diplomatic service and Minister in Washington, obtained information, which seems reliable, that, by 1933, the total debts of the NSDAP and its organizations had soared roughly to $40,000,000, or to about 130,000,000 marks at the rate of exchange in that year.[39] These debts appear to have been covered—though probably not wholly—by the Reich Government and by individual Germans.[40] One of these was Fritz Thyssen, who also mentioned to Mr. Emery Reves, the editor of his book *I Paid Hitler* (New York, 1941), that Sir Henri Deterding was one of the foreigners who gave financial aid to Hitler.[41]

In view of the fact that Franz von Papen's decisive meeting with Adolf Hitler on January 4, 1933, took place at the home of the banker, Baron Kurt von Schröder, in Cologne, the surmise has been publicly expressed that his banking house,

J. H. Stein, solicited financial contributions from friends abroad, and that the banking houses of Schroeder in London and New York themselves made large contributions. None of these assertions are true.[42]

On the other hand, it is remarkable that, in the early thirties, official and political circles in Austria were convinced that Hitler was being financed from abroad.[43] In this matter, there is a sweeping statement on record by the publicist, Pierre van Paassen. He was well acquainted with the chief Nazi leaders during the years of the Party's rise to power, and he declared in 1946, on the strength of the knowledge he had acquired in contacts with them: "It never was a secret that Hitler was the creature of international finance." He states as a fact that financial contributions had come "from Dutch, French, Czechoslovak, British, Belgian, and other industrialists, munitioneers, and bankers." [44] Yet Pierre van Paassen has so far not published any evidence to prove his contention. He would do well to submit his material.

In conclusion, a curious incident should be mentioned. After the *Reichstag* elections in September, 1930, the Prussian State Secretary, Herr Weismann, told the British Ambassador that the funds for the Nazi election campaign, running into millions, "must come from Russia." He argued that it was obviously in the interest of the Soviets to create a state of confusion in Germany. In his report on the conversation, the Ambassador added that Weismann, speaking of Moscow funds for the NSDAP, thereby confirmed a statement to that effect alleged by the press to have been made by Besedovski, the former Counsellor of the Soviet Embassy at Paris.[45] This would have been quite in accord with the Kremlin's calculation "After Hitler, Our Turn" (see below, p. 139).

The idea that Hitler, once in power, would, in the prevailing difficult times, soon have "mismanaged himself out of office," was then widespread. This idea animated millions of Germans opposed to Hitler, who believed that the surest way of getting rid of him speedily, was to let him have a try at the helm, with all the responsibilities attached to it. The idea also stimulated foreign statesmen and politicians who thought, as Dr. Brüning has observed, that Hitler's advent would foment disorder in Germany and weaken the country. It was a plausible speculation, considering Hitler's violent ways and his inexperience in diplomacy and statesmanship. The idea also appears to have inspired certain French actions.

The reader will recall that Ambassador William E. Dodd learned soon after his arrival in Berlin that the French munitions makers had helped Hitler to power. This may well sound incredible because Hitler in his book, *Mein Kampf,* had frankly proclaimed France to be Germany's mortal enemy. But Mr. Dodd recorded, moreover, on April 20, 1937:

The French Ambassador, whose country did most to start Germany on its military course, seemed miserable, although a part of his fortune had come to him from huge sales of arms during the early Hitler régime.[46]

Unaware of these statements, Louis P. Lochner, for many years Bureau Chief of the Associated Press in Berlin, wrote:

If there was one foreign statesman who thoroughly misjudged Hitler and his movement, it was André François-Poncet, the French Ambassador to Berlin. From what I know of behind-the-scenes activities toward the end of the Brüning era in 1932, I am forced to conclude that no other diplomat is more directly responsible for the elevation to power of Adolf Hitler than this brilliant, for-ever-wisecracking French politician.

According to François-Poncet, the incorruptible Chancellor Heinrich Brüning was too brainy and experienced in the wily game of international politics. Hitler, on the other hand, was a fool and a political dilettante—as he expressed it to the late American Ambassador William E. Dodd. With the Nazi leader in power, he thought, it would be much easier to effect deals which would be favorable to France. Therefore, it would be better to have Adolf Hitler in the chancellor's chair rather than Heinrich Brüning.

The French Ambassador to Germany was a weighty personality in those days. His opinion influenced not only the Quai d'Orsay but Downing Street and the foreign offices of numerous satellites that had hitched their wagon to the French star. So it is not too much to say that François-Poncet is a partial answer to the question, "Why Wasn't Hitler Stopped?"[47]

In the passages quoted there are two statements relevant to the present chapter, namely, that of Ambassador Dodd to the effect that the French munitions makers had helped Hitler to power, and the other by Mr. Lochner asserting that the French Ambassador was partly responsible for Hitler's elevation to power. Since these statements were made by distinguished Americans who had abundant opportunities for gathering information, they have to be carefully examined in an effort to establish real facts.

The opinions expressed by the two foreign observers have to be considered in their proper setting. They are connected with the economic depression of the thirties and with two major causes within the depression which contributed largely to the fall of the Brüning Government on May 30, 1932. They were the wrecking of the projected German-Austrian Customs Union and the frustration of the disarmament problem, both of which have been described in the foregoing chapter.

We have also to consider M. André François-Poncet's political career as it may be traced from available sources. He had early links with French heavy industry. In 1919, he was attached to the *Comité des Forges* when the Allies sent an economic mission to the United States. In 1922, he founded the *Société d'Études et d'Information Économiques* in Paris, and was in 1923, during the Ruhr occupation, economic adviser to the Commanding General there. Later, in the twenties, he directed the newspaper *L'Avenir,* which represented the interests of the *Comité des Forges,* "embracing all the important units of the heavy industry." In André Tardieu's Cabinet, 1930, he was Under-Secretary for Foreign Affairs, and Under-Secretary for National Economy. Subsequently, he was Under-Secretary of State to the Prime Minister's office in Pierre Laval's Cabinet, in 1931. In September of that year, he went to Germany as Ambassador. Through his marriage he had, according to some reports, acquired substantial holdings in the Lorraine steel industry.[48]

It is said that François-Poncet was selected for the post in Berlin because of his knowledge of business and finance.[49] But he was also a recognized expert on German affairs, with a complete mastery of the language. When once, among the staff of *L'Avenir,* the name of Adolf Hitler was mentioned and someone remarked that his movement was not to be taken seriously, M. François-Poncet replied, dryly, "not to be taken seriously for the moment. No more so than the name of Jesus Christ was to be taken seriously—a year before his death." [50]

Of some significance is François-Poncet's appointment to the Cabinet of Tardieu because of the latter's unrelenting attitude towards the Weimar Republic which had been a strongly retarding factor in the disarmament movement. In a recently published biographical study, Franklin L. Ford points out that François-Poncet had been identified with a policy of toughness toward Weimar Germany, because of his criticism of Briand in the Chamber and his known hostility toward the German-Austrian Customs Union.[51] Moreover, Ambassador Dodd recorded that his French colleague stated to him in 1933: "We must annex German territory to the Rhine. Wilson defeated us in this," namely at the Paris Peace Conference in 1919.[52]

Hence, there was understandable apprehension in the Brüning Government when Laval, who had been a lawyer for the *Comité des Forges,* proposed François-Poncet as Ambassador to Germany. German statesmen were gaining the impression that influential elements in the French Army and at the Quai d'Orsay rather welcomed the rise of the Nazis, partly to justify their own armaments claims, and partly in the belief that Hitler would disrupt the country internally. The German Foreign Office thought that it was reliably informed that François-Poncet belonged to that group.[53]

It is on record that French political circles meant "to utilize the dynamism of the Hitlerites." [54] Tardieu and Jean Louis Barthou are reported to have believed at the end of 1933 that Germany was destined for an early dismemberment.[55] Their calculation had, in fact, a fairly sound basis, for in the early years of his regime Hitler offered the Western Powers several golden opportunities for active intervention which resolute and far-seeing statesmen would have promptly seized for the protection of legitimate national interests. It was the disunion between Great Britain and France in the years 1933-1936, their weakness, and ineffective leadership in both countries which led this calculation to miscarry.

When François-Poncet arrived in Berlin in September, 1931, the Brüning Government was thought by many diplomats and politicians to be "the last bulwark against the rising tide of National Socialism." [56] Hence, whoever helped to undermine that bulwark promoted Hitler's prospects. The stagnating disarmament problem worked in this direction, and France was felt to have the heaviest share in the deadlock, as the foregoing chapter has shown.

Franklin L. Ford states that the French Ambassador made no secret of the misgivings he felt about Brüning.[57] So did *Reichswehr* General von Schleicher, a notorious intriguer, who openly proclaimed an early fall of the Chancellor. Friendly relations between François-Poncet and General von Schleicher aroused suspicion in Berlin government circles where the impression gained ground that the General was under the influence of the French Ambassador.

The fall of Brüning's Government did not, however, necessarily mean that Hitler would actually seize power. Indeed, in the end, he was lifted into the saddle at a time when the Nazi Party was losing voters, when it was in financial straits, and much discouraged. Nevertheless, the fall of Brüning marked a turn toward increased political tension, toward disorder, and toward possible explosions. A woman journalist in Berlin, Bella Fromm, who enjoyed good connections with international society, recorded her feeling that François-Poncet had foreseen the coming of the Nazis "approvingly." [58] This should not be misunderstood as meaning that he had any predilections for them. He has himself stated in his *Memoirs:*

In fact, I have always felt the most vivid aversion toward the National Socialist régime. . . . I did not let these sentiments appear too much. . . . I did not have bad relations with them [Nazis]. To be more exact, it came about that with some of them I had rather good relations.[59]

Before a parliamentary investigating committee, François-Poncet testified that the burning of the *Reichstag,* February 27, 1933, four weeks after Hitler had become Chancellor, made him realize the dangerous nature of the new regime.[60] In accord with this, Bella Fromm noted on March 7, "now, however, he recognizes the danger." [61]

Indeed, the *Reichstag* fire and the subsequent terror practised by the Nazis opened the eyes of many millions. Henceforth, François-Poncet warned his government frequently of the menace to peace presented by Hitler-Germany.[62] In a conversation with his American colleague, Mr. Dodd, on September 12, 1933, he "insisted that war is almost certain to come." [63] Moreover, as will be seen in a following book, he made early proposals to his government which, if adopted, would easily have curbed Hitler and given history a different turn.

If we assume that M. François-Poncet welcomed Hitler's advent, an explanation will be found in the economic field. His ambition was, as a well-informed Frenchman declared, to build up France as an economic power; and he would, therefore, have sought to bring about an association of the great French-German industrial interests.[64] In fact, in his initial press conference upon reaching Berlin he spoke with enthusiasm of an alliance between the French and German industries, the former rich but technically inferior, the latter well-equipped but lacking capital.[65]

Some kind of industrial cooperation between the two countries had already been envisaged by Brüning's Government. A prominent German supporter of such a plan was Arnold Rechberg, the Potash King, who even advocated an eventual military alliance with France aimed at the Soviet Union. It is reported that, in the spring of 1932, there was a conference at Luxemburg, attended by representatives of the *Comité des Forges,* which reached an agreement, in principle, that—under specific safeguards for France's national interests—the German Army, after 1919 limited to 100,000 men, might be raised to a force of 300,000, equipped with heavy arms.[66] For the munitions makers this would obviously mean the end of the disarmament menace, and a general boom for their trade in practically all European countries, because the armaments industry is one that profits by foreign competition.[67]

Bertrand de Jouvenel states that, in the autumn of 1931, the French *métallurgistes* were adherents to an intimate French-German *rapprochement.*[68] That was the time when M. François-Poncet became Ambassador to Germany. He was regarded as "the man of confidence" of the French steel magnates, representing "the two hundred ruling families of France." [69] The "alliance" between French and German industries which he advocated was in line with the Rechberg plan, and, one may add, in line with the post-war Schuman plan. On the face of it, there was nothing objectionable about the proposed "alliance." But the time was not propitious for the German side.

In the Great Depression France suffered much less than other countries, so that in those years "the franc controlled Europe." On the other hand, Germany's financial situation was desperate. She was, therefore, from the outset at a grave disadvantage which the French were keen to exploit. B. de Jouvenel has made this clear. He wrote:

To become the profiteers [*rentiers*] of German labor, that is the grand idea of the French capitalists. That is what one calls the policy of participation in German industry. The crux is, in short, to bring to life again the tribute which German industry paid under

the Dawes Plan, for the benefit, no longer of the French State but
of private interests. Since the German associations lack funds they
will necessarily be open to the French proposals.[70]

Evidently, Germany was to be the horse and France the
rider. It was quite natural that the French desired to be the
dominant partners. It was equally natural that the Germans
were distrustful of the promoters of a scheme which would
perpetuate France's economic and, consequently, her political
preponderance.

The author does not wish to suggest that M. François-
Poncet himself contemplated that Germany's share in the
"alliance" he envisaged should be that of the working horse.
In our study we are chiefly concerned with presenting the
available evidence for elucidation of the Ambassador's attitude
towards Hitler and his rise to power. He has himself stated the
vivid aversion he soon felt toward the Nazi regime, and there
is no reason to cast any doubt on it. Yet, there are contradictory statements in the record. An American student has referred to the Ambassador's "known enthusiasm for the National Socialist system." [71] A well-informed German declared
that François-Poncet was for his government an ironical critic
of Nazism, and for Berlin society "the greatest admirer of
Hitler." [72] Finally, there is a statement that Dr. Alfred Etscheit,
a prominent lawyer, once asked M. François-Poncet: "Where
in Berlin would Your Excellency wish to see your monument
erected that National Socialism owes you?" The explanation
given for this remark was that Dr. Etscheit was originally on
friendly terms with the Ambassador but later on became
sceptical as to the part he had played in 1932. The lawyer was
murdered by the Nazis toward the end of the war, and so far
there is no evidence on hand to show what particular motive
induced him to make the remark.[73]

The fact is that, in 1933, M. François-Poncet's relations
with Hitler were by no means friendly and that they became
very strained in 1934 when, after the massacre of June 30,
the Chancellor asserted that General von Schleicher had entertained treasonable contacts with the representative of a
Foreign Power, unmistakably meaning France. There was no
truth in that allegation. It was only in later years that M.
François-Poncet was favored by the *Fuehrer*.

Another fact is that Hitler's amazing diplomatic successes
in the mid-thirties aroused widespread admiration for him in

Germany as well as abroad, and not the least in France. A patriotic Frenchman has suggested as the main reason for this that France's Two Hundred Families "gazed with envy across the Rhine. They accepted Hitler, just as German big business before them had done, as the crusader and savior of Europe from Bolshevism." [74] This notion may best explain the astounding fact that, shortly after Hitler's accession, French armaments firms (supposedly Schneider-Creusot) furnished Germany with 400 modern tanks which were shipped through Holland to evade suspicion. [75]

The author considered it proper to submit to His Excellency M. André François-Poncet the foregoing presentation of evidence which it was his duty to use, and to suggest that he would make a statement with regard to the passages quoted from Ambassador Dodd's diary and from Mr. Louis P. Lochner's book. His Excellency has been kind enough to comply with my request, and I am very pleased to reproduce the following letter in translation:

Bad Godesberg, January 11, 1954

Monsieur,
I have already had occasion to let you know, through the intermediary of M. Pierre-Etienne Flandin, that I contest absolutely the truth of the assertions which you produce, here and there, and which would make me chiefly responsible for the fall of Chancellor Brüning and for the advent to power of Adolf Hitler and National Socialism.

Don't you think it absurd to attribute such an influence to an Ambassador quite new at his post who arrived in Berlin at a moment when National Socialism had already acquired an irresistible strength?

The fall of Brüning was the consequence of maneuvres by certain Junkers of East Prussia who made him suspect in the eyes of Marshal Hindenburg, and by Chiefs of the *Reichswehr* who did not forgive him for retaining contacts with Social Democracy, instead of forming together with the Right that national majority, for the constitution of which he had been called to the chancellorship.

My relations with Hitler were for a long time very bad. He had even denounced me, after June 30, 1934, from the tribune of the *Reichstag,* as one of Roehm's accomplices. Subsequently our relations improved, it is true, but they never bore an intimate character. As I have already said, I have from the beginning in my communications to the Quai d'Orsay announced and denounced the Hitlerian danger. That is the reason why, when these docu-

ments were seized, at the time of the German invasion of France, I
was forbidden to stay in Paris, was arrested by the Gestapo and
was interned at a Vorarlberg village for 21 months.

The allegations according to which I was said to have been the
man of confidence of the French iron [*métallurgique*] industry,
charged with defending the interests of merchants of cannons, have
never been raised but by the Communists.

I have enjoyed complete material independence; I have never
served any particular interest; I have never had any participation
in metallurgic enterprises. My wife is the daughter of an officer and
not of a Lorraine metallurgist; the *Société d'Études et d'Information Économiques,* which I founded in Paris in 1920, has in no way
been the instrument of the *Comité des Forges.* Besides, I resigned
from it in 1924, seven years before I was nominated Ambassador
to Germany.

The informations you have gathered emanate from pure calumny. How could a sensible person who knows me, believe the
ridiculous fable according to which I danced the *cancan* at
Roehm's, after having put on a SA uniform?

I have met Roehm only twice in my life; I have related exactly
under what conditions.

By the way, I advise you to turn your attention to the book I
have written, *Souvenirs d'une Ambassade à Berlin, 1931-1938*
(Paris, Flammarion). That is the faithful summary of the reports
which I have addressed to the Quai d'Orsay during the seven years
of my stay in Berlin.

If it had been otherwise, if I had played the role which some
people, impelled by malevolence or stupidity, attribute to me,
would it then be conceivable that the French Government would,
in 1949, again have entrusted me with the duty of High Commissioner in Germany at Chancellor Adenauer's?

I authorize you to publish this letter if you wish to do so, *et je
vous prie d'agréer, Monsieur, l'expression de mes sentiments dis-
tingués,*

                                    signed: André François-Poncet [76]

Mr. Louis P. Lochner, after having taken cognizance of
this letter, informed the present writer that he still adheres to
the conclusions he came to during his long service in Berlin.
But he points out that in his book he merely said that François-
Poncet was a "partial answer" to the question, Why wasn't
Hitler stopped? [77]

Frenchmen were by no means the only foreign industrialists
who endeavored to promote the interests of armaments manu-

facturers during Hitler's rise to power. They received vigorous assistance from the largest British armaments firm, Vickers-Armstrongs Limited, London. Irrefutable proof for this fact is furnished by the two accompanying illustrations, reproducing advertisements which covered the whole back page of the Berlin *Militär-Wochenblatt,* an independent weekly for the *Deutsche Wehrmacht.* The headlines of both advertisements read: WAR EQUIPMENTS OF ALL KINDS. In No. 7 of the weekly, published on August 18, 1932, a field howitzer is offered. The same advertisement appeared in No. 15 of October 18, 1932. In No. 11, and in No. 19, published on September 18, and November 18, 1932, respectively, "The world famous Vickers-Carden-Loyd Armored Car" for patrolling is offered.

These advertisements appeared shortly after the fall of Brüning, and at a time when the Conference at Geneva was discussing *disarmament,* not rearmament. It was not until December 11, 1932, that the Conference acknowledged, in principle, Germany's equality of rights in armaments, under specific restrictive conditions. The advertisements were, therefore, an open challenge to the official policy of the Western Powers.[78] And they were, above all, the strongest possible encouragement to militaristic and nationalistic forces in Germany. It is significant that, at the moment of Hitler's seizure of power, these advertisements vanished completely from the *Militär-Wochenblatt* and were replaced by advertisements for field tractors, manufactured by the same firm. Of course, with Hitler at the helm, war equipment did not need to be offered any longer.

In 1932, there were persistent rumors in Germany that the Berlin representative of Vickers-Armstrongs Limited was one of the financial backers of the NSDAP, and no wonder in view of the advertisements reproduced. Nor can there be any doubt that one of the armaments firms abroad which General von Schleicher had in mind when he spoke of the scandal of the Nazis' revenues, was Vickers-Armstrongs.

The spirit in certain British circles toward Hitler-Germany in 1933 is glaringly revealed in a speech which Sir Arthur Balfour, the Chairman of Capital Steel Works, made in October of that year. After having expressed the view that Hitlerism was preferable to Communism he declared:

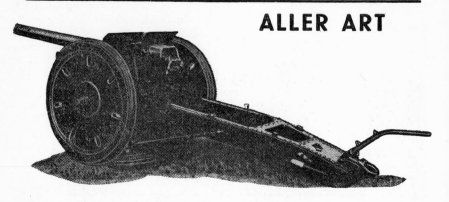
Verantwortlich für den redaktionellen Teil: Generalleutnant a. D. von Altrock, Berlin W15, Fasanenstraße 60, Fernruf: Oliva 975.
Verantwortlich für den Anzeigenteil: Hugo Hertel, Berlin-Schöneberg, Thorwaldsenstraße 11.
Druck von Ernst Siegfried Mittler und Sohn, Buchdruckerei G.m.b.H., Berlin SW68, Kochstraße 68—71.

KRIEGSAUSRÜSTUNGEN
ALLER ART

VICKERS - CARDEN - LOYD
PATROUILLE-KAMPFWAGEN

Der weltberühmte Vickers-Carden-Loyd Panzerkraftwagen mit verstärktem Motorbetrieb und Panzerturm mit Richtfeld von 360°.

Allgemeine Angaben:
Bemannung ... ... 2 Mann.
Bewaffnung   Vickers-M.G., mit 3500 Patronen.
Geschwindigkeit ... ... 48 km Std.
Steigung ... ... 25°
Drehkreis ... ... 4 m.
Höhe ... ... 1,65 m.
Breite ... ... 1,75 m.
Länge ... ... 2,59 m.
Gewicht ... ... ca. 2,000 kg.

Verantwortlich für den redaktionellen Teil: Generalleutnant a. D. von Altrock, Berlin W15, Fasanenstraße 60, Fernruf Oliva 973.
Verantwortlich für den Anzeigenteil: Hugo Berkel, Berlin-Schöneberg, Thorwaldsenstraße 11.
Druck von Ernst Siegfried Mittler und Sohn, Buchdruckerei G. m. b. H., Berlin SW68, Kochstraße 68—71.

Will the Germans go to war again? I don't think there is any doubt
about it, and the curious thing about it is that I am almost persuaded that some day we shall have to let the Germans arm, or
we shall arm them. With the Russians armed to the teeth, and the
tremendous menace in the East, Germany unarmed in the middle is
always going to be a plum waiting for the Russians to take, and
which we should have to defend if the Germans could not defend
themselves. One of the greatest menaces to peace in Europe today
is the totally unarmed condition of Germany.

Recalling this remarkable speech in 1937, the Labour Party
stated officially that "from the outset a large part of the City
has given every support and encouragement to German rearmament." [79]

Reviewing the evidence presented in the matter of the material support given by foreigners to Hitler during his rise to
power, it is plain that they were prompted by various motives.
Some backers expected, as Heinrich Brüning has stated, that
Hitler's advent would bring about disorder in Germany and a
more or less prolonged weakening of the country. Others expected handsome profits from an expansion of the armaments
trade. Others, again, wanted to be merely in the good graces
of the prospective master of Germany and neighboring states.
The Soviets hoped for the spread of Communism as the result
of Hitler's mismanagement. Apparently the largest and most
influential group of Hitler's backers supported him as the
crusader and a bulwark against Communism.[80] No doubt, some
contributors were animated by two, or even three motives
combined.

Further research will be needed for clarifying the question
of foreign financial aid given to Hitler in the years 1930 to
1933. Though non-Germans did contribute considerable sums,
it is evident, in view of the immense outlay of the NSDAP and
its organizations in those years, that by far the larger part
was provided by, or extorted from, Germans.

Two more hidden factors played a role in Hitler's rise.

It will be recalled from Chapter Two the circumstances
under which the Weimar Republic came into being. Stephen
King-Hall is right in saying that the Allies forced the Germans
to adopt a form of government with which they were unfamil-
iar.[81]

In an instructive chapter, "The Follies of the Victors," Winston S. Churchill wrote:

Wise policy would have crowned and fortified the Weimar Republic with a constitutional sovereign in the person of an infant grandson of the Kaiser, under a council of regency. Instead, a gaping void was opened in the national life of the German people . . . and into that void . . . strode a maniac of ferocious genius, the repository and expression of the most virulent hatreds that have ever corroded the human breast—Corporal Hitler.[82]

David Lloyd George came to the same conclusion. In 1918, he had been an ardent advocate of "Hang the Kaiser." Conveniently forgetting his own prominent part in that campaign, he said in the mid-thirties to one of Emperor William's grandsons, Prince Louis Ferdinand, that "we over here," in Britain, never expected or intended the fall of the Hohenzollern dynasty. It would have been impossible, of course, to conclude peace either with the Prince's grandfather or with his father. But, Lloyd George asserted,

we all thought that a regency for your brother Wilhelm would be set up under your mother and one of your uncles. If your family had remained in power in Germany, I am certain that Mr. Hitler would not be giving us any headaches right now.[83]

Lloyd George's belated regret was shared later on by men like Ernest Bevin.[84]

Prince Louis Ferdinand has correctly pointed out that not even the bulk of German Socialists wanted the dynasty abolished.[85] A regency would have been accepted by a large majority of the people, and the present writer is convinced that, under such a regency—which Reich President von Hindenburg wished to introduce—a Nazi triumph would have been absolutely impossible in Germany.

The other factor accounting for Hitler's rise was the effect of the blockade and of the Versailles spirit on the German youth. Sir Horace Rumbold, recollecting his term as British Ambassador to Germany in the transition years from the Weimar Republic to the establishment of Hitler's regime, wrote in April, 1938:

It must be remembered that Hitler was appealing to a generation which had either been born during the war or which had been quite young when the war broke out. In both cases that generation had been undernourished during the early years, and doctors have told me that, owing to undernourishment, such a generation could not be normal and properly balanced. Hence the effect of Hitler's hysterical appeals.[86]

Independently of Sir Horace, this estimate is confirmed by Arthur Bryant.[87] On his part, the writer who lived through the starvation years and their aftermath in close contact with numbers of families having young children, can vouch for the accuracy of those statements.

Indeed, the Hitler movement has been aptly described as a "mass rebellion" of disappointed and hungry youth.[88] H. R. Knickerbocker realized this clearly. He calculated that, in 1932, there were 13½ million Germans from 20 to 32 years old who had not served in the war. They explain many things, he wrote, "first of all Hitler." Knickerbocker even thought that without this frustrated body of youths the Nazi Party would have remained obscure.[89]

These young people argued: If a few responsible Germans in an autocratic regime bungled the country into war, and if some military men waged it ruthlessly, why on earth should we, wholly innocent by every standard of ethics, be made to suffer from an admittedly unjust treaty and its evil consequences? So they joined forces with the Communists, with reactionaries, with Nazis and with chauvinists for the overthrow of the hated and despised Republic that had accepted the onerous peace terms of 1919. Or, as Frederick Palmer—recalling General Tasker Bliss' forecast that "the devil will be to pay all over the world"—put it: "Young Germany rose in racial frenzy and blatant nationalism with its 'Heil Hitler' of vassalage to absolute autocracy." [90]

2. OBVIOUS AND DIRECT FACTORS

The consensus of informed international opinion is that the main factors that account for Hitler's *rise* to power, from 1919 to the end of 1932—as distinct from his *seizure* of power— were, in chronological order: Germany's defeat, 1918; the Treaty of Versailles, 1919; the invasion of the Ruhr, 1923; Germany's inflation, 1923; the economic depression, 1930-1932; and fear of Communism, all through the years 1919-1932.

There are, however, some notable exceptions. Several authorities attribute Hitler's advent exclusively, or to a decisive degree, to one of the following factors:

1) German character and history;
2) Germany's defeat;
3) the Treaty of Versailles;
4) economic causes (inflation and depression);
5) the disarmament failure;
6) demagogy and propaganda;
7) fear of Communism.

The leading exponent of the first theory was Sir Robert—later Lord—Vansittart, who declared that Hitler was "the natural and continuous product of a breed which from the dawn of history has been predatory and bellicose." [91] Concentrating on more recent times, J. Hampden Jackson concluded that the sources of Hitlerism lie not in reaction from Versailles and Weimar "but in Bismarck's Germany." [92] Mildred S. Wertheimer, having expert knowledge, also traced the roots of National Socialism back into the history of Germany where extreme nationalism and the doctrine of the superiority of the German-Aryan race were features of German ideology even before the First World War.[93] It is true that Pan-Germanism, chauvinism, and militarism did play their part in the rise of Hitler, but as undercurrents rather than as main factors, as Dr. Wertheimer made clear in her study.[94]

Theory two has been upheld by a leading British historian, Ernest—later Sir—Llewellyn Woodward, who stated in 1940 that "the rise of Hitlerism was not due to the Treaty of Versailles, but to the military defeat of Germany." [95] Similarly, a Swiss historian, Leonhard von Muralt, contends that the theory that Versailles caused National Socialism, is "entirely wrong." [96] In fact, Germany's defeat in 1918, artfully distorted and embellished by the complacent "stab in the back" legend, did nourish in Hitler personally and in a considerable section of his younger followers a strong desire for revenge, powerfully stimulated by the humiliations to which the German nation was subjected in 1919 and for years afterwards.

Theory three, the Treaty of Versailles, has been given prominence by numerous authorities. Sir Nevile Henderson, British Ambassador to Berlin from 1937 to 1939, wrote during the Second World War that the Versailles Treaty "created" Hitler.[97] His countryman, Sir Bernard Pares, likewise thought that in 1919 "we made him; the French rather more than we did." [98] This view was widely shared by American observers. Vincent Sheean is of the opinion that Adolf Hitler was "the inevitable product" of the Versailles *Diktat*, which was easily represented to the German masses as "a gigantic swindle inflicted upon the German people." [99] For Henry C. Wolfe there is no escaping the fact that Hitler was "the illegitimate offspring" of the Treaty, and he even considered it certain that the world would never have heard of Hitler had the treaties of 1919-20 been less severe on the Weimar Republic.[100] A well-informed Frenchman, Paul Ferdonnet, diplomatic correspondent in Berlin from 1928 to 1934, also stated that the Third Reich was the German people's retort to Versailles.[101] This view is confirmed, in an official way, by Sir Horace Rumbold, British Ambassador to Berlin, who, discussing the elections for the *Reichstag* of March 5, 1933, reported on the 21st: "In so far as the revolution has been a revolt against the Treaty of Versailles, the whole country may be said to be united in sustaining it." [102] Finally, an eminent psychologist, Dr. William Brown, particularly well qualified to render an accurate judgment, explained that the result of the humiliations heaped at Versailles upon a proud defeated nation "has been the advent of Nazi psychology." [103] The gravest of these humiliations for the German people was, as we have seen, the war guilt charge. With sound reason, therefore, American, British and French authors have stated that probably no single item of the Treaty of Versailles has been so useful to Hitler in destroying the morale of his democratic opponents as "that damnable War Guilt Clause." [104]

Narrowing down theory three to personal influences, some prominent publicists have declared that Georges Clemenceau, the "Tiger" of the Peace Conference in 1919, or alternately Raymond Poincaré as the invader of the Ruhr, was "the spiritual father of Herr Hitler," a *bon mot* which gained currency in some French circles.[105]

As to the fourth theory, economic causes, it is interesting to note that Sir Norman Angell doubted whether the world would have heard of Hitler if he had not been able to exploit the miseries which the inflation of 1923 entailed.[106] In the foregoing chapter the impact and significance of that event have been described. German recollection of the 1923 inferno played a large role during the Great Depression.

The notion, once widely held, that the "economic blizzard" was directly or solely the result of the peace settlements of 1919-20 was not correct. The basic causes appear to have been: the First World War itself; industrial overproduction; high protectionist tariffs; and overexpansion of credit.[107] Yet, the intensity of the financial crisis of 1930-33 was to a large extent the consequence of the reparations system.[108]

A distinguished Englishman looked upon the depression as the greatest disaster in world history since the destruction of the Roman Empire.[109] In any case, it was "assuredly the turning-point of the twenty years' truce" between the two wars.[110]

After 1930, hunger and despair spread over Germany. The number of unemployed increased rapidly, and so did the number of inscribed members of the NSDAP, the National Socialist German Workers Party, as will be seen from the following table.

	Unemployed	*Inscribed members of the NSDAP*
End of 1929	2,850,000	176,426
End of 1930	4,380,000	389,000
End of 1931	5,660,000	806,294 [111]

At the end of 1932 there were at least six and a half million unemployed, and by then the Weimar Republic had reached, in the words of an expert Frenchman, "a degree of misery and disorganization such as no other European nation has reached before." [112] Another eye-witness, Robert Boothby, wrote in 1932 of the German people:

They are terrified of another bout of inflation. . . . My impression is that they are spiritually done, and that Hitlerism is the expression of their despair. . . . The most remarkable thing about them is their staying power. There is no doubt that they are suffering like hell economically, but they never let you see it.[113]

In those years the votes for the National Socialists more than doubled. In the elections for the *Reichstag* Hitler's Party obtained: in May, 1928, 12 mandates out of a total of 491; in September, 1930, 107 out of 577; in July, 1932, 230 out of 608. In view of this trend a group of authorities contended that the economic crisis was the predominant factor in Hitler's rise,[114] and some assert that it was practically the sole factor.[115]

Interesting is the comparison John Gunther drew between the situation in Germany and that in the United States in 1932-33:

Several of the forces propelling Hitler into power were much the same as those that put Mr. Roosevelt into office—mass despair in the midst of unprecedented economic crisis, impassioned hatred of the *status quo,* and a burning desire by the great majority of people to find a savior who might bring luck.[116]

Theory five, according to which the failure of disarmament was the real cause for Hitler's rise, has been stressed by British statesmen. David Lloyd George, the "Welsh wizard," eager to saddle responsibility on his successors, stated tersely: "British Ministers put up no fight against the betrayal of the League and the pledges as to disarmament. Hence the Nazi Revolution. . . ." [117] One of these Ministers, the Marquess of Londonderry, in his turn, argued that the French, having deliberately wrecked every chance of accommodation at Geneva, "are mainly responsible for Hitler and his regime." [118] Taking a broader view, George Gilbert Armstrong declared that the Allies' disregard of their disarmament pledge "gave Hitler his greatest chance." [119]

The role of demagogy and propaganda, theory six, has been set forth by some authorities who have had psychological contact and experience with Germans. G. M. Gilbert thus attributes the rise of Nazism chiefly to Hitler's shrewd demagogy.[120] Similarly, Mildred S. Wertheimer believes that the Nazi movement would probably never have achieved success without the unceasing, well-organized propaganda of Hitler and his lieutenants.[121] Prominent amongst the latter were Dr. Joseph Goebbels, propaganda chief, and Captain Ernst Roehm, the organizer and leader of the SA, *i.e.,* the Storm Troopers, which numbered at least 300,000 men in January, 1933. Well-informed Germans attribute to Roehm and his SA a decisive role in Hitler's advent.[122]

There is no doubt that Adolf Hitler had the seductive gift of a veritable spellbinder. This greatly facilitated promoting his assumed role as a Messiah sent by Providence for the Glory of his People, a role which gradually took firm possession of his maniacal mind as an unshakable reality. No doubt, many persons of even more than average intelligence succumbed to his hypnotic-magnetic influence. In Joseph Goebbels, the Party had a superb and utterly unscrupulous master of the art of demagogy and propaganda. The peace settlements of 1919-20 and the spirit in which they were conceived, constantly provided these seducers of the populace with rich material. But the question may be raised whether, in general, the Germans were, and are, more susceptible to clever propaganda than other European nations? And, more important still, whether the German masses have learned their lesson, or whether they are likely again to fall prey to the siren songs of another Messiah, from their own midst, or possibly from the East?

Theory seven, fear of Communism, offers particular interest in view of the present situation in Europe. Otto Braun, the former Prime Minister of Prussia, used to answer the question how Hitler rose to power with but three words: "Versailles and Moscow." [123] An American observer put the same idea picturesquely this way:

If two Furies, rising out of the Great War, had said, one to the other, "You go to Paris and I will go to Moscow and together we will wreck the world," that would have adequately explained the havoc, the rise of the Reign of Force in Europe.[124]

The predominant spirit at Paris in 1919 has already been sufficiently treated in the present book and is perfectly clear. But the role of Moscow in our drama is much disputed and still obscure. It falls into two parts: German fear of Communism, and the Moscow-directed tactics of the German Communist Party.

The Great Depression provided an ideal soil for the spread of Communism. The Communists polled for the *Reichstag* 77 seats in September, 1930; 89 in July, 1932; and 100 in November, 1932, when the seats of the Nazis were reduced from 230 to 196. In fact, the German Communist Party was the only one that enjoyed a steady growth during those years.

Hitler never tired of claiming that he was the Savior of Europe from Bolshevism. As late as February, 1942, while waging war against the Soviet Union, he declared: "If Germany had not had the good fortune that I seized power in 1933, Europe would now not exist any more." [125]

Sir Horace Rumbold, British Ambassador to Germany from August, 1928, to May, 1933, took quite a different view. He was a keen observer on the spot and had unusual facilities for sizing up the situation. On January 24, 1933, a week before Hitler was put into power, ex-Chancellor Franz von Papen told the Ambassador it would be a disaster if the Hitler movement collapsed or were crushed, for, after all, the Nazis were the last remaining bulwark against Communism in Germany. Sir Horace contested this. He did not believe that the German people as a whole were receptive to Communist ideas, and he thought that the increase in Communism was largely due to bad economic conditions. But Papen replied that the Ambassador would be surprised if he knew how many "intellectuals" had imbibed Communist ideas; Communism was receiving recruits from the ranks of young men who had passed difficult examinations but could find no posts. Soon after this conversation, Sir Horace believed that he saw his opinion confirmed by the elections for the *Reichstag* on March 5 which furnished the proof, he reported, that the Communist menace was "largely a myth." [126] This is corroborated by Hermann Rauschning, President of the Danzig Senate at that time, who emphasized that in 1932-33 "no fate was farther removed from the German Reich than a Bolshevist Revolution." [127] The historian, Max Beloff, also dismisses Hitler's pretension that he saved Germany from Bolshevism, as a "legend." [128]

Well-informed Germans admit that the Communist danger was highly exaggerated and was cunningly exploited by Hitler.[129] On the other hand, we have the testimony of former Communist adherents whose opinion carries the weight of experience and authority. A former active Communist, Ruth Fischer, stated that there was "a real and not at all imaginary danger of Germany's russification." [130] Another authority, Alexander Weissberg, declared that the economic crisis of the thirties "would obviously bring either Fascism or Communism" to Germany.[131] Indeed, neutral observers during the Great Depression felt this menace very acutely.[132]

These contradictory statements about the actual danger of Communism in Germany in the early thirties are bewildering. The author heard at that time the same contradictory views expressed by German politicians in various parts of the country. The explanation seemed to be that, in rural areas, there appeared to be no serious danger; whereas people in contact with industrial districts were very apprehensive.

Whichever view was the right one, the fact is that, in the years 1930-32, the spectre of Communism swelled the ranks of the National Socialists to a very considerable extent. Some observers even maintain that, without this fear, Hitler would never have come to power.[133]

With regard to the Moscow-directed tactics of the German Communist Party, well-informed authorities stress the following points which decided Soviet action:

Germany was to have a leading role in the spread of Communism; the German Communist Party was, outside the Soviet Union, the strongest and best organized in the world;

Fascism represented, in the Kremlin's opinion, the last stage of capitalist development;

Hitler, in power, would operate like an "ice-breaker"; he would crush the *bourgeoisie* and disrupt the country;

Hitler's regime would, therefore, be a swiftly passing episode; and then—after Hitler—would come "our," the Communists', turn.[134]

Guided by such arguments the German Communists, in 1932, even joined forces occasionally with the Nazis for the overthrow of the Weimar Republic. The Social Democrats were then the mainstay of the Republic, and they endeavored repeatedly to induce the Communists to coordinate their action against their common chief enemy, Adolf Hitler. A determined effort for this purpose was made by Friedrich Stampfer, editor-in-chief of the Social Democrat *Vorwärts*, toward the end of 1932. In agreement with the Party executive, he approached the Soviet Ambassador in Berlin who designated a member of his staff, Vynogradov, to negotiate with Stampfer. But, after several discussions, Vynogradov told him in January, 1933: "Moscow wishes Hitler's advent for it is convinced that Germany will only go Communist after Hitler has been in power." Further negotiations would, therefore, be useless.[135]

There is, however, another story on record. According to "Ypsilon," the Soviet Ambassador in Berlin did not believe that the future belonged to Hitler. He expected Chancellor von Schleicher and the *Reichswehr* generals "to carry the day." Stalin is said to have shared this view. When the Comintern favored cooperation with the German Social Democrats against Hitler, Stalin remained adamant. He decreed:

The National Socialists will not attain power! They already lost many hundreds of thousands of votes in the last election while the Communists were still gaining. The National Socialists cannot seize power against the will of the Army. General Schleicher, the new Chancellor [December, 1932], is their determined enemy. . . . The main enemy is and remains the Social Democracy.

"Ypsilon" adds: "Stalin derived his assurance from contacts his Berlin representatives were maintaining with General von Schleicher and other *Reichswehr* generals." [136]

This recorded Soviet argument was in some respects well founded. It was known that Schleicher meant to split the NSDAP or, failing this, to crush it. There did exist not only contacts between the *Reichswehr* and the Red Army, but a friendly collaboration. At the head of the *Reichswehr* was General von Hammerstein, nicknamed the "Red General" because of his Socialist inclinations. He was openly hostile to the Nazis who had suffered a reverse in the elections of November, 1932, losing 34 seats in the *Reichstag*. It was also true that the Communists had then gained 11 seats. The fact which does not seem to fit into the picture was the Soviet stand against the German Social Democrats. If Schleicher had had his way, the position of the Social Democrats would have been much strengthened, and so would have been that of the Republic. Such an outcome was not desired by the Kremlin whose interests were evidently better served by Hitler's actual advent, in the comfortable expectation that he would really operate as "ice-breaker" for the coveted world revolution.

Whatever view is taken of "Ypsilon's" record, one fact is indisputable, namely, that the tactics of the German Communists, directed from Moscow, helped Hitler into power.[137] To what degree it is impossible now to establish. In any case, a first-rate authority, the historian Max Beloff, believes that the share of the Comintern in bringing about the rise of Hitler must be accounted "a very considerable one." [138]

CONCLUSIONS

The foregoing sections of this chapter provide sufficient material for a sound evaluation of the main factors in Hitler's rise to power. The author may claim to be qualified for a fairly accurate estimate in virtue of the following reasons.

By 1919, I had fifteen years' experience in politics. Residing in Munich, I was a careful observer of the National Socialist movement from its beginning. Munich, being "Capital of the Movement," offered special facilities for obtaining firsthand information. I was in continuous close contact with leading politicians, and with representatives of foreign countries, particularly with the Consuls of the United States and of Great Britain. Because of my work, I was also in close contact with German political and official circles in Berlin.

The main factors accounting for Hitler's rise (stated more or less chronologically) were: the military defeat, 1918, distorted by the "stab in the back" legend; the Treaty of Versailles, 1919; the invasion of the Ruhr, 1923; the inflation, 1923; the Great Depression, 1930-32; fear of Communism, 1919-32; internal strife and weakness, 1919-32; demagogy and propaganda, 1919-32; and the failure of the victors to redress grievous wrongs in time, 1919-32. Along with these basic causes a factor of considerable importance was foreign moral and material support for Hitler and his Party, especially in the years 1930-32.

Of these various factors the *prime* one was the Treaty of Versailles, and above all the *spirit* in which it was conceived—the spirit that inspired the document of June 16, 1919, branding the Germans a criminal nation, outside the pale of European civilization; the spirit which prompted Prime Minister Lloyd George in 1921 to declare in the name of the Allies that Germany's sole responsibility for the war was a *chose jugée, i.e.,* a closed case; the spirit which kept the victorious Powers from submitting this vital question of responsibility to neutral arbitration; the spirit that prevented them from heeding General Smuts' admonition in 1919, and in later years, that the Statesmen's peace should be changed into a real peace of the Peoples.

In the years 1930-32, the mounting social misery, hunger, despair and hopelessness, particularly amongst the German youth, and the correlated increasing fear of inflation and of Communism, played their part as main factors in Hitler's rise. Nevertheless, there can be no doubt whatsoever about the *decisive* role "Versailles" played from 1919 onward. Hitler's *Mein Kampf* and the bulk of his speeches clearly show the

use he made of it. We have also noted the opinion expressed
by the British Ambassador to Germany, in March, 1933,
namely, that practically the whole country was united in sustaining the Nazi movement in so far as it was a revolt against
the Treaty of Versailles. Significantly, Germans of quite different political creeds maintain that this Treaty provided *the*
fertile soil from which Nazism arose.[139] Therefore, the statement made by Mr. John Foster Dulles in 1938 (reprinted in
Chapter One) remains true, namely, that it was, above all,
the guilt charge in the Treaty which laid the foundation for
Hitler-Germany.

A Round Table Conference held around 1930 for a reasonable revision of the Peace Treaty, as the Weimar Government
had modestly requested in 1919, would have made a tremendous impression on the German masses. It would have taken
the wind out of Hitler's sails. Raymond Moley rightly pointed
out that earlier "appeasement," before 1933, "would have
made the growth of Fascism impossible in the first place." [140]
The tragic failure to revise the Treaty convinced the Germans
that only "Force and Might" would bring them justice.[141]

It is noteworthy that the chief author of the covering letter
of June 16, 1919, Philip Kerr, declared in 1936, as Marquess
of Lothian, that the Hitler regime "was largely the result of
the unfair treatment which Germany had had from her neighbors." [142] This was at that time a widespread impression
among statesmen and politicians all over the world. Likewise,
the eminent psychologist, Dr. William Brown, after thorough
studies occupying many years, came to the conclusion that
the Nazi revolution "was the direct result of the post-war
policy of England and France." [143]

At the Nuremberg trials of the Nazi leaders the Treaty of
Versailles became the subject of animated controversy between
the Defense and the Prosecution. On March 26, 1946, Dr.
Alfred Seidl, counsel for the defendant Rudolf Hess, Hitler's
Deputy for Party affairs, submitted to the Tribunal a volume
of documents which contained statements and quotations
taken from books and speeches of foreign statesmen, diplomats, and political economists, regarding the origin and history of the Versailles Treaty. Sir David Maxwell-Fyfe, the
British Deputy Chief Prosecutor, at once protested. He maintained that the issues of the terms of the Treaty were not a

relevant, nor an evidential, matter for the Court. Dr. Seidl, generally supported by two other counsels for the defense, declared:

> The Prosecution has submitted extensive evidence on the development of the NSDAP. Numerous document books were submitted to the Court to show the growth in membership, to demonstrate the increase in the *Reichstag* mandates. Now, if this evidence was relevant, it is my assertion that also the circumstances and the facts that first enabled this rise of the Party at all must be relevant, if only from the viewpoint of causal nexus.

However, the upshot of the lengthy controversy was that the President, Lord Justice Lawrence, member for the United Kingdom of Great Britain and Northern Ireland, announced that same day, March 26, 1946: "The Tribunal rules that evidence as to the injustice of the Versailles Treaty, or whether it was made under duress, is inadmissible." The volume of documents mentioned above was therefore rejected.

When, on July 5, 1946, Dr. Seidl, beginning a speech, referred to Wilson's Fourteen Points, the President of the Tribunal objected: "[T]he question of the Fourteen Points and the question of the justice of the Treaty of Versailles is irrelevant." The Tribunal, he added, was not prepared to listen to it. Dr. Seidl replied:

> I cannot leave the Tribunal ignorant of the fact that the Versailles Treaty and its consequences, especially the causal relationship with the seizure of power by National Socialism, form a considerable part of my speech,

and, having again been reminded of the ruling of the Tribunal, Dr. Seidl continued:

> Then I must construe the attitude of the Tribunal to mean that I will not be permitted to speak of the consequences of the Versailles Treaty, and particularly about the connection which these consequences had with the rise of the National Socialist Party and with the seizure of power by Adolf Hitler. . . .

That was actually the case. But it should be borne in mind that the Nuremberg Tribunal was set up to pass judgment on acts of aggression and crimes against humanity which were committed *after* the Hitler regime was *established*. It was not called upon to determine the factors accounting for Hitler's *rise to power*.

Reviewing the proceedings at Nuremberg, Sir Hartley Shaw-cross, the British Chief Prosecutor, observed on July 26, 1946:

The so-called injustice of Versailles, so cunningly exploited to provide a popular rallying point under the Nazi banner, had succeeded in uniting behind the Nazis many Germans who would not otherwise have supported some of the rest of the Nazi program. And the effect of that propaganda can be judged from the repeated efforts here made by the Defense to develop the alleged injustice of the Treaty.[144]

This statement brings out the essential points at issue, namely, the real nature of the Treaty of Versailles, the large part it played in the growth of the National Socialist movement, and the use the *Fuehrer* and his propagandists made of it in their rise to power. The proper assessment of these essential points will be a fitting task for a neutral commission of historians as is proposed in Part Two of this book.

Part Two

A Plea for Neutral
Collaboration

Sir Edward Grey, later Viscount Grey of Fallodon, felt justly outraged that, during the war of 1914-1918, official German circles declared that British foreign policy had brought about the war. He had no doubt that at least the German people believed it. So Sir Edward, while Secretary of State for Foreign Affairs, told the United States Ambassador in London, Walter H. Page, in 1916, that he would like to see it imposed as a condition of peace that the German Government should agree to submit to an impartial—neutral—commission or court the question, "Who began the war and who is responsible for it?" His idea was that all the governments concerned must submit to the tribunal all their documents and other evidence bearing on the subject; and that, of course, the finding of the tribunal must be published.[1]

Sir Edward Grey left the Foreign Office in 1916. There is no record that, in 1919, he submitted his idea to the Paris Peace Conference. But he laid down the principle, as Viscount D'Abernon has stated, that it is of "vital importance for the world" that the causes of the Great War should be examined minutely in the light of the fullest knowledge obtainable.[2] This proposal is now generally recognized as an urgent necessity by all those who sincerely wish to avoid another conflagration.

Lord Grey's desire for a neutral investigating commission became known only in 1922. Quite unaware of it, the German Government, on November 29, 1918, shortly after the conclusion of the Armistice, requested the Belgian, British, French, Italian and United States Governments to have the responsibility for the war investigated by a neutral commission. On March 7, 1919, the British Government rejected the proposal on the ground that, in the opinion of the Allies, German responsibility was proven. The German Government, however, gave its delegation to the Peace Conference the instruction: "We refuse to accept this enemy decision; no one can be at the same time prosecutor and judge." [3] This is, indeed, an old rule in common law.

Consequently, Foreign Minister Count Brockdorff-Rantzau said on May 7, 1919, in his ill-received speech: "The measure of guilt of all those who have taken part can be established only by an impartial inquiry, a neutral commission. . . . We have asked for such an inquiry and we ask for it once more." [4]

On May 24, the Allied and Associated Powers were informed that the question of responsibility for the war was one "of life or death for the German nation."

On May 27, the commission of four German experts rightly contended that this question cannot be decided by one side which was itself a party to the war. Their observations were transmitted to the Conference on the 28th.

Finally, on May 29, the German delegation reiterated its demand for a neutral examination of the responsibility for the war. [5]

The Belgian, British, French, Italian and United States Governments ignored or refused the German request of November, 1918. The twenty-seven Allied and Associated Powers represented at the Paris Conference were deaf to the three German requests and demands enumerated above.

Instead, on June 16, 1919, they declared themselves "prepared to stand by the verdict of history as to the impartiality and justice with which the accused will be tried." These accused had not only committed crimes in the war, they were also the alleged sole authors of the war, above all the former Emperor William II, as is evident from Article 227 of the Treaty of Versailles. [6] Yet, there was never a trial to establish the responsibilities for the war.

The Allied declaration just quoted was made in good faith. The governments concerned were then convinced that they could prove their charges.

Nevertheless, there is no denying the fact that the repeated Allied refusal of the German requests was a flagrant violation of an elementary principle of justice which forbids anyone to be judge in his own cause. The refusal was also a contradiction of point three of President Wilson's Four Points of July 4, 1918, which decreed:

The consent of all nations to be governed in their conduct towards each other by the same principles of honor and of respect for the common law of civilized society that govern the individual citizens of all modern states in their relations with one another; to the end that . . . a mutual trust [may be] established upon the handsome foundation of a mutual respect for right.[7]

The German Government did not invoke this particular item of the basis for peace agreed upon by all belligerents. Yet, it is obvious that it has a direct bearing on our subject. Since it was proclaimed by the President of the United States, it seems most fitting that the American people should be the first to take cognizance of it because, in the case of Germany, it was utterly disregarded in 1919 to the detriment of the indispensable mutual trust among nations.

In the years after the conclusion of peace, various German Governments made numerous efforts to secure an Allied revision of the war guilt charge. The first endeavor was made by Foreign Minister Walter Simons early in 1921, only to be told by Premier Lloyd George on March 3, that the question of responsibility "must be treated by the Allies as a *chose jugée.*"

Thereupon, Simons stated in the *Reichstag* on March 12:

There is no man and no woman in this House who believes that Germany was the sole cause of the war. I am very far from asserting that we were guiltless, but the world must gradually learn that it is wrong to say that Germany alone was guilty. It is our duty to do all we can to clear up this question.[8]

Many Germans did this, individually and through organizations. It was a popular movement in which virtually all Germany was united. The author took an active part in it from 1919 onward. In July, 1924, I issued, on my own initiative, *An Appeal to British Fair Play,* signed by 120 prominent Germans of all ranks and professions. It was a solemn declaration for the policy of fulfillment and for peace, but also an emphatic protest against the moral defamation of the German people. Most of the signers were representative supporters of the Weimar Republic. Amongst them were 27 leaders of the Social Democrats, 21 of the Democrats, 6 active pacifists, 7 active advocates of the League of Nations, 13 clergymen and theologians, and 7 women. The following men who enjoyed international reputation in their specific fields may be mentioned: (1) of statesmen, diplomats and civil servants: Bernhard Dernburg, ex-Secretary of State for the Colonies, Minister of Finance; Count J. H. von Bernstorff, pre-war Ambassador to the United States; and his Counsellor at the Embassy, Haniel von Haimhausen; Walter Simons, ex-Minister for Foreign Affairs, President of the Supreme Court, Leipzig; Rudolf Wissell, Minister of Economics; and Arnold Brecht who emigrated to the United States in 1933; (2) of leading Social Democrats (apart from Rudolf Wissell): Paul Löbe, for many years President of the *Reichstag;* and Wilhelm Hoegner who fled Germany in February, 1934 (after the war Prime Minister of Bavaria, 1945-47, since then Minister of Justice, Minister for Home Affairs, and Deputy Prime Minister); (3) of pacifists: Professor Ludwig Quidde, President of the Peace Society; (4) of clergymen and theologians: D. Adolf Deissmann; Dr. Ludwig Kaas who rose to an honored rank in the Vatican; Monsignore Dr. Kreutz; and Dr. Georg Schreiber; (5) of scholars: Dr. Moritz J. Bonn, as emigrant visiting professor in the United States, 1935, 1939-46; Dr. Christian Eckert, dismissed by the Nazis from the university; and the famous surgeon Ferdinand Sauerbruch; (6) of literary men: Wilhelm Hausenstein (May, 1950, appointed German Consul General in Paris, until recently Ambassador to France); Thomas Mann, emigrant, United States citizen; and Theodor Wolff, editor-in-chief of the *Berliner Tageblatt;* (7) of businessmen: Robert Bosch, a staunch Swabian Democrat and active opponent of the Hitler regime.

The *Appeal* logically concentrated, not on Article 231 of the Versailles Treaty, but on the all-important Allied Note of June 16, 1919. The booklet, written in English, had a distribution in Great Britain of about 8,000 copies. Its reception by the British public was much better than could have been expected at that time.

In the *Appeal,* twenty German historians and experts on historical matters declared their readiness to meet British and other foreign historians for a discussion of the origins of the recent war. By the time the Hitler regime was established, six of these twenty signers had died. Of the remaining fourteen no less than eight were dismissed from their positions or emigrated, namely: Ludwig Bergsträsser (1945-48, President-Governor of Darmstadt by appointment of United States authorities); Martin Hobohm; Ernst Jäckh, emigrated (since 1940 professor at Columbia University); Albrecht Mendels-sohn-Bartholdy, co-editor of the German documents, 1870-1914; Hermann Oncken; Paul Rohrbach, emigrated to the United States; Walther Schücking, co-editor of the German documents on the outbreak of the war; and Veit Valentin, emigrated. None of the remaining six signers played a role in the Third Reich. In fact, the only one of the 120 signers who did this, was Hjalmar Schacht, President of the Reichsbank, who had stopped the disastrous inflation in the autumn of 1923 and was a leading member of the Democrats all through the twenties.

It was in pursuit of this *Appeal to British Fair Play* that I met in England the chief author of the Allied Note of June 16, Mr. Philip Kerr. But the *Appeal* failed in its ultimate purpose: to pave the way for an official revocation of the charges in that Note.[9]

In that summer of 1924, the German Government believed that it could, with some prospect of success, once more raise the war guilt question. After an agreement had been reached on the Dawes Plan, the following proclamation was published in Berlin on August 29, 1924:

The Government cannot let this important occasion . . . pass without defining in plain and unambiguous terms their attitude in the war guilt question which since 1919 weighs upon the soul of the German people with heavy pressure. The declaration imposed on us by the Treaty of Versailles under the pressure of overwhelming force that Germany caused the outbreak of the World War by her aggression is contrary to historical fact. The Government of the Reich therefore asserts that it does not accept that declaration. The demand of the German people to be emancipated from the burden of this false accusation is a just demand. Until this has been done, and so long as a member of the community of nations is branded as a criminal to humanity, a real understanding and reconciliation between the peoples is impossible of realization.

The words "branded as a criminal to humanity" referred, of course, particularly to the Note of June, 1919. The proclamation expressed the feeling of the *whole* German nation, which was especially gratified to read that the Government would bring this pronouncement to the knowledge of foreign Powers.[10] But, immediately, a bitter disappointment followed.

The Quai d'Orsay declared in an official *Communiqué,*
published on August 31, 1924, that the German thesis runs
counter not only to the factual evidence but also to the formal
terms of the Versailles Treaty, *i.e.,* to the *chose jugée* as Lloyd
George expressed it in March, 1921.[11] In the next few days
the German Government was showered with protests from
foreign countries and with admonitions on the part of their
representatives. Prime Minister MacDonald informed Berlin
that, if this war guilt proclamation was officially submitted,
everything that had been accomplished so far to alleviate Germany's situation, would be annihilated; that France and her
satellite states were determined to have the war guilt verdict
confirmed anew; and that Germany's proposed step would be
"a catastrophe for her and for the world." [12]

The reaction of France was especially vehement. That British leaders close to official circles had some sympathy for the
German case was apparent to the present writer from the reception the *Appeal* had received a few months before and
from what he learned in May, 1925, in England.

Meanwhile, the German Government waited for a more
favorable opportunity for carrying out its intention of August,
1924.

On September 15, 1925, Germany was invited by the British, French and Belgian Governments to attend a conference
for the discussion of a security pact, the conclusion of which
was to precede her entry into the League of Nations. Accepting the invitation, the German Government, on September 26,
1925, submitted to the three Powers a "Verbal Memorandum"
in which it recalled its former declaration of September, 1924,
that Germany's entry into the League would not imply her
admission of a moral charge, and quoted the entire proclamation of August 29, 1924. The Government believed, so the
Memorandum stated, that this proclamation promoted the aim
of an understanding between the peoples and of their sincere
reconciliation. The Government expressly identified itself with
the proclamation "in the wish of creating thereby the condition of mutual esteem and inmost equality of rights which is
essential for the success of the confidential conversations now
contemplated." [13]

On September 29, 1925, the British Government replied
that the negotiation of a security pact "cannot modify the
Treaty of Versailles or alter their judgment of the past." The

answers of the French and Belgian Governments were similar.[14]

The German Government, in its turn, issued on October 3, 1925, a semi-official article in the press stating that the German people did not feel morally bound by the Versailles confession of guilt.[15]

Another year went by. The German people constantly urged their Government to take more determined action. At a rally of the People's Party at Cologne on October 2, 1926, Foreign Minister Gustav Stresemann declared:

We are ready to appear before any impartial court that inquires into the origins of the World War. Whoever has the same good conscience as we have, should follow our example. Mankind has a right to learn the truth, and no one will be able permanently to oppose this desire of humanity for an impartial arbitrament.[16]

On September 18, 1927, Reich President von Hindenburg, inaugurating the Tannenberg National Memorial, said that the German people unanimously reject the war guilt charge, and he repeated Germany's readiness at any time to prove before impartial judges that, for her, the war was essentially a war of defence.[17]

A week afterwards, Stresemann told Jules Sauerwein, the Berlin correspondent of *Le Matin,* that the German people consider the war guilt charge as the gravest insult inflicted upon them, and that they would not accept a verdict by prosecutors who were at the same time judges. Again, the reaction in the French press was violent.[18]

On the tenth anniversary of the conclusion of peace, June 28, 1929, Reich President von Hindenburg and the Cabinet of the Government issued a manifesto stating that the accusation of having caused the war does not give any peace to the German people and disturbs the trust amongst the nations; "we are at one with all Germans in repudiating the contention of Germany's sole guilt." [19]

Finally, in the summer of 1932, at the Lausanne Conference, Chancellor von Papen appealed personally to the Prime Ministers of Britain and of France for cancellation of the war guilt clause since its link with the reparations was now meaningless. This time, Premier MacDonald was willing to act but his French colleague refused.[20]

Apart from these official efforts there were plenty of private endeavors made by Germans to bring about a revision of the Versailles charges.

We have noted Sir Edward Grey's proposed condition of peace in 1916. This was exactly what various German Governments from November, 1918, all through the Weimar period, persistently asked for. Lord Grey's change of attitude in this matter is illuminating. His biographer, George Macaulay Trevelyan, tells us that Viscount Grey thought the refusal to allow the Germans to be heard at the Paris Peace Conference was "an outrage without precedent." [21] In later years, Grey explicitly disapproved of the war guilt clause in the Treaty and rejected the doctrine of Germany's sole guilt.[22] On the other hand, he warned in his Memoirs against devoting too much attention to the question of war guilt.[23]

Lord Grey was generally held in high esteem at home as well as abroad, and he could have wielded an enormous influence on public opinion, particularly in Great Britain and the United States, if, after 1919, he had advocated the implementation of his 1916 desire for a neutral investigation. With this view in mind, the author published in 1927, in German, and in 1928 in English, an *Appeal to Lord Grey and His Country* in which I stated that the German nation will never rest content with the misjudgment of Versailles. The sooner that was recognized outside Germany the better. I reminded Lord Grey of his own wish in 1916 for an impartial investigation of the war guilt controversy as a condition of peace, and I asked why he now advised against devoting too much attention to it—to *this question which, in the interval, was made the expressed basis for the treaty of peace?* I urged that "Europe's moral problem" should be determined by an impartial tribunal, and I closed the *Appeal* with the following passage:

So long as the German demand for the most elementary justice is not completely satisfied, the longing of our best Europeans will remain unsatisfied. How can good come out of the lie of Versailles? True peace between nations cannot be based on self-righteousness, only on universal righteousness.[24]

I have good reason to believe that this *Appeal* was duly brought to Lord Grey's attention and that he privately ac-

knowledged that there was justification for making it. Yet
there was no response from him. It appears that, from the end
of the war until his death in 1933, Grey persistently ignored
his own former judicious desire for arbitration although he
was convinced that any impartial verdict would establish the
fact that, in 1914, he strove for peace to the best of his ability
and that he hated the very idea of war. Why then this striking contradiction?

When I wrote the specific *Appeal to Lord Grey* I believed
that, in this matter of paramount importance for the world, a
gentleman of the rank of Viscount Grey could not well ignore
it. For, in 1916, when accused by Germans of being responsible for the war, he wanted a neutral commission set up for
his own vindication. Now, the situation was reversed: Germany was the accused, and she naturally wanted what he himself had desired. But he never intervened to advocate for Germany—although she was charged with much greater offences
than he had ever been—the same course he had wished for
his own protection.

The case is an instructive illustration of the notorious difference between statesmen's and politicians' conduct in personal matters and their conduct in public affairs. In point
three of July 4, 1918, President Wilson aimed at preventing
such discrepancies, and Cordell Hull denounced them in his
Memoirs.[25]

There is no doubt whatsoever that, in a private matter, Lord
Grey, like any other gentleman, would have insisted on justice being done by an impartial court. There is, also, no doubt
whatsoever that he was sincere in his condemnation of the refusal to grant the Germans a hearing at the Peace Conference
as "an outrage without precedent." But he felt that, as a politician, he could not go farther, although in his heart he wished
to be at liberty to take publicly such action as honor would
demand.

The explanation for Grey's inconsistent conduct is that he
found himself in a painful quandary. The Allies had based
the Treaty of Versailles on Germany's sole responsibility for
the war. He knew that a neutral verdict would deprive the
Treaty of this basis. He also knew that, for this reason, his
Government, and even more so the French Government, was
dead set against a neutral investigation. He knew, as every
politician has known since 1919, that the assertion of Ger-

many's exclusive guilt was an *instrument of power politics,* pure and simple. So as a British patriot, Lord Grey, although unhappy over the Treaty, followed the honored motto, "Right or Wrong: My Country!" Most politicians, in similar situations, have taken the same course.

There were, for instance, David Lloyd George and his former secretary, Philip Kerr-Lord Lothian. Both recognized by the mid-twenties the wrongs they had done in 1919; both developed a "guilt complex," as did many other leading Britons. Yet, they would not apply the only really effective remedy. Their half-hearted steps are clearly revealed in an article, entitled "War Guilt," which J. L. Garvin, editor of the *Observer,* published in the *Encyclopaedia Britannica* in 1929 and which ran through all its editions up to the Second World War. "The present situation is a moral deadlock," Garvin wrote, "and Germany as a whole desires some formal withdrawal of Article 231 in the Treaty of Versailles." Garvin thought "this form of moral triumph" impracticable. It would have a one-sided effect, he argued, and would by itself "be interpreted as an admission of the ex-Allies—with or without their former associates—that they were chiefly in the wrong. This, their peoples do not admit now, and never will admit hereafter." Instead, Garvin declared, "Article 231 is already a dead-letter in the moral sense, and the futility of Article 227 is only remembered with ridicule." When he wrote this, he was hopeful that there would not be another great war.[26]

Integral parts of Garvin's "War Guilt" article were two sections dealing with the historical events that led to the outbreak of the war in 1914, one written by the French historian Pierre Renouvin, the other by the present writer. From this fact, it has wrongly been inferred that I was in agreement with J. L. Garvin's lines of reasoning. If I had known them before the article was printed, I would have raised the following objections:

In 1929, Article 231, in the commonly accepted interpretation, was far from being a dead-letter in the moral sense. The argument that a withdrawal of the Article would be regarded as an admission of the Allies that they were *chiefly* in the wrong, was unsound. Above all, Garvin failed entirely to refer to the Allied document of June 16, 1919. The charges of the document were, and remain, the *main* issue, being the core of the whole matter. For Article 231 is but a weak and condensed, as well as distorted, symbol for the plain and sweeping verdict of June 16.

On the other hand, I was in complete agreement with Garvin's statement that "Germany as a whole" desired a formal withdrawal of the war guilt charge. I, personally, have never swerved from the stand I took in 1919 that only neutral arbitration would offer a satisfactory solution of the knotty problem which the Allied and Associated Powers bestowed on the world in 1919.

Garvin's move in 1929 was a well-meant endeavor to discard the war guilt controversy. If his contention that the peoples of the Allies will never admit having been partly in the wrong should turn out to be true, the inescapable conclusion would be this:

The German people were forced at the point of the bayonet to admit, against their firm conviction, a horrible guilt of the gravest, dishonoring kind;

The peoples of the Allies, despite abundant evidence disproving the charge, will never admit having been in the wrong.

I reject absolutely such a conclusion. I retain an unshakable faith in the fundamental sense of fairness which distinguishes the Anglo-Saxon peoples. Garvin's contention only confirms the indispensable necessity for a settlement of the war guilt controversy by a court of neutral experts.

Suppose that, in the late twenties, such a court had been set up to decide merely two practical questions: (1) have the German people, as distinct from their Government, any responsibility for the outbreak of hostilities in 1914? And (2), were the German armies defeated in 1918? The easily reached finding of the court would have been:

(1) The German people "did not originate or desire this hideous war," as President Wilson stated in June, 1917, because they were not initiated into the course of the diplomatic negotiations in July and August, 1914, and were not a party to them.

(2) The German armies were beaten in 1918 and would have fought a steadily losing battle if they had continued the fighting.

Had these two simple verdicts been proclaimed by 1932, Adolf Hitler and his cleverest propagandists would have been deprived of the vicious use they continually made of the "stab in the back" myth and of the war guilt accusations levelled against the German people. Both points were major weapons in the Nazi armory. Both procured for Hitler and his movement millions of followers. Quite apart from that, the readiness of the victors to submit such questions of vital importance to arbitration would have made a tremendous impression on the German masses, would have rekindled their faith in the fairness of the victors, and would have enormously strengthened the democratic elements in the country. What such action would have meant in 1932 becomes evident from the elections figures in that year. In July, the Nazis obtained 230 seats in the *Reichstag* out of a total of 608, in November, 196 seats out of 584. That is, at best, less than 30 per cent.[27] In view of this fact, the writer, on the strength of his intimate knowledge of the situation in Germany, asserts with absolute conviction that the formation of a neutral commission to decide the pending issues, and the proclamation of those two provisionary verdicts, would have prevented Hitler and the Nazis from making themselves masters over Germany.

We have a remarkable British testimony to this effect. Sir Horace Rumbold, reporting to the Foreign Office on February 22, 1933, criticized the German leftists for their slackness in the matter of educational policy and stated: "Had they insisted on teaching the true facts of the history of the war, the immature supporters of Hitler would not be so easily misled today." [28]

Chapter Two of the present book has shown that, in 1919, the victors claimed to have placed the Treaty of Versailles on a moral basis. Prime Minister Raymond Poincaré explicitly confirmed this in the *Chambre des Députés* on July 6, 1922. Defending himself from attacks, chiefly by Communists, on his own pre-war policy, he declared: "The authors of the Treaty of Versailles wished above all that it should rest on a moral idea," namely Imperial Germany's exclusive and total guilt for the war.[29]

The good faith of the Principal Allies in 1919 should not be doubted, since Russia was not a member of the Conference. But subsequent historical revelations gradually undermined that moral basis. It was a recognition of this fact which prompted Harold Nicolson, in 1933, to speak of the "appalling hypocrisy" of the Paris Conference. An apparent act of morality in 1919 thus turned little by little into an act of gross immorality.

The great calamity was not the victors' display of morality in 1919. The great calamity was that, when the self-chosen foundation for that comforting morality was visibly cracking up and was seen to rest on shifting sand, no Allied statesman in power had the moral courage officially to admit the fallacy of the historical verdict propagated in 1919 and to advocate a revision of that verdict through arbitration. Such a course would obviously have been in accord with President Wilson's point three of July 4, 1918. It would not only have been the honorable one to take: it would have been the wise and the safe course. For peace cannot be built upon a fallacy—the Versailles verdict—nor on the persistent denial of elementary justice—neutral arbitration—to a nation. In 1919, the Allies had stressed the sound principle that "reparation for wrongs inflicted is of the essence of justice." [30] The failure of Great Britain and France (since the United States withdrew in 1920) to live up to their own lofty principles—this moral failure was the great evil that essentially determined the fate of Europe. This evil is still virulent and, until it is expurgated, all efforts for constructing a peaceable Western world are likely to miscarry in the end.

This applies especially to the indispensable basis for a solid foundation of the United States of Europe: a friendly understanding between the French and the Germans and their gradual genuine reconciliation. They have now, for decades, been abysmally separated by the notion that Germany forced the war of 1870 on an innocent France and that Germany alone caused the First World War.

Salvador de Madariaga, an indefatigable worker for international peace, truly observed, in 1938, that the antagonism between France and Germany "has become one of the psychological laws within the soul of Europe." [31] The transformation of this antagonism into definite friendship must be mainly a psychological process based on the mutual recognition of the historical facts which shaped the events of the last ninety years and, above all, the events that produced the war of 1914-18, and brought about the triumph of Adolf Hitler.

With a clear vision, Alfred Fabre-Luce emphasized in 1924: *"No doubt, only the official version of the origins of the war stands between us and an irresistible movement of pacifism"* in France and Germany.[32] Likewise, in the inter-war period, the *League des Droits de l'Homme* held that friendship between the two Rhine countries would prove one of the greatest of all factors for world peace.[33] That is truer today than it has ever been. Indeed, in September, 1954, both Premier Pierre Mendès-France and Chancellor Konrad Adenauer officially declared that the organization of Europe must be based on lasting German-French reconciliation.[34]

From personal experiences in France and amicable ties with numerous Frenchmen extending over more than forty years, the author is firmly convinced that, under proper conditions, friendly understanding between the French and the German peoples can be developed without great difficulty. In 1901-02 I was witness to the fact that the French masses were quite ready to forget Imperial France's defeat in 1870 if Germany had shown willingness to revise the Treaty of Frankfort, say by giving autonomy to Alsace-Lorraine, or by allowing a plebiscite to decide the fate of the two provinces. I was also witness in the following years to the fact that French sentiment gradually underwent a radical change, so that by 1913 there was general animosity toward Germany. I was in Normandy from September, 1940, to July, 1942, and again for seven months in 1944, and I was a witness to the fact that, by a liberal policy, Hitler-Germany could have concluded an honorable peace with the French on terms acceptable to both sides. Indeed, up to 1942, there was sincere gratitude amongst the French for German reconstruction activities and for German aid in the revival of French industry. There was widespread admiration for German efficiency and, in the early years of the occupation, many true friendships were formed which have endured to the present day. I, therefore, underscore with all emphasis the assertion that the possibilities for a genuine understanding between the two peoples are plainly given.

The main prerequisite is, essentially, the unbiased teaching of history. The Germans and the French alike need to be enlightened about the origins of the war of 1870, about the Peace of Frankfort in 1871, about the war scare of 1875, about the underlying and immediate causes of the First World War, about the peace settlements in 1919-20, and about the main factors accounting for Hitler's rise to power.

With deep insight, Alfred Fabre-Luce, this truly European-minded Frenchman, wrote in 1940:

French-German friendship . . . will come to life on the day when on both sides of the Rhine some solemn step is taken. To make this step possible it will be necessary to reform educational textbooks, to distribute equitably the responsibilities for the war of 1914—

to which he added in a footnote: "For 1870 that is done. What a delay!" [35] This annotation refers to a remarkable German-French collaboration in historical revision which deserves to be generally known.

In the autumn of 1935, a meeting took place in Paris between two German and eight French historians who came to a number of conclusions concerning Franco-German history. These conclusions were published rather widely in the French press in 1937, but very little in Germany because, apparently, they did not suit Nazi policy at the time.

In May, 1951, there was another meeting, consisting of eight German historians and a French commission, at the Sorbonne in Paris, followed by a third meeting at Mayence in October, 1951, both for a revision of the conclusions drawn up in 1935. Forty "Recommendations" were formulated, partly by the French and partly by the Germans, for use by teachers of history in the schools of the two countries. For the present book the following excerpts from the forty recommendations are particularly noteworthy:

VII B. Bismarck's Policy

Bismarck's aspiration to found a German National State corresponded to the policy which the Western European states had pursued for centuries. He was therefore fully justified in regarding Napoleon's policy in the question of annexing South Germans as well as in that of territorial "compensations" as an obstacle to German vital interests. He was determined to remove this obstacle, if necessary by resorting to war—without, however, striving from the outset for a war as the only means for attaining his national policy.

. . . .

Bismarck counted on the possibility that the internal difficulties which the regime of Napoleon III had to face, would induce the

French Government to allow German unification to come about peaceably. But he was determined, in case this prospect did not materialize, to break French opposition by force.

VIII

A justly balanced account of the *outbreak of the war of 1870* must stress the fact that both sides contributed to aggravate the existing tension:

1) Bismarck by secretly encouraging the Hohenzollern candidacy for the Spanish throne hoping thereby to out-maneuvre Napoleon and to drive him diplomatically into such a tight position that the downfall of the Imperial regime could be the consequence. Perhaps he also intended to weaken France militarily in case of war by the creation of a front in the Pyrenees.

2) Napoleon and his Cabinet by overstressing their diplomatic-political counter-offensive from the 6th of July on, above all by demanding from King William a guarantee by which they put themselves in the wrong in the eyes of Europe, although Napoleon and most of his Ministers really feared rather than desired war.

3) Finally Bismarck by the well-known condensation of the Ems telegram which undoubtedly does not constitute a "falsification" but a conscious aggravation with the purpose of forcing France to accept a grave diplomatic defeat or to declare war.

It must be acknowledged that the German as well as the French peoples went to war in the honest conviction of having been provoked by the other side, both without exact knowledge of the diplomatic circumstances which were cleared up only very much later.

IX

On the subject of French-German relations between 1871 and 1890 the members of the Commission are in agreement:

1) that during this period Bismarck's aim was to assure to the German Empire the maintenance of the situation reached and that he did not attempt to provoke a new conflict; there is no proof that in 1875 or in 1887 Bismarck wanted war, despite the misgivings aroused in France by certain German press campaigns. . . .

X

French school-books often exaggerate the importance of the Pan-German movement. Like all active minorities the Pan-German group was able in diverse circumstances to affect public opinion; but it had no determining influence on the Government's policy, and it was combated by the democratic parties (Social Democracy, Center Party). . . .

XVIII

Documentary sources do not warrant attributing to any Government or to any people in 1914 a premeditated will for a European war. Distrust was at its peak, and in governing circles the idea prevailed that war was inevitable; everyone attributed to the other aggressive designs; everyone accepted the risk of war and saw a safeguard for his security only in the system of alliances and in the expansion of armaments.

XIX

1) Certain circles in the German General Staff believed Germany's chances of success were better in 1914 than they would be in the following years; yet it cannot be inferred that these considerations determined the course of the German Government's policy.

2) The great majority of the German as well as of the French peoples did not want war; in Germany, however, especially in military circles, there was more inclination than in France to accept the outbreak of a war. This readiness is attributable to the position of the army in German society; moreover, the German people, because of their geographical situation in the center, have always felt themselves to be more seriously threatened by opposing alliances.

3) The former conception according to which Poincaré pursued an active war policy is also no longer endorsed by German historians. But through the entanglement of the European alliances a situation was created in which on the German side French-Russian cooperation was felt to be a direct danger.

XXVII

In 1914, German policy did not aim at provoking a European war; it was determined above all by the obligations toward Austria-Hungary in virtue of the alliance. In order to counter-act this state's disintegration which was considered dangerous, assurances were given to the Vienna Government which were tantamount to a blank check. The German Government was dominated by the idea that it would be possible to localize the conflict with Serbia as was done in 1908-09; nevertheless, it was ready, if the necessity arose, to run the risk of a European war. Consequently it failed to exercise a restraining influence on Austrian policy in time. Only from July 28th on did Bethmann-Hollweg take steps in this direction. On the other hand Moltke, as Chief of the General Staff, under the impression that the European conflict was inevitable, urged on July 30th for purely military considerations the speeding of the order for general mobilization in Austria-Hungary.

The Russian general mobilization ordered on July 30th necessarily entailed a German decision for mobilization. From July 31st on the conduct of the German Government as well as that of the other continental Powers was determined by military considerations which put the political considerations into the background. The German measures were based on the firm conviction that in a German-Russian war France would under no circumstances remain neutral, and that a war on two fronts could be waged successfully only if it was opened by a march through Belgium for the envelopment and the speedy crushing of the French army.

This military situation led generally to a fateful precipitation of mobilizations, in Germany also of the ultimatums and declarations of war.[36]

These Franco-German recommendations for teaching history in both countries are of great importance. They reveal some of the serious misconceptions discussed in the first chapter of the present book, concerning the events in 1870, in 1875, and in 1914. They also reveal similar serious misconceptions among Germans regarding the wars of 1870 and 1914-18.

M. Fabre-Luce demands that Franco-German reconciliation be brought about by repudiation of war propaganda and by the joint writing of history.[37] The Franco-German recommendations presented above show that such joint writing of history is feasible. But they lack precision; they lack compulsory acceptance; they lack neutral status and authority. No French, or German, or foreign statesman, politician, or publicist is compelled to heed any of these recommendations. The urgent necessity is, therefore, to find means which will in the future prevent the dissemination of historical untruths and distortions. This can only be achieved through the formation of neutral commissions, composed of competent experts and endowed with sufficient authority to make their findings obligatory for all concerned.

The great Spaniard, Salvador de Madariaga, rightly pointed out, in 1938, that "a Court of Justice is an inevitable necessity on the road to real peace." [38] The world sorely needs such a court for the purification of the political atmosphere from the ever-virulent poison of historical falsehoods. Hitler-Germany spread such poison in large quantity. But Chapter One made it clear that, in this respect, Germany was by no means solely guilty. An additional example may be mentioned.

Lindley Fraser, since 1946 Head of the German and Austrian Services of the British Broadcasting Corporation, published a book in 1944, "primarily intended to be read by Germans—as a means of showing them how they had been misled by their own propagandists both before and during the National Socialist regime." But the book was also designed to assist British and American officers to understand the intellectual background of the German people. Fraser stated in this book that the Treaty of Versailles

neither departed from the principles of the Fourteen Points in any particular of major importance, nor was it unjust on its merits, except in so far as it pinned a share of the responsibility for the war on to Germany without submitting the whole question of war guilt to a thorough and impartial analysis.[39]

Mr. Fraser certainly did not mean to pervert historical truth. Yet, in that one sentence there are several glaring untruths on a matter of highest importance. The impression of such statements on German intellectuals, most of whom know the Treaty of Versailles far better than any of their opponents, can only have been devastating.

It is gratifying, however, that Fraser thought Germans had legitimate grounds for protest because they "felt" they were branded as war criminals without being given any chance to state their case.[40]

Over the years prominent Britons have made various proposals for settling the war guilt controversy. The first one was E. D. Morel, a far-sighted politician, a true humanitarian, and an indefatigable champion of justice. Exposing, in 1922, the fallacy of one-sided responsibility for the recent war in a brochure *The Poison that Destroys,* he gave it the significant subtitle *The Case for a National Inquiry into the Causes of the War and the Disaster of the Peace.*[41] Morel, whose father was French, was thoroughly hated in those years by millions of Englishmen and even more so by Frenchmen. In reality, both countries should be proud of him. Few truer forecasts were made than those by "E. D. M." in regard to the dire consequences in store for Europe if the war guilt charge and the Versailles Treaty were not revised.

In 1932, when Hitler's seizure of power was apprehended,
B. G. de Montgomery pleaded the cause of Germany "before
the mightiest of all tribunals, the public opinion of the world,"
in a book *Versailles: A Breach of Agreement,* which is particularly noteworthy because of the fact that its author believed the German Government was really guilty in 1914. But,
he declared, "even a guilty nation is entitled to justice, especially on the part of those who preach the sanctity of international agreements." De Montgomery felt the lurking fear of
a fresh conflagration. Since justice, "even-handed and dispassionate," was not done to Germany at Versailles, he demanded
that an effort must be made to right the wrongs done to her.
Germany's case should be "thoroughly revised in the light of
fresh and impartial evidence." [42]

Next came Professor Gilbert Murray, one of the most distinguished British scholars. He felt in 1933 that it was a mere
piece of insolence for the victors to say that the war was entirely due to the crimes of the vanquished, and a cruel mockery
to hold the vanquished down and starve them until they were
forced to admit the charge. "It ought to be stated clearly, publicly and officially," he urged, "that Germany and her Allies
are no longer thought guilty of having 'plotted to bring about
a world war.' " [43]

In 1938, the prominent British historian, R. W. Seton-
Watson, penned five chief criticisms of the Versailles Treaty.
In point three he stated:

. . . the charge of exclusive "War Guilt" sometimes levelled
against Germany is as absurd and untenable as the charge once
levelled by German opinion against Sir Edward Grey as the real
author of the war, and now universally abandoned as ridiculous. . . .

With regard to the "War-Guilt Clause" (Article 231),
Seton-Watson recommended a statement distinguishing between the immediate and the ultimate causes of the war, and
"declaring this to be a fitting matter for investigation by an
international committee of historical experts." He thought the
time was surely ripe for public admission of his five points.
And he added, very judiciously: "It would not be a sign of
weakness, but of strength and sanity of judgment." [44]

Seton-Watson's plea is particularly noteworthy because of
his well-known contacts with British official circles. In fact, it

appears that for some time in the mid-thirties leading members of the British Government were contemplating such a step as Seton-Watson advised. On April 15, 1936, Prentiss Gilbert, the United States representative at the League of Nations, Geneva, reported to Secretary of State Cordell Hull that, as a friendly gesture towards Germany, the British Cabinet would be willing to "remove the 'guilt clauses' from the Treaty" if Germany gave up claims for colonial mandates; and that Britain would not "permit Germany to be put again in the 'dock.' " [45]

This was a highly significant development, coming at the time of Hitler's regime, when compared to the hostile attitude adopted toward the Weimar Republic.

World War II has complicated the problem but, if anything, it has made the unbiassed establishment of the principal responsibilities for the First World War more imperative than ever.

We have had the trials of the criminals of World War II. Their worst feature was that, among the judges, sat representatives of Josef Stalin who, by his Pact of August, 1939, deliberately encouraged Hitler to make war on Poland. The defendants at Nuremberg were, as we have seen, forbidden by the Prosecution to discuss the nature and consequences of the Treaty of Versailles.[46] Yet, Hitler was mainly the bitter fruit of Versailles. Moreover, World War II was the direct outcome of the First World War and therefore the latter cannot be bypassed.

An outstanding critic of the Nuremberg trials, Lord Hankey, exclaimed: "I am horrified at the idea of future Anglo-German relations being poisoned by false history" [47]—a very pertinent observation. But the poisoning had already made itself felt by the beginning of our century; it increased its vigor with each crisis, from 1905 to 1914; and it has been virulent in *both* camps ever since 1919, perniciously affecting the relationships of the Great Powers.

The author's public appeals, in 1924 and in 1927-28, addressed by a German to Britons, failed in their chief aim. Now I venture to issue a third public appeal, this time as a United States citizen, addressed, in the first place, to the peoples of the United States, of Great Britain, and of France, but also more broadly to the peoples of the other twenty-four states whose governments, as Allied and Associated Powers, endorsed the document of June 16, 1919.

The essential facts, strictly within the limits of the present study, may be summarized as follows:

The refusal of the Allies to grant the German delegation at the Peace Conference in 1919 a proper hearing was, in Lord Grey's words, "an outrage without precedence."

The peace terms were partly in flat contradiction to President Wilson's program as agreed upon by all belligerents.

The German people of the Weimar Republic were betrayed.

The persistent refusal of the Allies to submit the fundamental question of responsibility for the war to neutral investigation was contrary to President Wilson's point three of July 4, 1918, and constituted a continued flagrant violation of an elementary principle of justice, aggravated by the Allies' claim that they acted as guardians of civilization.

Allied and neutral expert research has, since Versailles, proved the fallacy of the war-guilt verdict.

This verdict by the victors in their own cause has acquired a particularly obnoxious and odious flavor by the fact that two of the Five Principal Allies, Japan from 1931 onward, and Italy from 1935 onward, themselves became convicted aggressors.

It is plain that these facts will provide any skilful agitator and demagogue with highly inflammable material for arousing passionate emotions against the Democracies. The contempt which Nazi leaders heaped upon the Democracies stemmed largely from those facts.

The Bolsheviks were no party to the Versailles verdict. On the contrary, soon after 1919, they spontaneously supplied Germans with documentary material for combating the arbitrary Allied charges. This helped, as was stated in Chapter Three, to pave the way for Rapallo in 1922 and to inaugurate an intimate collaboration between the *Reichswehr* and the Red Army up to 1933, a collaboration clearly for the benefit of both sides and one which would have given history quite a different turn if Chancellor Hitler had pursued the course urged by the *Reichswehr* generals, instead of making a pact with Poland's Marshal Pilsudski in 1934.

We are living in a rapidly changing world. Some Allies in

the First World War were bitter enemies in the Second. Now, Germany's turn has come. She is being wooed into the Western European Union as an indispensable force for the preservation of the Free World. At the same time, the Kremlin has made a *volte-face* in its former attitude towards past German history. As recorded earlier, the Soviet Foreign Ministry has now revived the Allied 1919 verdict on German aggression during the last fifty years in order to frustrate West Germany's rearmament, thus using against the Democracies the very weapon which they themselves forged against Germany in 1919!

An important point for serious consideration is that rearmament is vehemently opposed by the German youth destined to build up the new army. On November 11, 1954, General Günther Blumentritt, a wholehearted Westerner, wrote the author that anyone in contact with Germans of all walks of life would quickly establish the fact that "at the most 25 per cent of the young people are willing to serve." Several American scholars who contributed to the remarkable symposium "Germany's Foreign Policy" in *Current History,* April, 1955, have stressed this aspect. Karl Loewenstein put the matter bluntly:

Nobody in Germany favors remilitarization, with the exception of some former military professionals. Of the responsible strata . . . none sees any advantage in it. . . . Heavy industry likewise visualizes rearmament with deep misgivings. Production of armaments would cut into the profitable export trade. . . . For the first time in history, the German nation in its vast majority is anti-militaristic if not outright pacifist.[48]

Indeed, the Germans live in fear of another war in Europe that would make a desert or graveyard of their country. Instead, every German patriot desires, above all, the reunification of his Fatherland which can be achieved without war only with the cooperation of Soviet Russia who is holding East Germany, with a population of some eighteen million, firmly in her grip. For the Soviets, on their part, it is of vital interest to prevent effective German rearmament, and they will employ all means to impede it. We do not know what kind of development, or evolution, the Soviet Union may undergo; what kind of attraction it may, some day, offer to Germany. Economically and industrially, Germany and Russia complement each other in a marvellous way. Both Powers combined would easily dominate continental Europe and most of Asia. The French politician, Paul Reynaud, observed recently with good reason:

Germany is not a peril in itself. But should she turn to the East, we are lost. For . . . it is Russia who holds in her hands all that Germany wants: her reunification first. . . . Germany needs to export towards Eastern Europe, towards Russia, towards China. What would she not do to secure these markets? And even this is not all, for Russia can offer to Germany, as the supreme gift, the restitution of all or part of the territories which she holds. If Germany is once again dominated by her Great General Staff, can one be sure that she won't accept to change camps for a price like this? [49]

In this respect Karl Loewenstein voiced a serious warning:

A grave danger looms behind the issues of rearmament and unification . . . if the Soviets would offer as a package deal unification and the lost territories in return for a political and economic alliance, [German] industry and labor alike would wholeheartedly grasp this opportunity of access to the unlimited markets of the East. . . . Ideological scruples would not stand in the way of this grandiose scheme, privately much mooted about in Germany. . . . Understanding with Russia has been the pillar of German foreign policy for almost two centuries. . . . He who knows German history . . . should not dismiss lightly this fearful contingency of a future Berlin-Moscow-Peiping axis. If materializing truly, it would spell the *Untergang des Abendlandes*.[50]

Similar apprehensions tormented Chancellor Konrad Adenauer when the European Defense Community plan was wrecked by France. Fearing "the reviving game of European national states" he said to the Benelux Foreign Ministers:

I am 100 per cent convinced that the German national army that Mendès-France forces upon us will become a big danger for Germany and for Europe. . . . My God, I don't know what my successors will do if they are left to themselves, if they are not bound to Europe.[51]

To bind the Germans solidly to Europe—that is, indeed, the crucial issue. It must be the predominant, and continued, concern of the Democracies, as has been clearly realized in the United States. In 1954, George F. Kennan, an authority on the Soviet Union and European policy, recalled the truism that a combination of the physical resources and man-power of Russia and China with the technical skills and machine tools of Germany and eastern Europe might spell a military reality more powerful than anything that could be mobilized against it on its own territory from any other place in this world.

Kennan felt "that this combination was well on the way to fruition," and he properly stressed:

That leaves the relationship between Germany and Russia at the heart of our security problem . . . it means that the heart of our problem is to prevent the gathering together of the military-industrial potential of the entire Eurasian land mass under a single power threatening the interests of the insular and maritime portions of the globe.[52]

In the American estimate, Germany will have an army "which should prove the most formidable component of free Europe's defense." [53] As an experienced strategist, General Blumentritt, formerly Field Marshal G. von Rundstedt's Chief of Staff, also pointed out in letters to the author that the West could not be defended without France because the French harbors and communications are absolutely necessary for the steady supply of the armed forces operating eastwards; that, in fact, France represents the nucleus for an effective defense. Therefore, he insists, the French and the Germans *must* join hands. Enlarging on the subject, a leading article in *The New York Times* stated on October 10, 1954: "Europe can be defended politically only if the West European nations, and especially France and Germany, join in a common cause able to inspire a new idealism. . . ." Yet, so far, the existing situation does not offer a favorable prospect for the realization of such an idealism.

French distrust of Germany is deep-rooted, one might say, boundless. It must be expected that, concurrently with the progress of German rearmament, this distrust will progressively mount.

In Germany, the idea of the United Nations of Europe is widely appreciated, and many forces are at work to promote friendship with France. On the other hand, 20,000 officers and 150,000 men of the old German army will form the cadres of the new army. They have been taught the Nazi version of history, above all, the hard facts—and some distortions—of "Versailles," where France played the role of Ger-

many's "mortal foe." Besides, many of these old-timers are
sure to remember the bitter charge Field Marshal Montgomery
impressed on the Germans in 1945; and that the American
comrade-in-arms of "Monty," General George C. Marshall,
characterized them as a "criminal nation." Finally, there were
the Allied trials of leading German soldiers. On this subject,
Time wrote on October 18, 1945, "that U.S. representatives
then sat with Communist judges to try others on charges of
'crimes against humanity' is now recognized as a mockery of
justice." Is it to be expected that the 170,000 soldiers of the
old army—the backbone of the new one—will meekly forget
all that? Or that the parents and relatives of the 330,000 soldiers to be drafted, mostly quite against their wish, will do
so—the parents and relatives who lived through the humiliations and miseries of "Versailles"? Moreover, for five years
after Germany's surrender in May, 1945, the victors did all
they possibly could to wipe out in the Germans all military
spirit, persistently defaming the very profession of a soldier.
Consequently, there is widespread distrust amongst Germans
and a fear that their troops will be regarded merely as "paid
mercenaries." [54]

France, naturally, demands adequate safeguards against
German militarism. On this important question the American
General Alfred M. Gruenther has, as Supreme Allied Commander of the armed forces of the North Atlantic Treaty Organization, appropriately remarked: "The only real safeguards
that you are going to get are those that come from the heart." [55]
That is, in fact, the hard core of the matter.

The Soviet Russians have been building up a powerful army
in East Germany. Under present conditions, they would not
risk opposing it to a West German army. But, being dictators,
they can reverse their policy towards Germany overnight (as
they did towards Austria in April, 1955). It should be kept
in mind that, in the twenties, the Soviet Government sided with
Germany against "Versailles." It is safe to predict that they
will do so again when it suits their purpose. If, at an oppor-
tune moment within the next three or four years, the Russians,
together with numbers of Germans, were to launch a ferocious campaign against the Democracies, posing as true friends
of the Germans, recalling their betrayal by the victors in
1919, the constant Allied refusal to do the Germans justice in

a matter declared to be one of life or death for them—such a virulent campaign, carried on with the efficacious armory the agitators will have at their disposal, would inevitably create most serious complications with the West.

The surest safeguard against this potentiality, fraught with incalculable consequences, is to make the Germans immune from that kind of agitation by destroying the armory it would use. This may well be done in a short space of time by a determined effort of the Democracies to satisfy the Germans on the points summarized above by submitting them to arbitration. If that is done, the Democracies will forge *spiritual* ties, not only with the West Germans but also with most East Germans, which may well prove much more solid than economic, military, or any other ties. France, above all, should, in her own well-considered interest, be eager to foster such ties. For, if Paul Reynaud's alarming vision comes true, she—second only to Belgium and the Netherlands—will be inexorably drawn into the Russo-German orbit.

To the specious argument of those who still maintain that "the old war guilt controversy" offers no more than an "academic" interest for the historian, the following questions may be put in refutation:

Did not Adolf Hitler thrive on the battle-cries "November Criminals," "stab in the back," and "Versailles," astutely distorting some essential facts? Was not the war-guilt charge an instrument of power politics? Do not the Soviets make use of it now? Was not the implementation of the European Defense Community plan delayed for years because of France's boundless distrust of Germany in view of her alleged past? Is it seriously contested that a mutual understanding of past events in their true light would greatly facilitate the smooth incorporation of Germany into the Western European Union, and the forming of 500,000 Germans into a national army wholeheartedly devoted to the West? Above all: how is the officially proclaimed policy of reconstructing Europe on the basis of lasting Franco-German reconciliation to be achieved if the distrust-provoking historical past is not authoritatively cleared up?

These queries should make it obvious that the unbiassed establishment of historical facts has once more gained an eminently *practical* importance for the present, and even more for the future.

But there is also a clear *moral* feature involved. I am well aware that morality in politics is pooh-poohed, and openly ridiculed by many politicians as well as by some historians. Political immorality reigned supreme during the Hitler regime, with disastrous results for the Germans and for the world at large. I am not blind to the fact that diplomacy cannot be carried on solely by the standards of ethics which govern the internal life of all civilized nations. Yet, without due regard to morality, no sane and no safe international policy can be pursued. It is gratifying that, for years, American statesmen have stressed this fact. In 1946, William C. Bullitt wrote: "Those who would find world peace must seek an indispensable minimum of international morality." [56] Cordell Hull emphasized, in 1948, that international morality is as essential as individual morality.[57] Sumner Welles proclaimed, in 1946, the effective moral leadership of the United States.[58] John Foster Dulles, the present Secretary of State, actually leads his country on this way, inspired by the sound doctrine *Diplomacy with Morality*.[59]

It is equally gratifying to see that leading British historians have taken the same line. Edward Hallett Carr warned in 1939: "It is as fatal in politics to ignore power as it is to ignore morality." [60] Especially insistent was R. W. Seton-Watson. Prophetically, he declared in 1938:

If the statesmen of our age have not the courage of a Christian faith and fail to establish a direct connection between the errors of foreign policy and the neglect of moral values in the past, their failure may drag down our whole world in ruin.[61]

There is no doubt that the words "the errors of foreign policy and the neglect of moral values in the past" were aimed, above all, at the 1919 spirit of Versailles and its doleful consequences. For this all too obvious neglect of public morality in both camps Europe and the world had to pay a terrific price.

Appealing to fairness and common sense, the writer ventures to submit some proposals for an *authoritative* adjustment of the main historical controversies which have embittered and poisoned international relations in the nineteenth and in our present century. These controversies center on six closely inter-connected problems, namely—

1) The origins of the Franco-Prussian War, 1870-71;
2) The Peace of Frankfort, 1871;
3) The war scare in 1875;
4) The origins of the First World War, 1914-18;
5) The peace treaties concluded in the years 1918-20, viz., the Treaty of Brest-Litovsk, the Treaty of Bucharest, the Treaty of Versailles, the Treaty of St. Germain, and the Treaty of Trianon;
6) The causes of Hitler's rise to power.

The American Government having repudiated the Treaty of Versailles in 1920, would be best qualified to initiate action. It might approach the British Government stating:

The covering letter and reply of the Allied and Associated Powers of June 16, 1919, contain charges of the gravest nature against Germany which she deeply resented. Subsequent revelations have shown that the most important of these charges were ill-founded and misconceived. American, British and French historians have concluded that the verdict of June 16 needs revision. Among prominent Anglo-American historians, Professor Sidney B. Fay, Harvard University, and Dr. G. P. Gooch, both specialists on the subject, have reaffirmed this (see pp. 24, 62 of the present book). On political as well as on moral grounds, it seems advisable, as a reasonable act of justice, to reconsider the verdict mentioned, especially in view of the fact that West Germany is now an Ally of the Western Powers.

The British Government may be reminded of Viscount Grey's 1916 condition of peace, of Lord Lothian's recantation published in 1936, of the advice given in 1933 and 1938 by such leading men in British life as Professor Gilbert Murray and Dr. R. W. Seton-Watson; and particularly of the reported intention of the British Government in 1936 to remove the "guilt clauses" from the Versailles Treaty (see above, p. 167).

The French Government may be reminded of the admirable endeavors made by French historians and teachers of history, jointly with German colleagues, in 1935 and 1951, in which Professor Pierre Renouvin took part, the reputable "revisionist" author of the book *Les Origines Immédiates de la Guerre*.[62] The Quai d'Orsay may further be reminded of

the far-sighted suggestions which their excellent Consul
General in Cologne, M. Jean Dobler, submitted to it in
March and April, 1936, after the reoccupation of the Rhineland by German troops. Commenting on Hitler's proposals at
that time for establishing peace-assuring conditions in Western
Europe, Dobler repeatedly urged his Government to make "a
great moral effort" by immediately opening direct negotiations
with Berlin for the eventual conclusion of "a very comprehensive treaty of non-aggression and obligatory arbitration." His
striking idea, based on intimate knowledge of German-French
sentiment, was that such a treaty could be placed "under the
guarantee of the future French and German generations." To
achieve this, the two Governments would engage to arrange
that "every year 20,000, 50,000, or 100,000 boys and girls
attending primary, secondary and high schools spend six weeks
of their vacation with families of the other nation." "Besides,"
Dobler recommended, "a mixed German and French commission would, by common consent, and in a spirit of international appeasement, revise the history text-books for use in the
primary and secondary schools of the two peoples." Dobler
was sure, he wrote, that his idea "would furnish the only basis
upon which some day a really sincere agreement between
France and Germany could be built," and he warned that
there was now, in 1936, "a chance that might not present
itself again." However, the French Government, outraged by
Hitler's provocative step, was then in no mood to entertain
such lofty ideas. M. Jean Dobler subsequently rose to the rank
of Ambassador, and when, in December, 1947, he informed
a Parliamentary Commission, investigating the events from
1933 to 1945, of the proposals he made in 1936, he was justified in feeling that they were sound and statesmanlike.[63] Indeed, they are singularly appropriate for the present situation
in order to create, "under the guarantee of the future French
and German generations," that cordial cooperation which is
indispensable for the maintenance of the Western European
Union.

The European countries not directly involved in the six
problems enumerated above are Denmark, The Netherlands,
Norway, Portugal, Spain, Sweden, and Switzerland. Of these,
The Netherlands and Switzerland might be asked to take a

leading part in the formation of Commissions composed of neutral experts on the specific questions at issue. Commission I, with its seat at The Hague, might deal with problems one to three; Commission II, in Geneva, might deal with problems four and five; Commission III, also in Geneva, with problem six. For Commission I, eight to ten members would probably be sufficient; for the Commissions II and III, ten to twelve members each. Attached to each Commission would be two representatives of each party directly involved as spokesmen for their respective countries. They would not be entitled to draw up conclusions or to vote.

The findings of a two-thirds majority of each Commission would be valid for all parties. The findings would be publicly proclaimed and distributed in print as widely as possible.

The United Nations Educational, Scientific and Cultural Organization would be a proper agency to cooperate in the matter. UNESCO has already taken an active interest in the work of the French-German Historical Commissions which met in 1951, and generally in the revision of history textbooks for various European countries.[64]

Since an improvement of German-French relations is most important, Commission I should be set up as speedily as feasible. To follow Alfred Fabre-Luce's sound suggestion recorded above (p. 161), for some solemn step it may be practicable to give the proclamation of the successive findings of the Commissions a particularly solemn character. "Potsdam" and "Versailles" have acquired an especially ominous meaning, the one for the French, the other for the Germans. The findings of the Commissions might be simultaneously announced in both places in an impressive form as milestones on the road to gradual French-German reconciliation. In time, "Potsdam" and "Versailles" might thus become symbols of French-German unity.[65]

Neutral Powers have often been the innocent victims of the policies of the Great Powers. The forming of Commissions, as here suggested, would give the smaller Powers a magnificent task to accomplish for the general benefit of Western Europe. They would powerfully contribute to that spiritual regeneration which General Marshall has justly proclaimed to be a necessity for the present and for coming generations.

The foregoing proposals will doubtless need modifications and amplifications. There are, of course, other means for attaining the same goal. The chief need is that something effective be done, and that without much delay.

It may be fitting to recall R. W. Seton-Watson's statement in 1938, that an *official* step taken by the Western Powers in the indicated direction *would not be a sign of weakness, but of strength and sanity of judgment.*[66]

Where there is a Will, there is a Way.

Appendix

UNTRUE ASSERTIONS AND FALSIFICATIONS CONCERNING AMERICAN FINANCING OF HITLER

(The original documents for the evidence presented below are deposited in the archives of the Hoover Institute and Library, Stanford University, Stanford, California.)

The importance of this appendix is evident from the following excerpts reproduced from the volume *Occupation of Germany: Policy and Progress, 1945-46,* Publication 2783, European Series 23, issued by the Department of State (Washington, 1947), dealing with German Denazification.

Directive to Commander in Chief of United States Forces of Occupation Regarding the Military Government of Germany, October 17, 1945:

Persons are to be treated as more than nominal participants in Party activities and as active supporters of Nazism or militarism when they have . . . (4) voluntarily given substantial moral or material support or political assistance of any kind to the Nazi party or Nazi officials and leaders.

This was repeated in the Control Council Directive No. 24, January 12, 1946 (pp. 112, 114).

On October 12, 1946, the Control Council approved Directive No. 38, designed to establish a uniform policy for the classification and punishment of war criminals, Nazis, militarists, and industrialists who supported the Nazi regime (p. 19).

The object of the Control Council Directive No. 38 was ". . . a) The punishment of war criminals, Nazis, Militarists,

179

and industrialists who encouraged and supported the Nazi regime" (p. 122).

Article I, Groups of Persons Responsible. . . . 1. Major offenders; 2. Offenders (activists, militarists, and profiteers). . . .

Article III. . . . Activists are in particular the following persons, insofar as they are not major offenders: 1. Anyone who substantially contributed to the establishment, consolidation or maintenance of the national socialistic tyranny, by word or deed, especially publicly through speeches or writings or through voluntary donations out of his own or another's property or through using his personal reputation or his position of power in political, economic or cultural life. . . . [p. 126]

A profiteer is: Anyone who, by use of his political position or connections, gained personal or economic advantages for himself or others from the national socialist tyranny, the rearmament, or the war [p. 127].

Non-membership in the NSDAP is, by itself, "not decisive to absolve one of responsibility" (p. 119).

Article IX, Sanctions against Offenders. 1. They may be imprisoned or interned for a period up to ten years in order to perform reparations and reconstruction work. . . . 2. Their property may be confiscated . . . either as a whole or in part. . . . 3. They shall be ineligible to hold any public office. . . . [p. 130]

These principles decreed by the victors in 1945 and 1946, lead logically to the conclusion that, for instance, Viscount Rothermere as an influential moral supporter, and Sir Henri Deterding as an outstanding financial supporter of the Hitler movement were Offenders, ranking as Activists, and would have been liable to the severe sanctions under Article IX.

It is, therefore, an obvious duty to clear all those who were falsely denounced in public as financial backers of Hitler and his NSDAP.

1. JOHANNES STEEL'S ASSERTIONS MADE IN 1933-1934 AND THEIR REFUTATION

Early in 1933, a young German refugee visited the American journalist Paul Scott Mowrer in Paris and told him that it had been his job to raise funds for Hitler. He offered to write an article describing the whole system by which the Nazis had for years been getting money from abroad, in England, America, France, "to stop Communism." His story seemed plausible to Mr. Mowrer, but when he saw the names of the alleged financial contributors—banks, automobile firms with worldwide reputation—he felt that without absolute evidence he could not deal with the matter. This refugee was Johannes Stahl.[1]

Stahl proceeded to London where he enlarged the article on foreign financial backing of the NSDAP into a book describing in general the "underworld of Hitlerism," that is, chiefly Nazi terror in Germany. For this book, *Hitler as Frankenstein,* the late economist Professor Harold J. Laski wrote a Preface in which he stated:

Another part [of the book] consists of a series of charges about the sources of Hitler's funds of which the gravity needs no emphasis. Of them I venture only to say two things: first, that the author's relations with eminent members of the Nazi movement gave him exceptional access to sources of information not available to ordinary persons; and, secondly, that, if the charges be untrue, in the interest of international relations they ought to be proven untrue by those against whom they are made. It is clearly a very serious matter if international financiers of the first rank have been concerned to subsidise a movement like that of Hitler. . . . It seems to me important that public opinion should have the means of pronouncing upon the validity of the charges here made. . . . It is because of my sense of their gravity that I welcome their submission to the test of public enquiry.[2]

The London School of Economics and Political Science, in which Professor Laski had played a prominent role, informed the present writer that no one at the School was able to make any pronouncement upon the reaction of the reading public to Stahl's book on its publication in England in 1933. Nor could the successors of the 1933 publishers.[3]

Stahl brought out *Hitler as Frankenstein* under the name of Steel. In 1934 he published another book, *The Second World War,* which conveyed, as the former one had done, an impressive warning of the grave troubles threatening Europe from Nazism. In his second book Steel stated that in August, 1931, he was "ostensibly attached to the German Embassy at Tokyo as Commercial Attaché." [4] But investigations carried out at the writer's request by the Foreign Office of West Germany and by the *Institut für Zeitgeschichte,* Munich, have established that no Johannes Stahl was known to have been attached in any capacity to the German Embassy at Tokyo.[5]

On the other hand, there seems to be no reason to doubt that Johannes Stahl was a member, and perhaps a director, of the German Industrial and Commercial Intelligence Service which took him to many foreign countries.[6] Certainly, both his books show much insight knowledge of the "underworld of Hitlerism" and of international finance.

In *Hitler as Frankenstein,* Steel claimed that "this book contains no opinions, but only facts"; and he declared that he "has confined himself to the reporting of a limited number of cases" of foreign financial contributions to the NSDAP, "for which he has been able to acquire unassailable proof in spite of all the difficulties." [7] Chapter II, "The Money," is devoted to Nazi financing, "one of the most interesting features of Hitlerism, one of the most illuminating." "For ten years," Steel says, "an army of paid agents has been collecting funds in Germany, Great Britain, Sweden, the United States and France."

The ground in these countries was first prospected by "contact men" who were not Nazis but men prominent in their own particular field and thus had access to industrial, commercial and other leaders abroad. "Paid agents" followed in their trail and gathered in the harvest prepared by the "contact men." The most important sums, Steel asserted, came from bankers, financiers, industrialists, and the like, in one word, "from the representatives of capitalism." Of especial interest are the following passages:

The American agents who worked under the supervision of Dr. Schacht were told to explain how National Socialism under Hitler would bring prosperity back to Germany, and how the return of prosperity implied protection of the large sums invested by Americans in German enterprises, the thawing of frozen capital. . . . These arguments evidently went home to the extent of several million dollars. One famous issuing house gave fifty thousand dollars in three instalments respectively of five thousand, ten thousand and thirty-five thousand dollars. The Morgan bank gave fifty thousand dollars once and thirty-five thousand dollars at another time. Another issuing house, at the instigation of Ivar Kreuger, also contributed generously. An American national bank whose President made frequent trips to Berlin, followed suit. Most of the cheques were drawn on other banks. When the contributions were in cash they were invariably sent on to Dr. Schacht by registered mail and he attended to the transfers. The largest individual contribution coming from America was not from a bank, but came from General Motors. In 1928 this corporation began to negotiate the purchase of the Opel Automobile concern in Germany. When the deal was concluded . . . American executives took charge of the organization. They soon discovered that in the calculation of production costs in Germany account must be taken of the social legislation sponsored by the Social Democrats at the bidding of the Trade Unions.

At that time Hitler was already looming as the eventual force to curb the Social Democrats. It was natural that General Motors should be interested in the Hitlerite movement. The assistance of the American corporation was solicited in the United States and it was furnished from the American offices of the General Motors Acceptance Corporation. Mr. R. was in charge of the transaction, after which he was sent to Germany, where he was in frequent contact with Dr. Schacht. In all, General Motors contributed two hundred thousand dollars.[8]

The present writer submitted copies of the passages quoted to the General Motors Corporation, and to Dr. Hjalmar Schacht for their comment. It was not necessary to submit a copy to the only other firm specifically mentioned by Mr. Steel, the Morgan bank, because in the Hoover Library's copy of *Hitler as Frankenstein* there is a printed slip affixed to page 31 which reads:

A DENIAL

The publishers are informed by Messrs. J. P. Morgan & Co. that this statement [of payments to the amount of eighty-five thousand dollars] is without the slightest foundation of fact, and that neither Mr. Morgan nor the firm of J. P. Morgan & Co., nor any individual partner of that firm, has ever made any contribution to the Hitler or any other German organization.

The General Motors Overseas Operations, New York 19, N. Y., replied that "General Motors made no contribution to the Nazi Party either before 1933 or thereafter"; and they stated, after the General Motors Acceptance Corporation had conducted a thorough search of their records, that

during the years 1929 through 1933 the few remittances made by them to Germany were entirely in the nature of normal financial transactions in the regular course of business. None of them was in any way connected with a contribution to the Nazi or any other German party or to any agent thereof.[9]

Dr. Hjalmar Schacht in his turn informed the writer:

All the assertions of Mr. Stahl are wholly fantastic inventions without any foundation. As regards me personally, I have never had connection with any agents of the Nazi Party operating abroad. . . . It is true that the Party got certain contributions from their groups abroad. The fact that these foreign sums were never delivered to the *Reichsbank* as should have been done in virtue of the Foreign Currency legislation, induced me in April 1936 to have the control of Foreign Exchange conferred upon Goering. I have never heard of any contribution of General Motors to the Nazi Party. I emphatically doubt also this contention of Stahl's.[10]

The other alleged contributors, namely, "One famous issuing house," "Another issuing house, at the instigation of Ivar Kreuger," and "An American national bank whose President made frequent trips to Berlin," could not be contacted because they are not named. Nor could "A German American brewer in New York who was one of the most successful bootleggers between 1926 and 1931," who paid $100,000 into the treasury of the Party.[11] It is the responsibility of Mr. Johannes Steel, American citizen, residing in New York City, to state explicitly whom he meant when writing in 1933.

Another contributor he did mention by name: Henry Ford. Steel declared:

Hitler's most important business connection in the United States, however, was that with Henry Ford. . . . The first link between Ford and Hitler dates back to the days when the automobile manufacturer's *Dearborn Independent* lambasted the Jews week after week. After the famous libel suit brought in Chicago and the subsequent cessation of publication of the *Independent,* Ford entered into conversation with the publishers of Hitler's Party literature, the firm of Fr. Eher Nachfolger in Munich. Ford's proposition was that they should reprint in the form of pamphlets a selection of articles from the *Independent,* translated into German, of course. He gave express permission for the joint use of the names Ford and Hitler in advertising the pamphlets, and he furnished the funds for the campaign. Henry Ford's offer was accepted with glee. It came at a psychological moment. The Nazi movement was still young, still "provincial" in the sense that little attention was yet paid to it outside Bavaria; . . . Hitler felt that with adequate advertising, the pamphlets would circulate throughout Germany and provide very welcome publicity. Fr. Eher Nachfolger received a cheque for forty thousand dollars to further the spread of anti-Jewish literature in Germany. This cheque represents the first financial support

of Adolf Hitler by Henry Ford. The pamphlets were a very qualified success. The restricted sale was out of all proportion to the
amount of the cheque . . . and dissatisfied him [Ford] to such an
extent that he temporarily severed his relations with Hitler. . . .

A few years passed, and the Hitler movement, steadily gathering
new followers, was still being watched by Henry Ford. Then in
1929 . . . Prince Ferdinand of Prussia . . . had taken up a post
in the engineering department of the Ford Works in Detroit. . . .
Prince Ferdinand was the link bringing Ford and Hitler into contact again. When I met the young Princes [August Wilhelm and
Ferdinand] at the Drake Hotel in Chicago . . . the fact was impressed upon me that so far as "selling Hitler" was concerned, Detroit was a special territory of Prince Ferdinand. . . . In Detroit,
Ferdinand Hohenzollern used much the same arguments that were
being used with bankers in New York—"the socialistic and com-
munistic menace in Germany will extend to the whole of Europe
if unchecked; socialism means the further impoverishment of nations; further predatory legislation in industry and finance," and
so on. . . .

To the world in general it was said that Prince Ferdinand proved
such a valuable asset in the Detroit Works that he deserved a large
salary, with important bonuses for "expert engineering services."
Ford valued the services rendered to him by the charming Prussian
Prince with three hundred thousand dollars. This money . . .
found its way into the Nazi Party chest through the intermediary
of "Auwi," otherwise Prince August Wilhelm, Nazi deputy in the
Prussian diet. . . .[12]

On this passage Professor Laski commented in 1933:

It is . . . a serious matter for Jews the world over, if it be true
that Mr. Henry Ford, having stopped his campaign against them
in the United States, then proceeded, as the author asserts, liber-
ally to endow a party in Germany devoted to a similar campaign
on a wider scale.[13]

These passages from *Hitler as Frankenstein* were sent by
the present writer to the grandson of Mr. Henry Ford and to
Prince Louis Ferdinand of Prussia. Before giving their reply,
it seems relevant to refer to public statements made elsewhere
with regard to Henry Ford's connections with Hitler.

George Seldes declared: "It was general knowledge in the
early 1920's, when it was not treason to aid Hitler, that Henry
Ford was one of his spiritual and economic backers." [14] In
those years it was rumored in Germany that Henry Ford be-

friended the Nazi Party.[15] In February, 1923, Vice-President
Auer of the Bavarian Diet stated publicly:

> The Bavarian Diet has long had information that the Hitler move-
> ment was partially financed by an American anti-Semitic chief . . .
> Henry Ford. . . . Herr Hitler openly boasts of Mr. Ford's sup-
> port. . . . A photograph of Mr. Ford hangs in Herr Hitler's
> quarters. . . .[16]

On February 5, 1930, Hitler swore in court, "with trem-
bling passion in his voice," that he had never made an attempt
to obtain money from Henry Ford. Yet a witness present could
have had him sent to prison for perjury by producing a certain
document.[17] The witness may well have been Kurt G. W.
Ludecke who, in quest of funds, was in Detroit and in contact
with W. J. Cameron, editor of Ford's *Dearborn Independent*.
Ludecke did not, however, say in his book that he obtained
any material support from either of them.[18] Konrad Heiden
pointed out, in 1936, that it was never denied by Ford or on
his behalf that he made financial contributions, directly or
indirectly.[19] But the lack of denial is no evidence for actual
support.

As regards German rumors of foreign support, the fact must
be kept in mind that they were exploited both by Nazi propagandists for the sake of winning followers, and by Nazi opponents in order to discredit the movement.

In 1937, Upton Sinclair repeated in his *Story of Ford-
America* as facts that the Hitler movement got $40,000 from
Ford to reprint anti-Jewish pamphlets in German translations;
and that, later on, a grandson of the ex-Kaiser had been the
agent through whom $300,000 were forwarded to the Party
treasury.[20] His source was probably Steel's book. Concerning
the assertions contained therein, the Assistant to the President
of the Ford Motor Company, Dearborn, after a thorough
search of materials bearing on the question had been made,
wrote to the author on February 1, 1954:

> This examination of the pertinent files has now been completed,
> and I can tell you without reservation (a) that there was no rela-
> tionship whatever between Adolf Hitler and Mr. Ford, as suggested
> by Mr. Steel; and (b) that Mr. Steel's charge that Ford used
> Prince Louis Ferdinand of Prussia as a means of channeling money
> to the Nazis is utterly false.
> Specifically, there was no business connection whatever between

Hitler and Ford. So far as we can determine from the files, Ford had no relationship whatever with the publisher, Fr. Eher Nachfolger. The accounting records of Mr. Ford and the Company for this period are quite complete and accurate. There is no evidence whatever that Mr. Ford gave a check for $40,000 or any other amount to this publisher or any other publisher.

On June 30, 1927, Mr. Ford retracted certain published statements that appeared in several issues of the *Dearborn Independent.* This statement was in the nature of a letter to Mr. Louis Marshall, then President of the American Jewish Committee. This letter was widely published, and I am sure was available to Mr. Steel at the time he wrote his book. Among other things, Ford directed various publishers to stop reprinting any articles that had appeared in the *Dearborn Independent.* So far as we can discover, only one German publisher was involved. On November 1, 1927, a letter was sent to him (Mr. Frisch) demanding cessation of publication and circulation of the articles printed in pamphlet form as *The International Jew.* Mr. Frisch in reply asked Mr. Ford for 40,060 marks as compensation for the withdrawal, but there is no record showing that Frisch was paid any money at all. All evidence indicates quite the contrary.

At that time, Henry Ford's General Secretary made a public statement that Mr. Ford was not interested in any political activity in Germany and had not nor *would* not make any contributions to any persons for that purpose.

As for the association of Prince Louis Ferdinand and Ford, all evidence shows that Mr. Steel's book is thoroughly wrong. The correspondence between Ford and Prince Ferdinand is quite complete, as are the Company accounting records. The only money Ferdinand received from Ford or the Ford Motor Company was a salary, the same salary that other Ford employees received for comparable work.

On October 2, 1929, Mr. Liebold, Mr. Ford's Secretary, wrote to Mr. F. F. Griffith, Manager of Ford Motor Company at Buenos Aires, advising him that no special consideration should be given to Ferdinand in his employment. Apparently, some question must have been raised in the press or elsewhere regarding Ferdinand's employment, as the Secretary continued in the letter, "There are no secret arrangements or understanding with him (Ferdinand) and he has no contacts or ties with us which will extend to him privileges not extended to the average employee." Mr. Ford did, however, give the Prince a car. This was a practice pursued by Mr. Ford and seems to have no special significance. The Secretary, however, does take note of this gift and refers to it thus: "Mr. Ford's contribution (to preserve Ferdinand's Royal position) in the form of a car was a mere gratuity, and he (Ferdinand) will have to pay the expense of its operation as I do not believe Mr. Ford is inclined to do so."

I have tried to give you here a complete answer refuting Steel's assertions. If there are other questions that you feel we may be able to help you on, do not hesitate to write directly to Mr. H. E. Edmunds, manager of the Ford Archives, Dearborn, Michigan.

Very truly yours,
signed: Allen W. Merrell [21]

Having no knowledge of the foregoing letter, Prince Louis Ferdinand replied to the author on December 7, 1953: "The allegations of Johannes Steel which you quote are in every respect untrue. More I have not to say on the matter."

It seems probable that the assertion of $40,000 having been paid to Hitler's publisher arose from Frisch's demand for 40,060 marks as compensation. It is interesting that this Mr. Frisch apparently thought he was entitled to a monetary compensation. Was he induced, without Mr. Ford's authority, by one of the latter's employees or friends to do some anti-Jewish publishing?

The fact that, in 1938, Mr. Henry Ford was presented with the Grand Cross of the German Eagle and that Ford accepted the decoration has naturally strengthened the belief that the *Fuehrer* had good cause to be grateful to Henry Ford. But it is on record that Ford's Secretary, Mr. E. G. Liebold, claimed at the time that Ford should accept the decoration for business reasons since the Company had a plant in Cologne.[22] Harry Bennett, who was very close to Henry Ford in those years, has given an explanation for Ford's general attitude towards Germany and towards Hitler. He stated:

Mr. Ford was definitely pro-German. He considered the German people were clean, thrifty, hard-working, and technologically advanced, and he admired them for that. During the early years of Hitler's rise to power, Mr. Ford stubbornly refused to believe the stories of Nazi violence and brutality, and put it all down to propaganda.

But, after Hitler had conquered Poland, in 1939, Ford said to Bennett: "Well, by God, we're through with him. He's just power-drunk, like all the rest of them." [23]

The flat denials of definite allegations made by Johannes Steel deprive his book of practically all credibility. Yet, there is no doubt that, in the years before he fled Nazi Germany, early in 1933, he had had unusual opportunities for gaining inside knowledge. Not a few of his general statements sound true enough, for instance when he says that financial contributions to the NSDAP came from Latin America, from Sweden, especially from Ivar Kreuger, from Great Britain and Poland, from armaments firms in various countries.[24] Chapter IV includes corroborative evidence for the truth of such statements.

Johannes Steel's prediction, *The Second World War,* published 1934 in New York, also contains material for our subject worthy of consideration. Relative to Sir Henri Deterding's connections with the NSDAP he asserts that Alfred Rosenberg suggested to the Oil King through Dr. Georg Bell:

A Polish-German understanding in regard to the Polish Corridor would be possible under Hitler if Poland would give Germany a free hand in the Baltic. In return, Germany would actively support any Polish attempt to regain the Ukraine, which had belonged to Poland in the days of the old kingdom. Sir Henri, as well as the directors of the Lena Goldfields . . . saw great possibilities in this plan and from that day on Deterding supplied the Nazis with money. This money was transmitted by Dr. Bell. . . . Two important results of this friendship . . . were the expulsion from Germany of the DEROP, the Russian competitor of Deterding's Royal Dutch Petroleum Company, and the signing on January 26 of this year [1934] of the Polish-German amity agreement.[25]

This is quite in accord with the evidence concerning Sir Henri Deterding's ties with the NSDAP, as presented above (pp. 114-17).

2. THE "SIDNEY WARBURG" FALSIFICATIONS, PUBLISHED 1933 IN AMSTERDAM, 1936, 1948, AND 1949 IN SWITZERLAND, AND 1952 IN BUENOS AIRES

A few months after Professor Harold J. Laski gave credence in London to alleged American financing of Hitler and the NSDAP, the same happened in Amsterdam. To all appearances both events occurred quite independently of each other. They constitute remarkable evidence for the fact that in 1933, and in later years, there was widespread belief outside of Germany that Hitler's movement received substantial financial support from abroad.

In the autumn of 1933, Mr. J. G. Schoup, a Dutch citizen, offered the esteemed publishing firm Van Holkema & Warendorf N. V., in Amsterdam, a booklet which revealed that American capitalists, with British and Dutch participation, had brought Hitler to power through huge financial transactions. Schoup declared that the author of the booklet was a personal acquaintance of his, Sidney Warburg, the son of one of the biggest bankers in the United States. To attest this, he submitted a file of papers which contained his correspondence with Warburg. The latter's communications were written on sheets with the printed letterhead "Warburg & Warburg, 5754 Fourth Avenue, New York." The manuscript, written in English, showed the same handwriting as the letters which were signed "Sidney Warburg." In one of these, Schoup was authorized to publish the manuscript in a Dutch translation under his own name because Warburg did not wish to appear as the author. The English original was to be destroyed as soon as the translation was set in type. On the strength of this evidence, Van Holkema & Warendorf undertook the publishing. Schoup left the whole correspondence with them, but it was, together with everything else connected with the booklet, destroyed by order of the German occupation forces in World War II.[26]

The booklet was the confession of a remorse-ridden gentleman of Jewish faith who had, acting on behalf of others, arranged payments for Hitler's movement totalling $32 million. The booklet of ninety-nine pages appeared late in 1933 under the title, translated, *The Financial Sources of National Socialism. Three Talks with Hitler by Sidney Warburg. Told by J. G. Schoup.*[27]

The essential contents were:

In July, 1929, Mr. Carter, President of the Guaranty Trust Co., New York, invited Sidney Warburg to a conference which was attended by the Presidents of the Federal Reserve Banks, by five independent bankers, by the "young Rockefeller" of the Standard Oil Co., and by Mr. Glean of the Royal Dutch. French policy was then giving Wall Street trouble. France wished to keep Germany economically in a weak condition, whereas other countries, above all America and Britain, desired a prosperous Germany. A national revolution in Germany would intimidate France, Wall Street people thought, and make her amenable to the wishes of the other Powers.

For this task, Hitler appeared to be the right man. Sidney Warburg, speaking German fluently, was requested to find out what sum Hitler would need for the envisaged revolutionary change of government.

In that summer of 1929, Warburg had his first interview with Hitler in Munich. The *Fuehrer* readily emphasized that "France is our enemy." He wanted 100 million marks. Carter granted $10,000,000, at German request payable through Mendelssohn & Co., Amsterdam. Upon his return to the United States, Warburg made a satisfactory report to the New York group, a new member of which was Mr. Angell, as English representative of the Asiatic Petroleum Co. At this meeting, Mr. Rockefeller displayed particular interest in Hitler's attitude toward Communism.

In September, 1931, Britain abandoned the gold standard. Wall Street felt that the dollar was endangered. France endeavored to weaken London financially and to induce President Hoover to give up his plan for a moratorium. At this time, Hitler inquired of Warburg on what further sums he could count for his rapidly growing movement. Carter, angry about France's conduct, convoked another meeting which was also attended by Montagu Norman, Governor of the Bank of England, who happened to be in New York. Rockefeller, Carter and Glean spoke up for Hitler. But Warburg was asked to explore the conditions in Germany first. There, he was much impressed by the tremendous increase of Hitler's followers. Even a Jewish banker in Hamburg (who was to play an unexpected role in a Swiss publication of 1948) assured Warburg that Hitler was the coming strong man whom Germany needed. Hitler told Warburg in Berlin that, for a real revolution, he would need half a billion marks, for a legal seizure of power 200 million. Carter granted $15,000,000, of which 5 million each were paid through Mendelssohn & Co., Amsterdam, the Rotterdam Bankvereiniging, and the Banca Italiana in Rome.

At Carter's wish Warburg went once more to Germany, in February, 1933. By that time Warburg had taken a strong dislike to the Nazi Party and thought his friends were doing wrong. The day after the *Reichstag* fire, he met Hitler who went "on a rampage against the Communists." He demanded another 100 million marks for his program. Carter granted $7,000,000. Two million were paid through the Rhenania

AG, the German branch of the Royal Dutch in Düsseldorf, and five million again through the Banca Italiana.

The notes which Warburg transmitted to Schoup closed as follows:

I have meticulously carried out my instructions. . . . Hitler's deeds will show whether he is an evil man what I consider him to be. . . . The world continues to suffer under a system which must make use of a Hitler in order to maintain itself. Poor world, poor humanity! [28]

Shortly after publication of the booklet, Van Holkema & Warendorf were informed that a banker "Sidney Warburg" did not exist. Subsequently, J. G. Schoup admitted this. He declared that he had disclosed his knowledge of Hitler's financial background in the guise of a translation.[29] The publishing firm withdrew at once all copies they could get hold of, and had them destroyed.[30]

If the publishers had suspected the accuracy of the alleged Warburg statements, they could have discovered the facts: there was no firm Warburg & Warburg in New York, and the address printed at the letterhead, "5754 Fourth Avenue," was impossible because this Avenue stops at No. 420; [31] several names of Germans and of localities in Germany were wrong.[32]

But the publishers, unaware of Schoup's shady past, did not imagine that anyone would dare falsely to impute to men of world-repute, like Rockefeller and Montagu Norman, huge transactions with Hitler; they did not suspect that the whole correspondence submitted by Schoup was faked on fraudulently printed sheets. Some of the detailed descriptions in the manuscript rang true enough. Besides, the alleged arguments of the Wall Street group had a real foundation. During the Great Depression which began in the autumn of 1929, the French franc controlled Europe, and the French press wrote with malicious joy of Britain's financial difficulties.[33] In those years, finance was made an instrument of policy to a degree and in a manner hitherto unknown.[34] It was notorious that in the United States and Britain there was hostility to French European policy. Besides, in the Netherlands it was well known that Sir Henri Deterding was a liberal supporter of the Hitler movement. The publishers may also have heard of Steel's book.

As regards J. G. Schoup, it appears that he had to pay with his life for his audacity. He was killed in 1944.[35]

While his booklet was in circulation, Counsellor von Alexich of the Austrian Legation at The Hague sent two copies to Vienna, one of which was passed on, two years later, to a Swiss publicist, René Sonderegger, who was then an ardent anti-Nazi. In 1948, Sonderegger publicly asserted that the Schoup booklet had been read by the Austrian Federal Chancellor, Dr. Kurt von Schuschnigg, and by some confidants of his Government.[36] In August, 1951, Sonderegger went further. In Zurich, he showed a representative of the Munich Institute for Contemporary History a photostat of the Dutch publication in which certain passages were underlined or marked in the margin. Sonderegger declared that these were made by the Federal Chancellor himself, from whom he had received the Dutch original, commissioning him to publish its contents in German, and that he did this, summarily, in 1936.[37]

However, minute investigations have established the following facts: the former Federal Chancellor von Schuschnigg does not know Dutch and therefore cannot have marked any passages in the booklet; in the archives of the Federal Chancellery, Foreign Office Department, Vienna, there is no trace of anything on the subject; in all probability the late Herr von Alexich sent the booklet to the Press Bureau of the Chancellery which was directed by the late Colonel Walter Adam. He alone, and not any member of the Austrian Government, would have approached Sonderegger who had published, in 1935, Otto Strasser's book *Die Deutsche Bartholomäusnacht*, a gruesome account of the massacre in Germany, June 30, 1934.[38]

It may be considered as certain that Counsellor von Alexich notified the Press Bureau in Vienna of the withdrawal of Schoup's *opus* from circulation as a mystification and hoax. On the other hand, in the same year, 1933, a brochure was published in Vienna which spoke of "rolling gold francs, gulden and dollars" for the Hitler movement.[39] Colonel Adam may also have known of Steel's *Hitler as Frankenstein*. Then, in April, 1934, Sir Henri Deterding's agent, Dr. Georg Bell, who knew of the subventions for the NSDAP, "going into the millions," as related earlier, was murdered in Austria. No wonder, therefore, that in the Austrian Press Bureau "all were firmly convinced that Hitler was being financed from abroad."[40]

In view of the Nazi agitation in Austria, culminating in the brutal murder of Federal Chancellor Dollfuss on July 25, 1934, it is quite comprehensible that Colonel Adam finally decided to use the Dutch publication as a weapon against the Nazis and that he selected Switzerland for it in order to avoid trouble for his country.

In the brochure, published in 1936, *Finanzielle Weltgeschichte,* with the subtitle (translated) *The Third Reich in the Service of International High Finance,* Sonderegger reproduced the gist of the Schoup story but added as foreign financiers, Deterding, whose contributions he estimated at 50 to 60 million marks, and John Pierpont Morgan. Of German financiers, he mentioned the banking house Schröder, 14 million, and the Stuttgart "Allianz," 10 million. As a new item, Sonderegger asserted that the Dutch original had been withdrawn by relatives of the author Warburg, and that Nazi agents had bought it up at the order of the German Propaganda Ministry.[41] The Amsterdam firm has declared that both these assertions are untrue.[42]

More important for the further development is that Sonderegger, in his brochure of 1936, annotated to the role of Sidney Warburg:

The silly attempts to obscure the existence of Sidney Warburg miscarry in view of an unintentional, frank testimony of an American lady of very high position—whose brother is Secretary of State—who was a childhood playmate of Sidney.[43]

Her alleged testimony marks the beginning of Sonderegger's later falsifications and inventions.

To the German translation of the Dutch booklet, which Sonderegger submitted to the Swiss State Library, Berne, he affixed a postscript, dated October, 1946, which shows his knowledge that Van Holkema & Warendorf themselves had withdrawn and destroyed the *Geldbronnen* booklet when they recognized it as a "gross mystification." Sonderegger declared that the Dutch publication was one of the most important documents of our epoch because it revealed the real cause of the Second World War and the innermost secrets of capitalistic world domination. He considered it, therefore, a duty to humanity to investigate the matter. And he claimed to be able to demonstrate that Schoup's fictional "Sidney" was the New York banker and publicist James Paul Warburg, son of

Paul Warburg, State Secretary in Wilson's administration, "though it is said that he denies the authorship." [44]

In 1948, Sonderegger published his chief *opus* on the subject, entitled *Spanischer Sommer*. In it he tells us that he derived his first "enlightenment" from a conversation he had in the thirties when he visited the Swiss Minister to Prague, Dr. Bruggmann. Talking about the "Warburg" booklet, Mrs. Bruggmann, sister of the former "State Secretary" Henry A. Wallace, "confirmed," Sonderegger asserts, that "Sidney" could be no other than a playmate of her childhood, who also went to school with her, namely, James P. Warburg; and she added further evidence in this direction. [45]

Mr. James P. Warburg has stated in an affidavit that he never knew Mrs. Bruggmann personally. [46] Dr. Charles Bruggmann, Swiss Minister to Washington, informed the present writer

that in a casual conversation Mr. Sonderegger asked Mrs. Bruggmann, whom he met in our Legation in Prague, whether she knew a Mr. Warburg in New York. Mrs. Bruggmann answered No, but that she had gone to school with a Miss Warburg who, according to her memory, may have a brother, whose name she does not know.

That is all, and whatever goes beyond these facts in Mr. Sonderegger's publication, is freely invented. [47]

In his embellishment of the Prague conversation Sonderegger explains—insinuating that his hostess agreed with him—that in familiar intercourse a common synonym for both Sidney and James is "Shimmy." In this respect, Sonderegger relates a striking experience he had as follows:

When the Swiss publisher and publicist with his mysterious truth and knowledge which was nowhere welcome, visited the well-known director of the American League for Rights of Man in New York, Roger N. Baldwin, he reached, smiling, for the telephone and connected himself with Warburg who evidently was as close to his radical movement as he was close to him in friendship. "Hallo, Shimmy," he called into the apparatus the moment Warburg announced his presence at the other end, "I have here that Swiss with me who is concerned about the story of the book. . . ." But he had hardly finished the sentence when an angry exclamation cut him short: "To the Devil with that Swiss, I don't want to have anything to do with him!" Overcoming the embarrassment which the presence of the man in question must have caused, he

[Baldwin] added, smiling . . . the query, "Why do you bother about such things, is it really astonishing, and is it not so that all dictators, Lenin as well as Hitler, got money from us?"

To this, Mr. Roger N. Baldwin, Chairman of the Board, International League of Rights of Man, has declared:

I state categorically that the statement attributed to me by René Sonderegger is wholly false. I have had occasion to deny this before.

So far as I recollect, I never knew any man under such a name, and never had a conversation of the character reported. If a man using another name called on me about some publication concerning Wall St. bankers, I certainly did not call up James P. Warburg, nor indeed, any other man connected with Wall St. I have called Mr. Warburg so seldom until recent years—the last two or three— that I would recollect any such reputed conversation.[48]

Mr. James P. Warburg has issued a corresponding denial.[49]

In order to demonstrate a Zionist world conspiracy under the leadership of the Warburgs, Sonderegger drags in Mr. James' German uncle, Max M. Warburg. The reader will recall that Schoup's "Sidney" learned with amazement from a Jewish Hamburg banker that Hitler was the man whom Germany needed. Now Sonderegger identified this unnamed banker with Max Warburg. Falsifying date and content, he quotes from an entry in Ambassador William E. Dodd's diary, Berlin, "July 28, 1938":

At the request of Rabbi Lazaron of Baltimore, Max Warburg, eminent Hamburg banker and brother of Felix Warburg of New York, came to see me in the Embassy. He showed me the effects of his troubled life in the last years and stood in danger of losing his life if his opinions would ever become known to the governing people here.

The second sentence, however, reads in the original:

He showed the effects of his troubled life the last year and now stands in danger of losing his life if he ever allows his opinions to become known to authorities here.[50]

The purpose of Sonderegger's falsifications—"in the last years" instead of "the last year," and "stood in danger" instead of "now stands in danger"—becomes manifest through the wrong date given, "July 28, 1938," for Dodd's entry is dated "August 9" of the year 1934. Max Warburg's "troubled life the last year" referred, of course, to the general prosecution of the Jews in Hitler's Germany. The change of date was to serve Sonderegger's imputation that, when Max Warburg left Hamburg in 1938, he had terminated "his economic-political mission in Germany," which "represented perhaps the shrewdest deception by which statesmen were ever fooled."

In 1949, Sonderegger drew even more out of Dodd's diary. He then asserted that Max Warburg turned to the American Ambassador in July, 1938, "to protect his escape to New York," and that he then admitted to Mr. Dodd, "how masterly he had deceived the Germans and had led them towards their prepared destiny." [51] It goes without saying that the American Ambassador never recorded anything of the kind. His last entry about Max Warburg is dated November 27, 1935.[52]

But how does Sonderegger explain the absurdity that the Jewish conspirators chose Adolf Hitler, one of the most ferocious Jew-baiters of all times, as their tool? Very simple, according to Sonderegger, because Hitler's anti-Semitism would exactly fulfill the Wall Street bankers' expectations by arousing world-wide sympathies for the Jews, thus enabling them to crush Germany, as the same forces before had crushed Tsarist Russia.[53]

For his demonstration of a Jewish conspiracy to dominate the world, Sonderegger declares the Dutch publication of 1933 to be the fundamental basis, the *pièce de résistance,* as he says.[54] We have seen that this basis was a daring piece of fiction in which no Jew appears as a financial supporter of Hitler; for the non-existent "Sidney" Warburg played only the role of an informer and mediator.

Over-hasty but in good faith, Werner Zimmermann inserted the Schoup-Sonderegger story of Hitler's financing by Americans to the amount of $32 million in his book *Liebet eure Feinde,* which was also published in Switzerland in 1948. When he realized his mistake he recanted and apologized publicly.[55]

Spanischer Sommer and *Liebet eure Feinde* attracted much attention in Germany. In 1948 and 1949, German denazification was still in progress, and former prominent members of the NSDAP used the material of the two Swiss authors in court as evidence that they were much less guilty than some Wall Street people who had financed Hitler's rise to power.

A part of the German press took up the matter, and an agitation ensued which gave the impression of a revival of anti-
Semitism in Germany. Therefore, Mr. James P. Warburg
drew up a detailed statement and a formal affidavit, dated
July 15, 1949, which he brought to the official attention of
the Swiss Government, the Government of the United States,
and the British and French High Commissioners in Germany.
The statement is entitled "Renascent Nazi Propaganda in
Switzerland," and the author declared:

There are clear indications that certain anti-democratic and chau-
vinistic groups in Germany are involved in what appears to be a
systematic effort to clear the German conscience of all guilt for
Nazism by proving that Hitler was put into power by foreign
capital and especially by a Jewish conspiracy.[56]

Despite the publication of Mr. Warburg's refutation and of
Zimmermann's recantation, assertions continue to be made,
and not only in Germany, that J. G. Schoup must have had
a sound basis for his allegations. The present writer has, therefore, submitted the matter to the alleged principal American
participants. The following communications were received:

From Mr. R. Gordon Wasson, Vice-President, J. P. Morgan
& Co., New York 8, December 8, 1953, in behalf of Mr.
Carter:

Neither our bank nor the individuals who shaped its policies took
part in any operations such as are described, and, in fact, they
sound quite absurd.

From Mr. David A. Shepard, Director, Standard Oil Company, New York 20, December 15, 1953:

During the period which you say Mr. Schoup referred to in his
pamphlet—namely, 1929-1933—and, indeed, for many years previously—no member of the Rockefeller family was an officer, director, or employee in any other capacity of Standard Oil Company (New Jersey). Further, it can be stated categorically that
neither this company nor any of its officers or directors as individuals ever contributed funds to the Nazi Party.

From Mr. William C. Potter, Albany, Georgia, December
17, 1953:

In July 1929 and for at least ten years thereafter I was President
of Guaranty Trust Company of New York. No Mr. Carter has as
yet occupied that office. To the best of my knowledge and belief

no such meeting took place as was described under Mr. Carter's auspices as an officer of Guaranty Trust Co., nor was any credit granted by such Trust Company at any time to or for the Hitler movement.

In 1949 René Sonderegger announced that he would bring out a new edition of *Finanzielle Weltgeschichte,* and that he was preparing a study describing "The Role of the Warburgs in Germany and Europe." [57] In 1952, he succeeded in having a second edition of *Spanischer Sommer* published in Buenos Aires. His fabrications, buttressed by impudent falsifications and by unscrupulous inventions, have now been completely exposed. The evidence presented implies a definite warning for the future.

Postscript—Section two of the Appendix was published, somewhat enlarged, in October, 1954, under the title, "Fälschungen zur Auslandsfinanzierung Hitlers," in *Vierteljahrshefte für Zeitgeschichte* (München). I had a copy sent to Mr. René Sonderegger. So far, he has not ventured to refute my exposure. But from several quarters—Swiss, Dutch, German and American—persistent attempts have been made to uphold the assertions published by J. G. Schoup in 1933, to the effect that a Wall Street group actually did make the alleged financial contributions to the Hitler movement. These circles base their conviction largely on the following statement made by A. Pokorski, a former member of General von Schleicher's Intelligence Service:

I knew that on January 4, 1933, at the discussion Hitler/Papen/ Banker Schröder, also Mr. John Foster Dulles was present, the present United States Foreign Minister [*sic*]. Allen Dulles, the present Chief of the American Central Intelligence, was at that time Director of the Henry Schroeder Banking Corp., New York. The international banker von Schröder worked together with Warburg/Hamburg, the Schroeder Corp. and the Dillon-Read group (Baruch). This will make you understand the connection. Foster Dulles was at the time head [*Inhaber*] of the firm of Attorneys-at-Law Sullivan and Cromwell, who took charge of the legal matters of the above mentioned High Finance group.

It is truly amazing that there are people who appear to believe that the presence of Mr. John Foster Dulles at the historical meeting of January 4, 1933, could have been kept

secret all these years, and, above all, would have been kept
secret by interested German parties, especially by the Nazi
bigwigs.

I am authorized to state on behalf of Mr. John Foster
Dulles (letters, December 2, 1955, and April 18, 1956):
"There is, of course, no slightest thread of truth in this alle-
gation."

As for Baron von Schröder, I refer to the record on pages
118, 227-28, note 42 of this book, which shows that the assertions of financial contributions made by the banking houses of
Schroeder in London and New York are not true.

Notes

PART ONE

CHAPTER ONE

1. *Black Record: Germans Past and Present* (London, 1941). The passages quoted are on pp. 1-3, 8, 16, 21, 30, 39. In his Preface, p. iv, Vansittart declared that if the Germans had had their way, there would have been a war every eight years for the last three-quarters of a century.—Sir Robert was "proud," he wrote, "to be able to dedicate the whole to Miss Dorothy Thompson, whose clear thinking and clear writing have long laid the world in her debt." However, he had not asked Miss Thompson's permission to dedicate his book to her. In fact, their views on Germany differed radically, as Miss Thompson pointed out to the writer, letter of March 16, 1954, referring to a transocean debate on the question of Germany, September 30, 1943, printed in *Town Meeting,* vol. 9, No. 22, published by American Education Press (Columbus, Ohio).— Victor Gollancz, in a reply to Lord Vansittart, *Shall Our Children Live or Die?* (London, 1942), p. 5, estimated that by 1942 at least three million persons had read *Black Record.*

2. *Germany's Record: A Reply to Lord Vansittart,* Parliamentary Peace Aims Group, House of Commons (London, 1941). On p. 4 the writers declared they had no doubt that the plain purpose of *Black Record* was to make plausible Mr. Duff Cooper's statement that the crimes of the Nazis were "the crimes of a whole nation," and that it would be "wishful thinking and dangerous thinking to believe that we could drive a wedge between the German Government and the German people."

3. Clearly demonstrated by Captain Russell Grenfell, R.N., in *Unconditional Hatred: German War Guilt and the Future of Europe* (New York, 1953), pp. 25-26.

4. *Lessons of My Life* (New York, 1943), p. 23. In a following brochure, *The German Octopus* (London-New York-Melbourne-Sydney, 1945), p. 3, Lord Vansittart maintained that the German's "spiritual home has been war."

5. *Bones of Contention* (New York, 1945), p. 158. *L'Eternelle Allemagne,* published under the direction of Wladimir d'Ormesson, Ambassador of France (Paris, 1945), p. 13.

6. Article in the *Sunday Chronicle,* October 25, 1953, and two letters to the *Daily Telegraph,* September 15 and 20, 1954.
7. *The Diplomacy of Imperialism, 1890-1902,* 2nd ed. (New York, 1951), pp. 561, 576. Cf. G. P. Gooch and J. B. H. Masterman, *A Century of British Foreign Policy* (London, 1917), p. 40; Grenfell, *op. cit.,* p. 29; Harold J. Laski, *Reflections on the Revolution of Our Time* (New York, 1943), p. 255; Leonard Woolf, *The War for Peace* (London, 1940), pp. 168-69, 171.
8. Edward Hallett Carr, *The Twenty Years' Crisis, 1919-1939* (London, 1939), p. 90.
9. Quoted by Norman Angell in *Must It Be War?* (London, 1939), p. 69.
10. Quoted by Langer, *op. cit.,* p. 566, from the London *Times,* November 14, 1898.
11. Quoted by Langer, *op. cit.,* pp. 507-08.
12. More fully quoted by Langer, *op. cit.,* p. 659. Chamberlain did not mean a formal alliance but a close understanding which should include the United States of America. Cf. Sir Raymond Beazley, *The Road to Ruin in Europe, 1890-1914* (London, 1932), pp. 10-11, 14-15, 34. Chapter I of this book gives a good description of Britain's change of attitude towards Germany at the turn of the century.
13. *Op. cit.,* p. 70. Cf. Carr, *op. cit.,* p. 90.
14. *The Origins of the War, 1871-1914* (New York-London, 1915), p. 3. Cf. Gooch and Masterman, *op. cit.,* p. 23.
15. *Grooves of Change: A Book of Memoirs* (Indianapolis-New York, 1946), p. 323.
16. *The Second World War * The Gathering Storm* (Boston, 1948), p. 5.
17. Gaston Bodart, *Losses of Life in Modern Wars,* Carnegie Endowment for International Peace (Oxford-London-Edinburgh-New York, etc., 1916), p. 56 for the war of 1864, pp. 57-64 for the war of 1866. The Lord Mayor of Dresden informed the writer by letter of August 28, 1953, that the officially acknowledged number of dead is 35,000. *Neues Deutschland* (Berlin), February 13, 1955, stated that 35,000 dead were "positively established" and that there were "some thousands more" whose bodies were torn to shreds or consumed by fire; quoted in *Dokumentation der Zeit* (Berlin), March 15, 1955, p. 6747. Other estimates run much higher. Axel Rodenberger in *Der Tod von Dresden* (Dortmund, 1952), p. 169, mentions 100,000 dead, and so does F. J. P. Veale in *Advance to Barbarism* (Appleton, Wisconsin, 1953), pp. 134-35. *Time,* June 8, 1953, p. 36, wrote: "Dresden (pop. 468,000) lost 250,000 civilian dead in three nights of air bombardment in February 1945."—For Nagasaki see *The United States Strategic Bombing Survey* (Washington, 1946), p. 15, where the number of dead is given as "over 35,000," and more than that injured.
18. Clara Eve Schieber, *The Transformation of American Sentiment Toward Germany, 1870-1914* (Boston-New York, 1923), p. ix.
19. *Where Are We Heading?* (New York-London, 1946), p. 79. See

also his book *Seven Decisions That Shaped History* (New York, 1951), p. xiv.

20. Paul Joseph Ferdonnet, *Face à Hitler* (Paris, 1934), p. 309; Salvador de Madariaga, *The World's Design* (London, 1938), p. 159. Cf. Robert H. Ferrell, *Peace in Their Time* (New Haven-London, 1952), p. 17.

21. *European Alliances and Alignments, 1871-1890* (New York, 1931), pp. 7-8.

22. *Ibid.,* pp. 8-9 (brackets in the original). Cf. Carlton J. H. Hayes, *A Political and Social History of Modern Europe,* 2 vols. (New York, 1924), vol. II, pp. 197-99; Rose, *op. cit.,* p. 92; Raymond James Sontag, *Germany and England* (New York-London, 1938), pp. 76-77, 82-88; Robert Strausz-Hupé and Stefan T. Possony, *International Relations in the Age of the Conflict between Democracy and Dictatorship* (New York-Toronto-London, 1950), p. 463. The British historian J. A. Cramb stressed in his book *Germany and England* (London, 1914), pp. 11-12, that the war of 1870 was for Germany a war of just revenge.

23. *Op. cit.* (Paris), pp. 826, 1598-99. For newer French evidence see Joseph Caillaux, *Mes Mémoires,* vol. I (Paris, 1942), p. 25 n.; Louis Lévy, *La France est une Démocratie* (London, 1943), p. 25; Geneviève Tabouis, *Jules Cambon par l'un des Siens* (Paris, 1938), p. 18.—Octave Aubry sets forth French responsibility in parts VI and VII of his book *Le Second Empire* (Paris, 1938). Cf. Edmond Rossier, *Du Traité de Westphalie à l'Europe de Versailles* (Paris, 1938), pp. 202-04.

24. Bodart, *op. cit.,* pp. 148-51; *Strategic Survey, op. cit.,* p. 15.

25. *Op. cit.,* p. 92.

26. *European Alliances, op. cit.,* p. 10.

27. Andrew Dickson White, *Autobiography,* 2 vols. (New York, 1905), vol. I, pp. 565-66.

28. *Seven Decisions, op. cit.,* p. xiv.

29. G. P. Gooch, *Franco-German Relations, 1871-1914* (London-New York-Toronto, 1923), p. 14. D. W. Brogan speaks in *The Development of Modern France* (London, 1949), p. 123, of "the mythical projected attack of 1875." Even C. Grant Robertson, very critical of the Iron Chancellor in his biography *Bismarck* (New York, 1919), p. 348, finds it difficult to believe that the Chancellor meant more than to drive Duc Decazes from office. Carlton J. H. Hayes in *A Generation of Materialism, 1871-1900* (New York-London, 1941), p. 24, presumes that Bismarck wanted to frighten France into halting her military preparations. Langer, *op. cit.,* p. 55, concluded that Russia and Britain had saved France from a danger "that did not exist, perhaps not even in the mind of the French Foreign Minister himself."

30. *Bulletin de la Société des Professeurs d'Histoire et de Géographie de l'Enseignement Public,* No. spécial 130 bis (Paris, March 1952), pp. 8, 26; *Deutschland-Frankreich,* ed. by Deutsch-Französisches Institut Ludwigsburg (Stuttgart, 1954), pp. 55, 70; *Deutschland-Frankreich-Europa: Die Deutsch-Französische Verständigung und der Geschichtsunterricht,* ed. by Professor Dr. Georg Eckert and

Dr. Otto-Ernst Schüddekopf (Baden-Baden, 1953), pp. 20, 40; *Internationales Jahrbuch für Geschichtsunterricht,* ed. by Arbeitsgemeinschaft Deutscher Lehrerverbände, Georg Eckert, vol. I (Braunschweig, 1951), p. 49; vol. II (Braunschweig, 1953), pp. 82, 98.

31. *Recent Revelations of European Diplomacy,* 4th ed., revised and enlarged 1940 (London-New York-Toronto, 1940), p. 7. This is endorsed by Sir Victor Wellesley, *Diplomacy in Fetters* (London-New York-Melbourne-Sydney, 1944), pp. 104, 106.

32. *Seven Decisions, op. cit.,* p. xiv.

33. *Op. cit.,* vol. II, p. 249.

34. *Conditions of Peace* (London, 1942), p. 211. Wellesley, *op. cit.,* p. 102, declared that the Germans as a nation have, on the whole, been neither more nor less aggressive than many other great nations. A good book on the subject is René A. Wormser's *The Myth of the Good and Bad Nations,* Foreword by Raymond Moley (Chicago, 1954).

35. *Security: Can We Retrieve It?* (New York, 1939), pp. 310-11.

36. *Failure of a Mission* (New York, 1940), p. x.

37. *The International Post-War Settlement* (London, 1944), pp. 13, 17-18.

38. Nora Waln, *Reaching for the Stars* (Boston, 1939), pp. 363, 371. Cf. the estimate of Martha Dodd, *Through Embassy Eyes* (New York, 1939), p. 133.

39. *American Diplomacy, 1900-1950* (Chicago, 1951), pp. 55-56.

40. Gustav Hilger and Alfred G. Meyer, *The Incompatible Allies* (New York, 1953), p. 341.

41. *Must, op. cit.,* p. 84. Cf. Evelyn Anderson, *Hammer or Anvil: The Story of the German Working-Class Movement* (London, 1945), p. 19, endorsing the view of F. P. Chambers, *The War behind the War* (London, 1939), pp. 6, 16.

42. Raymond Leslie Buell, *Poland: Key to Europe* (New York-London, 1939), pp. 3-4.

43. Allan Nevins, *Henry White: Thirty Years of American Diplomacy* (New York-London, 1930), pp. 325-26. Cf. Frederick Palmer, *Bliss, Peacemaker* (New York, 1934), pp. 402-03.

44. Thomas A. Bailey, *Woodrow Wilson and the Lost Peace* (New York, 1944), p. 35; Vera Dean, *Europe in Retreat* (New York, 1939), p. 237; G. P. Gooch, *Germany* (New York, 1925), pp. 113-14; Edgar Ansel Mowrer, *Germany Puts the Clock Back,* rev. ed. (New York, 1939), p. 104; Frederick L. Schuman, *International Politics* (New York-Toronto-London, 1948), p. 110; Frank H. Simonds, *How Europe Made Peace Without America* (Garden City, N. Y., 1927), p. 43; Alfred Fabre-Luce, *La Victoire* (Paris, 1924), p. 422.

45. *Le Relèvement de l'Allemagne, 1918-1938* (Paris, 1938), p. 28.

46. Frank P. Chambers, Christina Phelps Harris, and Charles C. Bayley, *This Age of Conflict,* rev. ed. (New York, 1950), p. 16. Cf. Carr, *Crisis, op. cit.,* p. 143; Jonathan French Scott, *Five Weeks: The Surge of Public Opinion on the Eve of the Great*

War (New York, 1927); K. Zilliacus, *Mirror of the Past* (New York, 1946), p. 137.
47. Roger Martin du Gard, *Les Thibault,* Septième Partie, *L'Été 1914,* 3 vols. (Paris, 1936). For this trilogy the author was awarded the Nobel Prize for Literature.
48. *European Diplomatic History, 1871-1932* (New York-London, 1933), p. 211.
49. See Chapter Two of the present book, p. 37.
50. George F. Kennan, *op. cit.,* p. 56.
51. Illuminating is Selig Adler's article "The War-Guilt Question and American Disillusionment, 1918-1928," *The Journal of Modern History,* vol. XXIII No. I, March 1951, pp. 1-28.
52. *Gathering Storm, op. cit.,* p. 85 n. 3. On p. 4 Churchill wrote that Germany, "the head and forefront of the offence," was "regarded by all as the prime cause of the catastrophe which had fallen upon the world." Cf. Grenfell, *op. cit.,* p. 24.
53. *The Time for Decision* (New York-London, 1944), p. 361.
54. Thomas A. Bailey, *The Man in the Street: The Impact of American Public Opinion on Foreign Policy* (New York, 1948), p. 2; and on p. 319: "Upon every citizen in our democracy rests a solemn obligation to inform himself so that he can direct our foreign policy—*his* foreign policy—along intelligent and far-visioned lines." E. H. Carr, *Britain: A Study of Foreign Policy from the Versailles Treaty to the Outbreak of War* (London-New York-Toronto, 1939), p. 9: "Public opinion has become a factor of the first importance." Herbert Hoover in a memorandum, April 11, 1919, for President Wilson: "The United States is the one great moral reserve in the world today," printed in *The Memoirs of Herbert Hoover. Years of Adventure, 1874-1920* (New York, 1951), p. 457.
55. *Lord Grey und der Weltkrieg* (Berlin, 1927); English and American edition, *Lord Grey and the World War* (London, 1928; New York, 1928); *Die europäische Politik in der Julikrise 1914,* published by an Investigating Committee of the Reichstag (Berlin, 1930); article "War Guilt" in *Encyclopaedia Britannica* (London-New York, 1929), vol. 23, pp. 350-54, reprinted in subsequent editions up to World War II.
56. *The Origins of the World War,* 2 vols. (New York, 1928, The Macmillan Company), vol. II, pp. 547-58.
57. *Recent Revelations of European Diplomacy,* 4th ed., revised and enlarged 1940 (London, 1940, Longmans, Green & Co.), pp. 465-70. Dr. Gooch considers the conclusions of 1940 to be his best on the subject, and he has authorized the present writer by letter of December 23, 1953, to state on his behalf: "I see no reason to withdraw or to modify the opinions I expressed on various occasions before the Second World War in reference to the responsibilities for the outbreak of hostilities in 1914." Cf. Gooch's *History of Modern Europe, 1878-1919* (New York, 1923), pp. 554-59; *Germany, op. cit.,* pp. 110-11; *Before the War: Studies in Diplomacy,* vol. II, *The Coming of the Storm* (London-New York-Toronto, 1938), pp. 284-85, 369-70, 445-46.

58. *The International Anarchy, 1904-1914,* new ed. with Foreword by Sir Arthur Salter (London, 1937), pp. 478-79. Cf. Yves Simon, *La Grande Crise de la République Française* (Montréal, 1941), English translation *The Road to Vichy, 1918-1938* (New York, 1942), pp. 19-22.

59. James T. Shotwell, *What Germany Forgot* (New York, 1940), p. 95: "Everyone now agrees that [Chancellor] Bethmann-Hollweg did not want war; nor for that matter did the Kaiser."

60. *Germany, op. cit.,* p. 353.

61. *Origins, op. cit.,* vol. II, p. 549.

62. Even during the war of 1914-18 there were men in all countries who refuted the charge of Germany's sole or primary responsibility. In England prominent leaders in this movement were the Parliamentarian Francis Neilson who published his notable book *How Diplomats Make War* in 1915, in New York, and the publicist E. D. Morel who rightly stressed Tsardom's part in the war. In France it was Georges Demartial, followed by Gouttenoire de Toury, Alfred Fabre-Luce, and others. There is a good summary of this "revisionist" literature in the Appendix to Harry Elmer Barnes, *The Genesis of the World War,* 3rd ed. (New York, 1929); and a more detailed treatment in his *World Politics in Modern Civilization* (New York, 1930). See also Alfred von Wegerer, *Bibliographie zur Vorgeschichte des Weltkrieges* (Berlin, 1934).

63. Cf. Hugh Dalton, *Hitler's War Before and After* (Harmondsworth, 1940), p. 49.

64. "The Secrets of Diplomacy," *The Times Literary Supplement,* April 12, 1947.

65. In a letter of December 26, 1953, to the writer, Professor Fay confirmed that the passage quoted exactly expresses his views. S. Adler, *op. cit.,* p. 23, declared: "Probably even today the overwhelming majority of American writers and teachers of history who concern themselves with this problem do not seriously differ from Fay's findings of over twenty years ago." Cf. Edward Norman Peterson, *Hjalmar Schacht: For and Against Hitler* (Boston, 1954), p. 33: "more and more historians . . . accept the thesis set down by Sidney B. Fay in 1928 that no one power was entirely to blame for the war, rather all the major participants must share the responsibility."

66. Regarding this matter see Harry Elmer Barnes' brochure *The Struggle Against the Historical Blackout,* privately printed, 9th ed. (Cooperstown, N. Y., 1953). Much of it is reprinted in Chapter I of H. E. Barnes *et al., Perpetual War for Perpetual Peace* (Caldwell, Idaho, 1953).

67. *Op. cit.,* pp. 97-98.

68. Alma Luckau, *The German Delegation at the Paris Peace Conference* (New York, 1941), Doc. 51, p. 272.

69. Foreword to Philip Mason Burnett's book *Reparation at the Paris Peace Conference from the Standpoint of the American Delegation,* abridged edition (New York, 1940), p. xi; see also pp. xii-xiii.—Letter to the writer, March 19, 1954.

70. *Op. cit.,* p. 86; see also pp. 45-46.

71. Victor Gollancz deals with this "amazing document" in *Our Threatened Values* (Hinsdale, Ill., 1948), p. 157.
72. *Der Kurier*, January 26, 1950, and detailed information given to the writer by letter of August 16, 1954. Cf. article by Alfred Fabre-Luce in *Écrits de Paris*, October 1953, p. 88.
73. Sir John Marriott, *The Tragedy of Europe* (London-Glasgow, 1941), p. 17.
74. Cf. Norman Angell, *For What Do We Fight?* (New York-London, 1939), p. 22; Vincent Sheean, *This House Against This House* (New York, 1946), pp. 21, 28-29. See Chapter Two of the present book.
75. Bailey, *Man, op. cit.,* p. 173.
76. In his Biennial Report, July 1, 1943, to June 30, 1945, General George C. Marshall, Chief of Staff of the United States Army, characterized Germany, Italy and Japan as the "three criminal nations, eager for loot and seeking greedily to advance their own self-interest by war"—published in *The War Reports* (Philadelphia and New York, 1947), p. 145.
77. *Conditions of Peace, op. cit.,* p. 235.
78. *The New York Times,* December 12, 1953, reproduced the text of the lecture.
79. *War and Peace* (London, 1939), and its 2nd enlarged ed. entitled *War and the Psychological Conditions of Peace* (London, 1942); *Oxford Essays on Psychology* (London, 1948), pp. 22-65, 74-76, 82-86.—General Eisenhower read *War and Peace* when he was the Royal guest at Balmoral just after the war, and expressed his approval of it, as Dr. Brown informed the writer by letter of May 16, 1951.
80. Simon, *op. cit.,* p. 83. Cf. E. H. Carr, *International Relations between the Two World Wars* (London, 1948), pp. 4-5; Dorothy Thompson, *Listen, Hans* (Boston, 1942), p. 12.

CHAPTER TWO

1. Published by the Columbia University Press (New York, 1941), 522 pages. The quotation is on p. v. Important for the topic of this chapter is also Professor James T. Shotwell's book *At the Paris Peace Conference* (New York, 1937).
2. *How Europe Made Peace Without America* (Garden City, N. Y., 1927), pp. 34, 39-40.
3. In the symposium *Prefaces to Peace* (New York, 1943), p. 234.
4. In 1938, David Lloyd George, one of the chief architects of the Treaty of Versailles, attempted to prove in *The Truth about the Peace Treaties,* 2 vols. (London, 1938), that the Treaty did not depart from the terms laid down before the war ended. In 1948, André François-Poncet, French Ambassador to Germany, 1931-1938, and again since World War II, asserted in his book *De Versailles à Potsdam* (Paris, 1948), p. 74, that the Versailles Treaty was not in flagrant contradiction to Wilson's Fourteen Points, except—perhaps—with regard to the German colonies.

5. Essential are the two books by Thomas A. Bailey, *Woodrow Wilson and the Lost Peace* (New York, 1944), and *Woodrow Wilson and the Great Betrayal* (New York, 1945). Cf. Hoover and Gibson, *op. cit.*, p. 236; *The Memoirs of Herbert Hoover. Years of Adventure, 1874-1920* (New York, 1951), p. 472; John Mackintosh, *The Paths That Led to War* (London-Glasgow, 1940), p. 7. Raoul de Roussy de Sales truly said in *The Making of Tomorrow* (New York, 1942), p. 193, that Wilson was closer to the soul of the common man of 1919 than any other leader of the time.

6. Luckau, *op. cit.*, Doc. 57, pp. 308-09.

7. The entire correspondence between Berlin and Washington from October 6th to November 5th, 1918, is printed in Luckau, *op. cit.*, Docs. 5-12, pp. 140-47. At the Peace Conference, the last sentence of the memorandum of the Allied governments, as quoted by Lansing on November 5, 1918, was misinterpreted by the Allies. In a Note of May 20, 1919, to the German delegation on responsibility for the war, G. Clemenceau, President of the Conference, drew attention to the words "Germany's aggression by land, by sea and from the air" contained in Lansing's Note, and contended that, since the German Government did not at the time make any protest against this allegation, it thereby recognized it as well-founded. He underscored this by adding: "Therefore, Germany recognized in 1918 implicitly but clearly, both the aggression and her responsibility. It is too late to deny them today." The German reply of May 24th demonstrated at length that the admitted aggression referred only to the violation of Belgian neutrality, not to Germany's alleged responsibility for the war, which was, the German Note added, "a question of life or death for the German nation"—see Luckau, *op. cit.*, Docs. 44, 51, pp. 254, 268-72. The Allies did not insist on their interpretation.

8. Numbers of authorities have acknowledged that the accepted terms were legally binding for both parties, for instance Bailey, *Lost Peace, op. cit.*, pp. 46, 240, 318; Paul Birdsall, *Versailles Twenty Years After* (New York, 1941), pp. 290-91; Collin Brooks, *Can Chamberlain Save Great Britain?* (London, 1938), pp. 120-21, 197; Professor Gilbert Murray in *The Intelligent Man's Way to Prevent War*, ed. by Leonard Woolf (London, 1933), p. 73; Harry R. Rudin, *Armistice 1918* (New Haven, 1944), p. 396; Maurice Baumont, *Peuples et Civilisations: Histoire Générale*, vol. XX, *La Faillitte de la Paix (1919-1939)* (Paris, 1945), pp. 45-46. The legally binding character must be stressed because dishonest attempts have been made to deny the fact, as George Gilbert Armstrong stated in *Why Another World War?* (London, 1941), pp. 28, 41.

9. Edgar Ansel Mowrer, *Germany Puts the Clock Back*, rev. ed. (New York, 1939), p. 102. Cf. James Murphy, *Adolf Hitler* (London, 1934), pp. 27-28; E. Alexander Powell, *Thunder over Europe* (New York, 1931), pp. 40-41; Simonds, *op. cit.*, p. 86.

10. *The Treaties of Peace, 1919-1923,* Carnegie Endowment for International Peace, vol. I (New York, 1924), p. 3.
11. Luckau, *op. cit.,* Doc. 27, p. 212.
12. *Memoirs, op. cit.,* pp. 456-57.
13. Luckau, *op. cit.,* Doc. 21, pp. 199-209. The Instructions terminated with section IX, "The Question of War Guilt."
14. *Ibid.,* Doc. 21, p. 208. According to Doc. 16, pp. 187-88, the proposal was rejected by the British Government.
15. *Ibid.,* pp. 82-83. The four were Hans Delbrück, Max Graf Montgelas, Max Weber and Albrecht Mendelssohn-Bartholdy. The latter signed the writer's *Appeal* in 1924—see pp. 149-51.
16. Stanley High, "The Momentous Aim of John Foster Dulles," *The Reader's Digest,* January 1955, p. 67.
17. Luckau, *op. cit.,* p. 119.
18. *Memoirs, op. cit.,* pp. 461-62.
19. Luckau, *op. cit.,* Doc. 30, pp. 223-24. W. Simons gained the impression that Clemenceau's sentences were thrown out as if "in concentrated anger and disdain," making any reply quite futile, *ibid.,* p. 66.
20. John W. Wheeler-Bennett, *The Nemesis of Power* (London-New York, 1953), p. 49 n. 2. Cf. James T. Shotwell, Foreword to Luckau, p. vii.
21. Vincent Sheean, *This House Against This House* (New York, 1946), p. 46. Cf. Esmé Wingfield-Stratford, *The Harvest of Victory, 1918-1926* (London, 1935), p. 65.
22. Sheean, *op. cit.,* p. 46. Joseph C. Grew relates in *Turbulent Era: A Diplomatic Record of Forty Years, 1904-1945,* 2 vols. (Boston, 1952), vol. I, pp. 387-88, that Wilson said to him "What abominable manners!" Cf. Shotwell, *Peace Conference, op. cit.,* pp. 46-49; *The Diplomats, 1919-1939,* ed. by Gordon A. Craig and Felix Gilbert (Princeton, 1953), pp. 132-48.
23. Frederick Palmer, *Bliss, Peacemaker* (New York, 1934), pp. 397-98. On May 1, when the credentials of the plenipotentiaries were exchanged, Henry White was shocked seeing the Count; he seemed to be at the point of collapse. "His face was chalky, his knees shook uncontrollably, and his hands trembled," as Allan Nevins recorded in *Henry White: Thirty Years of American Diplomacy* (New York-London, 1930), p. 443. Cf. Raymond James Sontag, *European Diplomatic History, 1871-1932* (New York-London, 1933), pp. 286-87.
24. Stewart Roddie, *Peace Patrol* (London, 1932), pp. 96-97.
25. Gustav Hilger and Alfred G. Meyer, *The Incompatible Allies* (New York, 1953), pp. 89-90. Edgar Stern-Rubarth, *Graf Brockdorff-Rantzau, Wanderer zwischen zwei Welten* (Berlin, 1929), pp. 16-17, confirms that the Count remained seated as a deliberate remonstrance in view of undignified treatment. Bertrand de Jouvenel, *D'Une Guerre à l'Autre,* vol. I (Paris, 1940), p. 92, interpreted the Count's conduct as "an effort of dignity on the part of the vanquished." Cf. Luckau, *op. cit.,* pp. 67-68.
26. Luckau, *op. cit.,* Doc. 29, pp. 220-23. Doc. 28, pp. 213-20, reproduces three preliminary drafts for the Count's speech in German.

27. *Lord Riddell's Intimate Diary of the Peace Conference and After, 1918-1923* (New York, 1934), p. 74.
28. *Op. cit.,* p. 444.
29. *Ibid.,* p. 445.
30. *The Peace Negotiations* (Boston-New York, 1921), pp. 273-74.
31. Salvador de Madariaga, *The World's Design* (London, 1938), p. 22.
32. *Op. cit.,* p. 274.
33. Luckau, *op. cit.,* pp. 71, 94.
34. *Ibid.,* pp. 97-100.
35. *Ibid.,* Docs. 31, 33, pp. 225, 233-34, for the exchange of Notes, May 9th and 10th. On p. 120 the bitter comments by W. Simons.
36. J. C. Smuts, *Jan Christian Smuts* (London, 1952), pp. 228-29, reprints the exchange of letters.
37. Lansing, *op. cit.,* pp. 274-75. The Secretary of State records that a prominent adviser to Wilson felt very bitterly over the terms of peace and had found the same feeling among the British in Paris.
38. The whole letter is printed in *The Bullitt Mission to Russia,* Testimony before the Committee on Foreign Relations, United States Senate, of William C. Bullitt (New York, 1919), pp. 96-97. Interesting details about Bullitt's resignation are described by Sisley Huddleston, *In My Time: An Observer's Record of War and Peace* (New York, 1938), pp. 156-57. See also Huddleston's Dedicatory Letter in *France: The Tragic Years, 1939-1947* (New York, 1955), pp. v-vii.—Ambassador Joseph C. Grew records in *Turbulent Era, op. cit.,* vol. I, pp. 396-99, that in November, 1934, he had a long conversation with Mr. Bullitt about his resignation. Grew wrote in his diary: "Bullitt was profoundly right in regarding the Treaty of Versailles as a disaster." Grew was inclined to admire Mr. Bullitt for his "extraordinary courage."— The broken faith of a member of the German delegation in Wilson is described by W. Simons, Luckau, *op. cit.,* p. 124.
39. Luckau, *op. cit.,* Docs. 37, 44, pp. 241-42, 254.
40. *Ibid.,* Docs. 48, 51, pp. 262, 268-72.
41. *Ibid.,* Doc. 52, pp. 272-87.
42. Cf. Sidney Bradshaw Fay, *The Origins of the World War,* 2 vols. (New York, 1928), vol. II, p. 549.
43. Luckau, *op. cit.,* Doc. 53, pp. 287-99.
44. *Ibid.,* Docs. 56, 57, pp. 302-406. See especially pp. 307-08, 310, 313, 319-20, 370-71, 376-78, 382, 385, 387. Italics in the original.
45. *Peacemaking 1919,* new ed. (New York, 1939), p. 350. In a letter to his father, June 8, 1919, *ibid.,* p. 359, Harold Nicolson repeated: "The real crime is the reparation and indemnity chapter, which is immoral and senseless."
46. Luckau, *op. cit.,* pp. 385, 387. Italics in the original.
47. *The Economic Consequences of the Peace* (New York, 1920), p. 350. Etienne Mantoux attempted a refutation in *La Paix Calomniée ou les Conséquences Economiques de M. Keynes* (Paris, 1946).

48. Bailey, *Lost Peace, op. cit.,* pp. 240-41, 243; Philip Mason Burnett, *Reparation at the Paris Peace Conference* (New York, 1940), p. 64.
49. Murray, *op. cit.,* pp. 78, 90.
50. Luckau, *op. cit.,* p. 127.
51. Palmer, *op. cit.,* p. 399.
52. Nicolson, *op. cit.,* p. 30.
53. Hoover, *op. cit.,* p. 463.
54. Nicolson, *op. cit.,* p. 30.
55. *What Germany Forgot* (New York, 1940), p. 87. Professor Shotwell was present at the Conference.
56. Lansing, *op. cit.,* p. 275.
57. Nicolson, *op. cit.,* p. 210. On June 5th, he entered in his diary, *ibid.,* p. 30: "Cannot understand Wilson. Here is a chance of improving the thing and he won't take it."
58. Hoover, *op. cit.,* p. 463.
59. Excellent on this subject are the two books by Professor Thomas A. Bailey mentioned in note 5. For tributes to President Wilson see *Ambassador Dodd's Diary, 1933-1938,* ed. by William E. Dodd, Jr., and Martha Dodd (New York, 1941), p. 442; Grew, *op. cit.,* vol. II, p. 389; Konrad Heiden, *Der Fuehrer: Hitler's Rise to Power* (Boston, 1944), p. 346; Madariaga, *op. cit.,* p. 22.
60. Luckau, *op. cit.,* Doc. 60, pp. 411-19, brings the entire letter; pp. 419-72 the Allied reply to the German observations of May 29th.
61. *Ibid.,* Doc. 60, pp. 411-72; Part VIII, pp. 438-42.
62. Quoted from the National Archives by Charles Callan Tansill, "The United States and the Road to War in Europe," in *Perpetual War for Perpetual Peace,* ed. by Harry Elmer Barnes (Caldwell, Idaho, 1953), p. 98.
63. *American Diplomacy, 1900-1950* (Chicago, 1951), pp. 55-56.
64. Camille Bloch and Pierre Renouvin, *L'Article 231 du Traité de Versailles, sa Genèse et sa Signification* (Paris, 1932). Their conclusions have been accepted by a number of authors but they are fallacious, as is clearly shown by Ph. M. Burnett, *op. cit.,* pp. 142-57.
65. *Schulthess' Europäischer Geschichtskalender, 1917,* ed. by Wilhelm Stahl (München, 1920), Part I, p. 722. Cf. Heiden, *op. cit.,* p. 241. The Peace Resolution of the Reichstag was followed by Lord Lansdowne's letter to the *Times,* November 27, 1917, in which this statesman urged the commencement of peace negotiations, as F. J. P. Veale recalled in *Advance to Barbarism* (Appleton, Wisconsin, 1953), p. 109.
66. F. Lee Benns, *Europe since 1914,* rev. ed. (New York, 1934), p. 149.
67. "The German People and the Postwar World. A Study based on Elections Statistics, 1871-1933" in *The American Political Science Review,* vol. XXXVII, No. 4, August 1943, pp. 614, 623.
68. G. P. Gooch, *Germany* (New York, 1925), p. 352; Edmond Rossier, *Du Traité de Westphalie à l'Europe de Versailles* (Paris,

1938), p. 255; Rudin, *op. cit.,* pp. 397-98. Cf. Sir Arthur Salter, *Security: Can We Retrieve It?* (New York, 1939), p. 16.
69. Viscount Rothermere, *Warnings and Predictions* (London, 1939), p. 155. See also Brooks, *op. cit.,* p. 114; Murphy, *op. cit.,* pp. 27-28; Lieutenant Colonel Seton-Hutchison, *The Truth about Germany,* in *Hitler,* ed. by F. K. Ferenz (Hollywood, 1934), pp. 26-27.
70. E. H. Carr, *International Relations between the Two World Wars* (London, 1948), p. 45.
71. Simonds, *op. cit.,* pp. 57, 59.
72. Sir Raymond Beazley, *The Road to Ruin in Europe, 1890-1914* (London, 1932), pp. 1-3, 6-7.
73. The expressions in this sentence may all be found in the following publications: Murray, *op. cit.,* pp. 86, 137-38; Roussy de Sales, *op. cit.,* pp. 178, 186-87; Simonds, *op. cit.,* pp. 40, 42, 86; Sontag, *op. cit.,* p. 299; Stephen King-Hall, *History of the War,* vol. I, *The Cause of the War* (London, 1939), p. 30; Sisley Huddleston, *War Unless——* (Philadelphia, 1934), p. 31, and *Popular Diplomacy and War* (Rindge, New Hampshire, 1954), pp. 99-101; Count Kurt Bluecher von Wahlstatt, *Know Your Germans* (London, 1951), p. 77. Cf. William Orton, *Twenty Years' Armistice, 1918-1938* (New York-Toronto, 1938), pp. 12-13; Robert Strausz-Hupé and Stefan T. Possony, *International Relations in the Age of the Conflict between Democracy and Dictatorship* (New York-Toronto-London, 1950), p. 4.
74. Quoted in *Time,* October 4, 1954, p. 30.
75. *Tass,* Moscow, September 10, 1954, reproduced in *Dokumentation der Zeit* (Berlin), October 15th.
76. Note of Oct. 23, and of Nov. 13, *Dokumentation der Zeit,* Nov. 15, and Dec. 1, respectively (see esp. p. 5967); Proceedings at the Moscow Conference, *ibid.,* Dec. 15, 1954 (see esp. p. 6069). Cf. Declarations of the Kremlin on the German question, Jan. 15 and Febr. 9, 1955, *ibid.,* Febr. 15, p. 6483, March 1, p. 6575.
77. *Germany, op. cit.,* p. 353. As early as 1915, Francis Neilson, Member of Parliament, demonstrated in his book *How Diplomats Make War* (New York, 1915), that there was divided responsibility for the outbreak of hostilities.
78. *Op. cit.,* vol. II, p. 549.
79. Luckau, *op. cit.,* p. 90. Cf. Burnett, *op. cit.,* p. 143, n. 8.
80. *Germany and the Rhineland,* The Royal Institute of International Affairs (London, 1936), pp. 45, 47, 64.
81. Luckau, *op. cit.,* Doc. 67, pp. 483, 488.
82. The speech is printed in *Geschichtskalender, op. cit.,* for 1919 (München, 1923), pp. 249-52. The passage quoted is on p. 251.
83. Luckau, *op. cit.,* Doc. 63, pp. 478-81.
84. A. L. Kennedy, *Britain Faces Germany* (New York, 1937), p. 20; Marquess of Londonderry, *Ourselves and Germany* (London, 1938), p. 26. Both authors attribute the proposal to Herr von Haniel [*sic*], who was then head of the German delegation. It was actually a proposal of the German Government, transmitted by

Herr Haniel von Haimhausen (who signed the writer's *Appeal* in 1924—see pp. 149-51).

85. *Waters under the Bridge* (London, 1945), p. 217. Brackets in the original.

86. Luckau, *op. cit.,* p. vii, end of Foreword.

87. *Ibid.,* Docs. 64, 66, pp. 481-82. Doc. 70, pp. 496-97, is an appeal of the Weimar Government to the German people, June 24th, stating that it had decided to sign "under the pressure of the most relentless power," and with but one thought: to save the defenseless people from having to make further sacrifices and endure added pains of hunger. It implored the people to bend every effort to fulfill the Treaty "so far as it can be carried out."

88. Count Brockdorff-Rantzau resigned on June 20th, Dr. W. Simons on the 22nd. In April, 1919, before going to Versailles, Simons said to a friend of Colonel House: "I am willing to accept obligations which will burden even my grandchildren. But I do not want to give them reason to be ashamed of the name I leave them." In this sense he wrote from Versailles on June 4th, Luckau, *op. cit.,* pp. 108-09, 130-31, and Doc. 69, pp. 495-96. Simons expressed the general feeling of the best Germans throughout the country. In 1924 he signed the writer's *Appeal,* see pp. 149-51. A defeatist activity was attributed to Mathias Erzberger, leader of the *Zentrum* (Catholic Party). He advocated signing the Treaty if the "points of honor," articles 227-231, were rescinded. As they were not, he voted against signing. However, the impression was left that he had undermined resistance. On August 26, 1921, Erzberger was murdered by two former officers, *ibid.,* pp. 102-06, 111.

89. *Why Europe Fights* (New York, 1940), pp. 6-7.

90. *International Relations, op. cit.,* pp. 4-5. Cf. Captain Russell Grenfell, *Unconditional Hatred. German War Guilt and the Future of Europe* (New York, 1953), p. 181; Simonds, *op. cit.,* pp. 40-41.

91. Quoted by Sontag, *op. cit.,* p. 292.

92. *Europe since 1918* (New York-London, 1923), p. 58. Gibbons relates there that a signatory, representing one of the British Dominions, told him on the evening of June 28th, that this had been the saddest day of his life. Gibbons does not give his name.

93. J. C. Smuts, *op. cit.,* pp. 234-37.

94. *Op. cit.,* pp. 370-71. As early as May 28th, Nicolson confessed that the more he read the Treaty, "the sicker" it made him, *ibid.,* p. 210.

95. Palmer, *op. cit.,* p. 401.

96. Quoted by Millis, *op. cit.,* p. 8.

97. Related by Nevins, *op. cit.,* p. 448.

98. H. C. Peterson, *Propaganda for War* (Norman, Oklahoma, 1939), pp. 326-27.

99. For instance by Arthur Ponsonby, *Falsehood in War-Time* (London, 1928); Peterson, *op. cit.;* Harold D. Lasswell, *Propaganda Technique in the World War* (New York, 1938); James R. Mock and Cedric Larson, *Words That Won the War* (Princeton, 1939).

Cf. Thomas A. Bailey, *The Man in the Street* (New York, 1948), pp. 141, 180, 204-05, 299; Robert W. Desmond, *The Press and World Affairs* (New York-London, 1937), pp. 161-62.

100. *Report on the Germans* (New York, 1947), p. 251.
101. Luckau, *op. cit.*, Doc. 8, p. 143.
102. *Ibid.*, Doc. 9, pp. 143-44.
103. *Ibid.*, Doc. 29, p. 221.
104. *Ibid.*, Docs. 51, 56, 57, pp. 270, 305, 349, 370-71.
105. *Ibid.*, Doc. 60, p. 442.
106. *Ibid.*, Docs. 51, 57, pp. 269, 348. Alcide Ebray recorded in an illuminating book, *Chiffons de Papiers* (Paris, 1926), numerous treaty violations by various European Powers.
107. *Germany, op. cit.*, p. 353.
108. Luckau, *op. cit.*, Docs. 51, 57, pp. 270, 363. Cf. Doc. 14, p. 178.
109. *Ibid.*, Doc. 60, pp. 418-19.
110. *Unfinished Victory* (London, 1940), pp. 3, 26. The figure of 800,000 victims, partly based on the findings of a Danish investigating commission, is accepted by Harry Elmer Barnes, *Modern World Politics*, ed. by Thorston V. Kalijarvi (New York, 1943), p. 344; J. Hampden Jackson, *The Between-War World* (London, 1947), p. 33; and by Tansill, *Perpetual War, op. cit.*, p. 96.
111. *Man in the Street, op. cit.*, p. 299. Cf. Bailey's *Lost Peace, op. cit.*, p. 305.
112. Armstrong, *op. cit.*, p. 28. Cf. B. C. de Montgomery, *Versailles, a Breach of Agreement* (London, 1932), pp. v, 61.
113. *Op. cit.*, p. 76. Cf. E. H. Carr, *Conditions of Peace* (London, 1942), pp. 218-19; Winston S. Churchill, *Step by Step* (London-New York, 1939), p. 141; William Harbutt Dawson, *Germany under the Treaty* (London, 1933), p. 81; Gibbons, *op. cit.*, p. 390; Hoover, *Memoirs, op. cit.*, pp. 334-52; Hoover and Gibson, *op. cit.*, pp. 227-28; Huddleston, *War, op. cit.*, pp. 29-30; John Maynard Keynes, *Two Memoirs* (London, 1949), pp. 11-71. Suda Lorena Bane and Ralph Haswell Lutz have collected the relevant material on the subject in *The Blockade of Germany after the Armistice* (Stanford-London, 1942).
114. *Diplomat between Wars* (New York-Toronto, 1941), p. 103. In Germany from old times rickets was popularly called *Die englische Krankheit, i.e.,* The English Sickness. In World War I the expression acquired a malignant meaning.
115. Luckau, *op. cit.*, Doc. 57, pp. 312, 340-43.
116. *Ibid.*, Doc. 60, p. 434.
117. *British Documents on the Origins of the War, 1898-1914*, ed. by G. P. Gooch and Harold Temperley, vol. I (London, 1926).
118. *The Long Roll on the Rhine* (New York, 1934), pp. 17-18.
119. *Op. cit.*, pp. 353-57. In an introduction to Mary Evelyn Townsend's study, *The Rise and Fall of Germany's Colonial Empire, 1884-1918* (New York, 1930), Carlton J. H. Hayes endorsed her belief "that Germany's colonial administration was neither better nor worse than that of any other colonial Power similarly circumstanced." "Her evidence," Hayes added, p. viii, "should be welcomed by all persons who desire to free themselves from war

myths." Sir Victor Wellesley of the British Foreign Office paid a fair tribute to German colonial achievements in *Diplomacy, op. cit.,* pp. 50-51. Stephen King-Hall wrote in *Our Own Times* (London, 1940), p. 959: "In South West Africa the German treatment of the natives was barbarous. In the other colonies the administration was good." Murray, *op. cit.,* p. 135, acknowledged the generally good administration in German East Africa. Harry R. Rudin, *Germans in the Cameroons, 1884-1914* (London, 1938), pp. 414, 419, praised German administration in that colony. Cf. Bailey, *Lost Peace, op. cit.,* pp. 165, 167; De Montgomery, *op. cit.,* pp. 70-72; Salter, *op. cit.,* p. 336; Tansill in *Perpetual War, op. cit.,* pp. 86-87. Viscount Grey deplored the retention of the whole of the German colonies, as recorded by George Macaulay Trevelyan in his biography *Grey of Fallodon* (Boston, 1937), p. 398.

120. Luckau, *op. cit.,* Doc. 60, p. 434.
121. Arthur Berriedale Keith, *The Causes of the War* (London-Edinburgh-Paris-Melbourne-Toronto-New York, 1940), pp. 63, 129-31.
122. It was chiefly thanks to a great humanitarian, the French-born British publicist E. D. Morel, that the atrocities in the Belgian Congo were exposed and subsequently stopped under pressure of Western public opinion; see Seymour F. Cocks, *E. D. Morel: The Man and His Work* (London, 1920), and Hermann Lutz, *E. D. Morel: Der Mann und sein Werk* (Berlin, 1925).
123. The Congo atrocities are mentioned by Bailey, *op. cit.,* p. 165, and by Dawson, *op. cit.,* pp. 355-56.
124. *Op. cit.,* pp. 353-57.
125. *Britain and the Dictators* (Cambridge, 1938), pp. 76-77.
126. For twenty years after the war the writer was in close contact with the late Dr. Heinrich Schnee, the last Governor of German East Africa. Through this association I gained an intimate knowledge of the sentiments that moved millions of Germans in the colonial question. Most of them felt that their alleged unfitness for colonization was a graver personal degradation than the war guilt charge. Recently the City of Berlin took over the *Heinrich Schnee Archiv* which his British widow, Mrs. Ada Schnee, has arranged. This donation will keep the memory of German colonization alive. (Heinrich Schnee signed the writer's *Appeal,* see pp. 149-51.) The strength of the colonial movement in Germany was duly emphasized by M. E. Townsend, *op. cit.,* pp. 386-87, 392-93.
127. *Op. cit.,* p. 167.
128. Luckau, *op. cit.,* Docs. 20, 21, 29, 32, 51, 57, 60, 68, pp. 198, 207-08, 223, 225-33, 314-15, 320-23, 363, 372, 376-77, 390, 400, 418, 423-24, 493.
129. Joseph King, *The German Revolution: Its Meaning and Menace* (London, 1933), p. 22; Simonds, *op. cit.,* p. 43.
130. Luckau, *op. cit.,* Docs. 16, 57, pp. 184, 330. In Doc. 20, p. 197, the German Foreign Office observed that the injustice of 1871 "is at any rate not greater than the wrong done by France under

Louis XIV when the territories of Alsace-Lorraine were separated from the German Reich."

131. *Franco-German Relations, 1871-1914* (London-New York-Toronto, 1923), p. 4.

132. *The Wreck of Europe,* rev. ed. (Indianapolis, 1922), p. 62. Geoffrey T. Garratt stated in *What has Happened to Europe?* (Indianapolis-New York, 1940), p. 177, that the Versailles Treaty was "considerably more drastic" than the Treaty of Frankfort.

133. Luckau, *op. cit.,* Docs. 51, 56, pp. 271, 306.

134. Bailey, *Lost Peace, op. cit.,* pp. 318-19. Robert Boothby, a prominent Member of Parliament, described in his noteworthy book *I Fight to Live* (London, 1947), p. 48 (German translation, *Europa vor der Entscheidung,* Düsseldorf, 1951, p. 63), the treaties of Brest-Litovsk and of Bucharest as "two of the most ruthless treaties ever signed." On the other hand, he declared *ibid.,* pp. 57, 234 (German edition, pp. 75, 311), that the characterization of the Versailles Treaty as a *Diktat* is a "fatal legend."

135. Quoted by Evelyn Anderson, *Hammer or Anvil: The Story of the German Working-Class Movement* (London, 1945), p. 65 and note. See also Bryant, *op. cit.,* p. 42; E. C. Helmreich in *Central-Eastern Europe, Crucible of World Wars* (New York, 1946), p. 243; Henry C. Wolfe, *The German Octopus* (New York, 1938), p. 3; Richard von Kühlmann, *Erinnerungen* (Heidelberg, 1948), pp. 518-50; Leonhard von Muralt, *Der Friede von Versailles und die Gegenwart* (Zürich, 1947), p. 89.

136. Luckau, *op. cit.,* Docs. 31, 38, 56, 63, 67, 68, 69, pp. 225, 242-44, 302, 379-90, 480-81, 488, 489-95, 495-96.

137. *Ibid.,* Doc. 64, p. 481.

138. *Ibid.,* Doc. 67, p. 488. Cf. Otto Braun, *Von Weimar zu Hitler* (New York, 1940), p. 70; Stern-Rubarth, *op. cit.,* p. 116.

139. *Op. cit.,* p. 145. Boothby, *op. cit.,* p. 234 (German ed., p. 311), wrote about Keynes' book: "It established irrevocably the legend of the Versailles *Diktat,* which, more than anything else, reduced the Western Democracies to paralysed impotence, and enabled Hitler, only twenty years later, to trample the continent of Europe underfoot."

140. *Op. cit.,* pp. 13, 39-41, 44.

141. *Op. cit.,* p. 471. John Foster Dulles stated in his book *War, Peace and Change* (New York-London, 1939), p. 82: "In consequence [of propaganda, intensified hate] the Treaty inevitably embodied many injustices. Some provisions were in themselves unfair or intentionally repressive. Others were unjust in that they contravened the pre-armistice agreement, in reliance upon which Germany had laid down her arms." See also *ibid.,* pp. 146-50.

142. *Op. cit.,* pp. 21, 49, 58. Cf. Brooks, *op. cit.,* pp. 120-21, 197. On the other hand, Duff Cooper (Viscount Norwich) wrote in his autobiography *Old Men Forget* (London, 1953), pp. 195-96, that to this day there are many people in Britain and America, who are "unaware" that the terms of the Treaty of Versailles "were generous to Germany."

143. *Op. cit.,* pp. 11, 23, 28. Cf. Brooks, *op. cit.,* pp. 53, 147; Keith, *op. cit.,* pp. 57-58; Dwight E. Lee, *Ten Years: The World on the Way to War, 1930-1940* (Boston, 1942), p. 38; Powell, *Thunder, op. cit.,* pp. 40-41; Simonds, *op. cit.,* p. 86; Wellesley, *op. cit.,* p. 60.

144. *Perpetual War, op. cit.,* p. 81; Dr. Harry Elmer Barnes, *ibid.,* p. 630. Cf. Baumont, *op. cit.,* pp. 45-46. Emery Reves, *The Anatomy of Peace* (New York-London, 1945), says, p. 2, that, American intervention having decided the outcome of the struggle in favor of the Allies, "the major Allied Powers—Britain, France, Italy and Japan—betrayed the common cause."

145. *Lost Peace, op. cit.,* p. 52. In *The Great Betrayal, op. cit.,* pp. 356-61, Bailey enumerates 14 various betrayals.

146. Luckau, *op. cit.,* Doc. 60, pp. 411-19, and in the text of the present chapter, pp. 54, 56. The estimate of seven million dead was much too low. According to Kirby Page, *National Defense: A Study of the Origins, Results and Prevention of War* (New York, 1931), pp. 160-61, the "known dead" were: of Russia: 2,762,064; Germany: 1,611,104; France: 1,427,800; Austria-Hungary: 911,000; Great Britain: 807,451; Serbia: 707,343; Italy: 507,160; Turkey: 436,924; Rumania: 339,117; Belgium: 267,000; United States: 107,284; Bulgaria: 101,224; Greece: 15,000; Portugal: 4,000; Japan: 300—a total of 9,998,771 dead.

147. Arnold-Foster, and Murray, in *Man's Way, op. cit.,* pp. 82, 346-47; Sherwood Eddy, *The Challenge of Europe* (New York, 1933), p. 29; Lee, *op. cit.,* pp. 421-22; Millis, *op. cit.,* pp. 17-18; Seton-Watson, *op. cit.,* pp. 76-77.

148. Luckau, *op. cit.,* Docs. 16, 21, 29, 53, 56, pp. 187-88, 208, 221, 288, 305. Some authors deplored the lack of a neutral verdict, for instance Lindley Fraser, *Germany between Two Wars* (London-New York-Toronto, 1944), pp. 54, 63, 65; Gibbons, *op. cit.,* p. 602; Keith, *op. cit.,* pp. 63, 129; De Montgomery, *op. cit.,* pp. vii-x; Salter, *op. cit.,* p. 322.

149. From twenty years' experience the writer has intimate knowledge of currents in the German movement against the war guilt charge which may easily surge to the surface whenever favorable conditions arise.

150. *Op. cit.,* p. 7. Cf. Mackintosh, *op. cit.,* p. 27.

151. Thomas A. Bailey, *A Diplomatic History of the American People,* 3rd ed. (New York, 1946), p. 665.

152. *Man's Way, op. cit.,* p. 45. Cf. G. D. H. Cole and Margaret Cole, *The Intelligent Man's Review of Europe Today* (New York, 1934), pp. 539-43.

153. Bryant, *op. cit.,* p. xii; Vernon Bartlett, *Intermission in Europe* (New York, 1938), pp. 27, 41.

154. Norman Angell, *Must It Be War?* (London, 1939), pp. 89, 119.

155. W. D. Herridge, *Which Kind of Revolution?* (Boston, 1945), p. 23. Nitti, *op. cit.,* p. 19, declared: ". . . the Treaty system . . . determines a state of permanent war."

156. Gibbons, *op. cit.,* pp. 73-74. Knox recognized that Germany could never acquit herself of the obligations imposed on her.

157. Jackson, *op. cit.*, p. 23; Mackintosh, *op. cit.*, p. 27; Gilbert Murray in *The Background and Issues of the War* (Oxford, 1940), p. 55; Harold Nicolson, *Why Britain Is at War* (London, 1939), pp. 145-46; Powell, *Long Roll, op. cit.*, p. 12; Shotwell, *Forgot, op. cit.*, p. 85; Wellesley, *op. cit.*, pp. 46, 59. Professor Bailey, *Lost Peace, op. cit.*, p. 310, aptly says that the Big Four at the Paris Conference were "but the servants and mouthpieces of their people."

158. R. T. Clark, *The Fall of the German Republic* (London, 1935), pp. 59-62.

159. Edward Hallett Carr, *The Twenty Years' Crisis, 1919-1939* (London, 1939), p. 79.

160. *Peacemaking, op. cit.*, pp. 122, 187. On p. 189, Nicolson speaks of the "ghastly hypocrisy."

161. Sisley Huddleston has shown this at length in his *Popular Diplomacy and War* (Rindge, New Hampshire, 1954).

162. *Geschichtskalender* for 1919, *op. cit.*, p. 211.

163. Erich Kordt, *Wahn und Wirklichkeit: Die Aussenpolitik des Dritten Reiches* (Stuttgart, 1948), p. 407; Carl H. Müller-Graf, *Irrweg und Umkehr* (Stuttgart, 1948), pp. 61, 117. Cf. Boothby, *op. cit.*, p. 70 (German ed., pp. 91-92); Clark, *op. cit.*, p. 61; Herridge, *op. cit.*, p. 23; Huddleston, *My Time, op. cit.*, p. 155; Nitti, *op. cit.*, p. 127.

164. Gibbons, *op. cit.*, p. 89. George F. Kennan said in *op. cit.*, p. 69: "Truly, this was a peace which had the tragedies of the future written into it as by the devil's own hand."

165. Bryant, *op. cit.*, p. 75; Burnett, *op. cit.*, pp. 144-45; Clark, *op. cit.*, pp. 59-62; Eddy, *op. cit.*, pp. 28-29; Hoover and Gibson, *op. cit.*, p. 227; Mowrer, *op. cit.*, p. 104; Frederick L. Schuman, *International Politics* (New York-Toronto-London, 1948), p. 114; Shotwell, *Forgot, op. cit.*, p. 119; Wingfield-Stratford, *op. cit.*, pp. 63-64; René A. Wormser, *The Myth of the Good and Bad Nations* (Chicago, 1954), p. 88; Louis Bertrand, *Hitler* (Paris, 1936), pp. 19-21.

166. Luckau, *op. cit.*, Docs. 29, 53, pp. 221, 287-99.

167. *La Victoire* (Paris, 1924), p. 396.

168. Hoover, *op. cit.*, p. 482.

169. The Shantung settlement was a significant factor in the rejection of the Treaty, see Russell H. Fifield, *Woodrow Wilson and the Far East* (New York, 1952), p. x and Chapter Three.

170. *International Conciliation* (New York), May 1921, No. 162, pp. 161-62.

171. *Papers Relating to the Foreign Relations of the United States, 1921* (Washington, 1936), vol. II, p. 40.

172. Luckau, *op. cit.*, Doc. 57, p. 309.

173. "The Challenge to Americans," *Foreign Affairs*, vol. 26, No. 1, October 1947, p. 6. Numbers of Americans have admitted United States moral responsibility, for instance Herbert Agar, *A Time for Greatness* (Boston, 1942), pp. 55-56, 289, 294; Bailey, *Betrayal, op. cit.*, pp. v, 357-61; Carlton J. H. Hayes, *This Inevitable Conflict* (New York, 1942), p. 15; Charles Seymour, *The Inti-*

mate Papers of Colonel House (Boston-New York, 1928), vol. IV, p. 489; A. L. Kennedy, *op. cit.*, p. 20; Henry R. Luce, Foreword to John F. Kennedy, *Why England Slept* (New York, 1940), p. xix; Bernadotte E. Schmitt, *From Versailles to Munich* (Chicago, 1938), p. 36; Sheean, *op. cit.*, p. 22. John Flournoy Montgomery, U. S. Minister to Hungary, 1933-1941, wrote in his record *Hungary the Unwilling Satellite* (New York, 1947), p. 7: "But having helped our allies to win, we had our share of responsibility in the results of victory. We should not have washed our hands of all the injustice committed in the name of national self-determination, and yet we did."

174. George Glasgow, *From Dawes to Locarno* (London, 1925), pp. 120-21, reproduces the German proclamation and the British answer.

175. Luckau, *op. cit.*, Doc. 60, p. 414.

CHAPTER THREE

1. Cf. Thomas A. Bailey, *The Man in the Street* (New York, 1948), p. 44.
2. *Germany Tried Democracy* (New York, 1946), pp. 152-53.
3. *Where Are We Heading?* (New York-London, 1946), p. 77.
4. G. P. Gooch, *Germany* (New York, 1925), p. 358; Gooch in *World Outlook* (London, 1939), pp. 130-31; J. Hampden Jackson, *The Between-War World* (London, 1947), p. 126; Stephen King-Hall, *History of the War*, vol. I, *The Cause of the War* (London, 1939), pp. 27-28; Frederick L. Schuman, *Germany since 1918* (New York, 1937), p. 27; Frank H. Simonds, *How Europe Made Peace Without America* (Garden City, N. Y., 1927), pp. 87-90; Otto Braun, *Von Weimar zu Hitler* (New York, 1940), p. 70.
5. Alma Luckau, *The German Delegation at the Paris Peace Conference* (New York, 1941), Doc. 57, p. 385. See the text on pp. 50-51 of the present book.
6. About Quidde see Hans Ernest Fried, *The Guilt of the German Army* (New York, 1942), pp. 248-49; John W. Wheeler-Bennett, *The Nemesis of Power* (London-New York, 1953), p. 147. Quidde was Nobel Peace Prize winner in 1927, jointly with Ferdinand Buisson, President of the *League des Droits de l'Homme*. Though an uncompromising pacifist, Quidde fought valiantly for his convictions. In 1924 he signed the writer's *Appeal*, see pp. 149-51.
7. R. W. Seton-Watson, *Britain and the Dictators* (Cambridge, 1938), pp. 77-78, 192-93. Cf. Theodore Abel, *Why Hitler Came to Power* (New York, 1938), pp. 31-32; Joan and Jonathan Griffin, *Lost Liberty?* (New York, 1939), pp. 5-6; Calvin B. Hoover, *Germany Enters the Third Reich* (New York, 1933), pp. 42-43; Louis P. Lochner, *What About Germany?* (New York, 1942), p. 16; Simonds, *op. cit.*, pp. 83-84; George Macaulay Trevelyan, *British History in the Nineteenth Century and After*, new ed. (London-New York-Toronto, 1941), pp. 483-84; W. L. White, *Report on the Germans* (New York, 1947), pp. 253-54.

220 GERMAN-FRENCH UNITY

8. *Diplomat between Wars* (New York-Toronto, 1941), pp. 96-98. On p. 115 the author speaks of the "incredible difficulties" the German Government had to confront, "financial chaos, unemployment, a people underfed for years and in despair."
9. Simonds, *op. cit.*, pp. 83-84; White, *op. cit.*, pp. 253-54.
10. Thomas A. Bailey, *Woodrow Wilson and the Lost Peace* (New York, 1944), p. 38. Cf. Paul Birdsall, *Versailles Twenty Years After* (New York, 1941), pp. 263, 296.
11. Arthur Salter, *The Dual Policy* (Oxford, 1939), p. 24.—Dr. G. P. Gooch wrote in *Contemporary Review*, October 1926, p. 346, about the American "Revisionists": "Among American students of the causes of the war of 1914 Professor Barnes, Professor Fay and Professor Bernadotte Schmitt are the best known; and no other American scholar has done so much as Professor Barnes to familiarize his countrymen with the new evidence . . . or to compel them to revise their war-time judgements in the light of this new material." Barnes' chief books on the subject are *The Genesis of the World War* (New York and London, 1926; rev. ed. 1929), and *In Quest of Truth and Justice* (Chicago, 1928). Prof. Bernadotte E. Schmitt's *The Coming of the War, 1914,* 2 vols. (New York-London, 1930), is admittedly very severe on the Central Powers. Sidney B. Fay's *The Origins of the World War,* 2 vols. (New York, 1928), remains a universally recognized standard work (see two American appraisals of 1951 and 1954 on p. 206, note 65). In a letter to the Hoover Institute and Library, July 18, 1955, Dr. G. P. Gooch declared: "I find myself in closer agreement with Professor Fay than with any other American writers on the origins of the war of 1914."—The most monumental work on the subject has been written by Luigi Albertini, *Le Origini della Guerra del 1914,* 3 vols. (Milano, 1942-43); English translation, *The Origins of the War of 1914,* published by the Oxford University Press (London-New York-Toronto, 1952 ff.).
12. Winston S. Churchill, *The Second World War * The Gathering Storm* (Boston, 1948), p. 12; Gooch, *Germany, op. cit.,* p. 269, and *Outlook, op. cit.,* p. 131; John Mackintosh, *The Paths That Led to War* (London-Glasgow, 1940), p. 54; Seton-Watson, *op. cit.,* pp. 192-93; Louis Bertrand, *Hitler* (Paris, 1936), p. 22.
13. Joseph King, *The German Revolution* (London, 1933), pp. 18-20. Cf. Birdsall, *op. cit.,* pp. 218-23, 300; G. E. R. Gedye, *The Revolver Republic: France's Bid for the Rhine* (London, 1930), pp. 150-240; Bertrand de Jouvenel, *D'Une Guerre à l'Autre,* vol. I (Paris, 1940), p. 332. Immediately after conclusion of the armistice there were French attempts to create a Rhine Republic, against which the German Government lodged a vigorous protest on June 3, 1919—see Luckau, *op. cit.,* Doc. 59, pp. 410-11. Cf. Pierrepont B. Noyes, *While Europe Waits for Peace* (New York, 1921), pp. 50-60. In the early 'twenties, Chancellor Wirth warned General Ch. Nollet, President of the Allied Military Control Commission: "With your system you will kill the German Republic," as recorded by Spectator in *Deutschlands Erwachen, von einem Ausländer Gesehen* (Genf, 1933), p. 59.

14. *Op. cit.*, pp. 114-15. Cf. Walter Phelps Hall, *Iron out of Calvary* (New York-London, 1946), p. 9; Arthur Berriedale Keith, *The Causes of the War* (London, 1940), pp. 89-90; Switzer McGrary, *The National Socialist State* (Dallas, 1935), p. 6.

15. *International Relations between the Two World Wars* (London, 1948), p. 58. Cf. Floyd A. Cave and Associates, *The Origins and Consequences of World War II* (New York, 1948), pp. 278, 280; Edward Norman Peterson, *Hjalmar Schacht: For and Against Hitler* (Boston, 1954), pp. 32, 38-46; F. H. Soward, *Twenty-Five Troubled Years* (London, 1944), pp. 147-48; Friedrich Lütge in *The Third Reich* (London, 1955), pp. 421-25.

16. *Die Versailler Friedens-Verhandlungen. Persönliche Erinnerungen* (Berlin, 1921).

17. Keith Feiling, *The Life of Neville Chamberlain* (London, 1947), p. 247; Colonel E. Alexander Powell, *The Long Roll on the Rhine* (New York, 1934), p. 29.

18. Bailey, *Lost Peace, op. cit.*, pp. 314-15, and *Woodrow Wilson and the Great Betrayal* (New York, 1945), pp. 357, 358; C. E. Black and E. C. Helmreich, *Twentieth Century Europe* (New York, 1951), p. 130; E. H. Carr, *Britain: A Study of Foreign Policy from the Versailles Treaty to the Outbreak of War* (London-New York-Toronto, 1939), p. 105; William Henry Chamberlin, *America's Second Crusade* (Chicago, 1950), pp. 42-43; Vera Micheles Dean, *Europe in Retreat* (New York, 1939), pp. xvii-xviii; *The Memoirs of Herbert Hoover. Years of Adventure, 1874-1920* (New York, 1951), p. 471; Herbert Hoover and Hugh Gibson in *Prefaces to Peace* (New York, 1943), pp. 267-68; Sisley Huddleston, *War Unless——* (Philadelphia, 1934), p. 271; Keith, *op. cit.*, pp. 29-30; Mackintosh, *op. cit.*, pp. 30-31; Dwight E. Lee, *Ten Years: The World on the Way to War, 1930-1940* (Boston, 1942), p. 46; Soward, *op. cit.*, p. 39; Welles, *op. cit.*, p. 3; Sir Victor Wellesley, *Diplomacy in Fetters* (London-New York-Melbourne-Sydney, 1944), pp. 64, 66.

19. Hugh Dalton, *Hitler's War Before and After* (Harmondsworth, 1940), p. 16; Soward, *op. cit.*, p. 122; *Survey of International Affairs, 1939-1946. The World in March 1939*, ed. by Arnold Toynbee and Frank T. Ashton-Gwatkin (London-New York-Toronto, 1952), p. 19. Cf. Lindley Fraser, *Germany between Two Wars* (London-New York-Toronto, 1944), p. 67; Sir John Marriott, *The Tragedy of Europe* (London-Glasgow, 1941), p. 8; Lord Vansittart, *Bones of Contention* (New York, 1945), p. 156.—Ambassador Hugh R. Wilson, *op. cit.*, pp. 333-34, contended that American participation in the League would not have altered Article XIX.

20. *The Truth about the Peace Treaties*, 2 vols. (London, 1938), pp. 1410-11. James T. Shotwell refers in *What Germany Forgot* (New York, 1940), p. 100, to the well known disaster which Poincaré's leadership brought to France and to Europe.

21. "The German People and the Postwar World. A Study based on Election Statistics, 1871-1933," *The American Political Science Review*, vol. XXXVII, No. 4, August 1943, p. 623. Robert A.

Brady declared in *The Spirit and Structure of German Fascism* (London, 1937), p. 20, that the extent and quality of the resurgence of the German people during the short period 1924-29 "is one of the greatest tributes to the human species known in the annals of written history."

22. *The Memoirs of Cordell Hull,* 2 vols. (New York, 1948), p. 356. Cf. Richard W. Van Alstyne, *American Diplomacy in Action* (Stanford-London, 1944), p. 373; J. A. Spender, *Between Two Wars* (London-Toronto-Melbourne-Sydney, 1943), p. 129.

23. Carr, *International Relations, op. cit.,* pp. 138-39; *Les Evénements Survenus en France de 1933 à 1945,* Assemblée Nationale (Paris), No. 2344, vol. III, p. 759; C. W. Guillebaud, *The Economic Recovery of Germany from 1933 to the Incorporation of Austria in March 1938* (London, 1939), p. 20; Halperin, *op. cit.,* pp. 463-64; Mackintosh, *op. cit.,* p. 72. Cf. M. Margaret Ball, *Post-War German-Austrian Relations* (Stanford-Oxford, 1937), Chapt. VII, VIII; Malcolm Bullock, *Austria, 1918-1938* (London, 1939), Chapt. IX; Julius Curtius, *Bemühung um Oesterreich: Das Scheitern des Zollunionsplans von 1931* (Heidelberg, 1947), and *Sechs Jahre Minister der Deutschen Republik* (Heidelberg, 1948), Chapt. VI and XII.

24. William Harbutt Dawson, *Germany under the Treaty* (London, 1933), pp. 391-92; James T. Shotwell, *On the Rim of the Abyss* (New York, 1936), pp. 212-13. Cf. George Gilbert Armstrong, *Why Another World War?* (London, 1941), p. 66; Marquess of Londonderry, *Wings of Destiny* (London, 1943), Chapt. III-V.

25. *Op. cit.,* p. 1408.

26. *Op. cit.,* p. 266.

27. *Op. cit.,* p. 176; cf. p. 50.

28. *Ibid.,* p. 195.

29. Black-Helmreich, *op. cit.,* p. 521; Carr, *Britain, op. cit.,* p. 152; Geoffrey T. Garratt, *What Has Happened to Europe?* (Indianapolis-New York, 1940), pp. 200-03; Hoover and Gibson, *op. cit.,* pp. 266, 269-70; John F. Kennedy, *Why England Slept* (New York, 1940), pp. 69, 82-83; John W. Wheeler-Bennett, *Munich: Prologue to Tragedy* (New York, 1948), p. 204; Herbert von Dirksen, *Moscow, Tokyo, London* (Norman, Oklahoma, 1952), pp. 103, 232-33; Albert C. Grzesinski, *Inside Germany* (New York, 1939), p. 363; Rainer Hildebrandt, *Wir sind die Letzten* (Neuwied-Berlin), p. 25; Rudolf Pechel, *Deutscher Widerstand* (Erlenbach-Zürich, 1947), p. 265; Hans Schlange-Schoeningen, *Am Tage Danach* (Hamburg, 1946), pp. 105, 126. Ernst von Weizsaecker declared in his *Erinnerungen* (München-Leipzig-Freiburg i. Br., 1950), p. 79, that German Democracy received its death-blow at Geneva.

30. Franz von Papen, *Memoirs* (London, 1952), pp. 176-83; Lutz Graf Schwerin von Krosigk, *Es Geschah in Deutschland* (Tübingen-Stuttgart, 1952), p. 144.

31. *The Social Policy of Nazi Germany* (Cambridge, 1941), p. 18. Cf. G. M. Gathorne-Hardy, *A Short History of International Affairs, 1920-1939,* 4th ed. (London-New York-Toronto, 1950), pp.

285-86; C. Grove Haines and Ross J. S. Hoffman, *The Origins and Background of the Second World War* (London-New York-Toronto, 1943), pp. 322-23.

32. *Op. cit.,* pp. 415-16. Cf. Carr, *International Relations, op. cit.,* p. 45; Harold J. Laski, *Reflections on the Revolution of Our Time* (New York, 1943), p. 107; Henri Lichtenberger, *The Third Reich* (New York, 1937), pp. 13-14; Robert H. Lowie, *Toward Understanding Germany* (Chicago, 1954), pp. 158, 328, 330; Gerhard Ritter in *Third Reich, op. cit.,* pp. 389, 405, 407, 411, and in "Vom Ursprung des Einparteienstaates in Europa," *Historisches Jahrbuch,* 74. Jahrgang (Freiburg-München, 1955), p. 580.

33. Schuman, *op. cit.,* pp. 28-29. Jackson, *op. cit.,* p. 35, declared: "Only the marvellous stamina of the German people could have succeeded in working that Constitution for a decade and more in spite of Versailles." Harold Picton, *Nazis and Germans: A Record of Personal Experience* (London, 1940, Preface by G. P. Gooch), p. 25, says: "On the whole it is surprising that the German Republic survived as long as it did."

34. *Documents on British Foreign Policy, 1919-1939,* Secd. Series, vol. IV, *1932-3,* ed. by E. L. Woodward and Rohan Butler (London, 1950), No. 266, pp. 462-63; cf. *ibid.,* No. 243, p. 427.

35. Londonderry, *op. cit.,* p. 194. Cf. Hoover and Gibson, *op. cit.,* pp. 251-52, 286-87; Seton-Watson, *op. cit.,* pp. 77-78; Arnold J. Toynbee in *Foreign Affairs,* vol. 17, No. 2, January 1939, pp. 316-17; Trevelyan, *op. cit.,* pp. 484-85. E. Alexander Powell shrewdly forecast in *Thunder over Europe* (New York, 1931), p. x, that French policy "will sooner or later bring France and Europe to the brink of disaster." In *Ambassador Dodd's Diary, 1933-1938,* ed. by William E. Dodd, Jr., and Martha Dodd (New York, 1941), p. 52, the Ambassador recorded in October 1933: "The German Social-Democratic movement was ruined by French policy."

CHAPTER FOUR

1. *Völkischer Beobachter, Reichsausgabe* (München), September 25th and 26th, 1930. Striking passages of Lord Rothermere's article are quoted by Konrad Heiden, *Der Fuehrer: Hitler's Rise to Power* (Boston, 1944), pp. 354-55, and by Kurt G. W. Ludecke, *I Knew Hitler. The Story of a Nazi Who Escaped the Blood Purge* (New York, 1937), pp. 344-45.

2. Viscount Rothermere, *Warnings and Predictions* (London, 1939); Ward Price, *I Know These Dictators,* rev. ed. (London-Toronto-Bombay-Sydney, 1938).

3. *Britain and the Dictators: A Survey of Post-War British Policy* (Cambridge, 1938), p. 211.

4. *Deutsche Rundschau* (Stuttgart), July 1947, p. 22. Cf. Charles Callan Tansill, *Back Door to War: The Roosevelt Foreign Policy, 1933-1941* (Chicago, 1952), pp. 33-34, with reference to a dissertation by E. J. Dunne. Dr. H. Brüning will enlarge on the subject in his forthcoming Memoirs.

5. Konrad Heiden in *Geschichte des Nationalsozialismus* (Berlin, 1933), pp. 143-47; in *Adolf Hitler: Das Zeitalter der Verantwortungslosigkeit* (Zürich, 1936), pp. 262-66; and in *Hitler: A Biography* (New York, 1936), pp. 220-23. Richard Lewinsohn (Morus), *Das Geld in der Politik* (Berlin, 1930), pp. 148-50.

6. *Internationale Presse-Korrespondenz* (Berlin), No. 49, June 1932. Johannes Steel, *Hitler as Frankenstein* (London, 1933), pp. 95-96, alleged that Abel was murdered after Hitler's seizure of power. According to Paul Reynaud, *La France a Sauvé l'Europe*, 2 vols. (Paris, 1947), vol. I, p. 148, Mussolini sent Hitler money and arms in 1930, 1931, and 1932. Alfred Fabre-Luce, *Histoire de la Révolution Européenne* (Paris, 1954), p. 114, states that under the Weimar Republic Mussolini made financial contributions to Hitler, but refused to give him his photograph and to grant him an interview.

7. *Arbeiterzeitung* (Wien), June 24, 1923; Ruth Fischer, *Stalin and German Communism: A Study in the Origins of the State Party* (Cambridge, Mass., 1948), p. 292; Heiden, *Adolf Hitler, op. cit.,* p. 264, and *Hitler, op. cit.,* p. 222; C. J. C. Street, *The Treachery of France* (London, 1924), pp. 135-45; Klaus Bredow, *Hitler rast: Der 30. Juni* (Saarbrücken), pp. 7-8.

8. *Le Quai d'Orsay* (Paris, 1938), pp. 199-213, section "Did the Quai d'Orsay subvention Hitler?" The passages quoted in the text are on pp. 207, 210, 212. Cf. Maurice Baumont in *The Third Reich* (London, 1955), p. 469.

9. *Op. cit.,* pp. 207, 209.

10. The version of Morel's revelation as given by Heiden in *Geschichte, op. cit.,* p. 146 (English ed., London, 1934, p. 92), in *Adolf Hitler, op. cit.,* p. 264 (American ed., New York, 1936, p. 223), needs rectification. Morel never spoke of "a member of the French Cabinet," but of a *former* Cabinet Minister, and he did not suggest that he was informed in Paris. Morel did not reveal his source but we were left under the impression that it was Joseph Caillaux. In 1925, I was witness in one of Hitler's lawsuits concerning French payments.

11. See *Korrespondenz* in note 6. It has been denied that Hitler ever foamed at the mouth when in rage, yet it is a fact.

12. *Op. cit.,* pp. 190-91. A similar authorization had been given to Ludecke on December 15, 1923, by the "National Socialist Party of Greater Germany, Vienna." In his book of 1937 Ludecke did not disclose the result of his endeavors. About Ludecke's role in the Party see Dr. Paul Schwarz, *This Man Ribbentrop: His Life and Times* (New York, 1943), p. 87.

13. Albert C. Grzesinski, *Inside Germany* (New York, 1939), p. 365. Johannes Stahl, another fugitive from Nazi Germany, has minutely recorded the methods employed for collections abroad. He had apparently unusual inside knowledge but the Appendix shows that he made several untrue statements of grave importance. Ludecke, *op. cit.,* chapt. xvii, describes his "Selling Hitler in America."

14. Letters from abroad, July 25, 1952, and January 5, 1954.

15. H. C. Engelbrecht and F. C. Hanighen, *Merchants of Death: A Study of the International Armament Industry*, Foreword by Harry Elmer Barnes (New York, 1934), pp. 196-97, and chapt. xv, "The Menace of Disarmament."

16. Jean Galtier-Boissière and René Lefebvre, *Les Marchands de Canons contre la Nation*, special issue of *Crapouillot* (Paris), October 1933, pp. 85-87; Richard Lewinsohn, *The Profits of War Through the Ages* (London, 1936), pp. 188-90, passage "Threats to Disarmament."

17. Speech on February 11, 1932, published in Faure's brochure *Les Marchands de Canons contre la Paix* (Paris, 1932). The same statement also in Faure's study *Eugène Schneider: Potentat du Creusot* (Paris, 1932), and reproduced by many American and British authors. According to *Fortune*, vol. IX, No. 3, March 1934, "Arms and the Men," pp. 53, 113-14, the French controlled 56 per cent of the Skoda stock, and the Directors "contributed millions of marks to Hitler's campaign."—About Schneider-Creusot, Skoda and Faure see also *Munitions Industry: Report of the Special Committee on Investigation of the Munitions Industry, United States Senate*. S. Res. 206 (73rd Congress) (Washington, 1936), pp. 252-54.

18. *Ambassador Dodd's Diary, 1933-1938*, ed. by William E. Dodd, Jr., and Martha Dodd, Introduction by Charles A. Beard (New York, 1941), p. 415, entry of June 4, 1937.

19. *The Berlin Diaries, May 30, 1932-January 30, 1933*, ed. by Dr. Helmut Klotz, Foreword by Edgar Ansel Mowrer (New York, 1934), pp. 250-51.

20. Rudolf Diels, *Lucifer Ante Portas . . . es spricht der erste Chef der Gestapo . . .* (Stuttgart, 1950), pp. 103-04.

21. Edgar Ansel Mowrer, *Germany Puts the Clock Back*, rev. ed. (New York, 1939), pp. 144-45.

22. For instance *The Brown Network: The Activities of the Nazis in Foreign Countries* (New York, 1936), p. 64; *Der Rote Aufbau* (Berlin), July 1, 1932, p. 594. Willi Münzenberg stated in *Propaganda als Waffe* (Paris, 1937), p. 235, that payments by Kreuger to the Party were proved.—On January 16, 1933, the British Ambassador to Berlin reported on statements in the German press according to which funds had been forthcoming from Sweden; the Swedish banker Marcus Wallenberg denied that he had furnished any funds, *Documents on British Foreign Policy, 1919-1939*, Secd. Series, vol. IV, *1932-3*, ed. by E. L. Woodward and Rohan Butler (London, 1950), No. 225, p. 387. (This publication hereafter referred to as *Brit. Docs.*)

23. Glyn Roberts, *The Most Powerful Man in the World: The Life of Sir Henri Deterding* (New York, 1938); Emil Rasche, *Die Sechste Grossmacht: Männer und Mächte um Erdöl* (Frankfurt a. M., 1951), pp. 123-41. See also *Brown Network, op. cit.*, pp. 64-65, 140; *Crapouillot*, July 1933, pp. 61-62; Lewinsohn, *Geld in Politik, op. cit.*, pp. 352-56. In *Nazism: An Assault on Civilization*, ed. by Pierre van Paassen and James Waterman Wise (New York, 1934), pp. 223-24, P. van Paassen declared that Messrs.

Coty, Deterding and Rothermere financed the "League for Ukrainian Independence."

24. Rasche, *op. cit.*, p. 135.

25. Roberts, *op. cit.*, p. 305; *Brown Network, op. cit.*, p. 65; Münzenberg, *op. cit.*, p. 235.

26. Dr. Erwein Freiherr von Aretin, *Fritz Michael Gerlich: Ein Märtyrer unserer Tage* (München, 1949), p. 120 n. "Quietus" stated in an article "Hitlers Finanzen" in *Die Weltbühne*, ed. by Carl von Ossietzky, XXVIII. Jahrgang, No. 16, April 19, 1932, p. 585, that Alfred Rosenberg and Dr. Nyland, Chief of the Nazi foreign propaganda office, had negotiated an agreement with Deterding the terms of which stipulated that the latter, in return for his subsidies to the NSDAP amounting to £1½ million, would get an oil monopoly in Germany upon Hitler's assumption of power. Some years later Ossietzky perished in a concentration camp.

27. *Ibid.*, pp. 114, 120 n.—Letter from Dr. J. Steiner, collaborator of Dr. Gerlich, to the writer, November 11, 1953.

28. *Von der Brandstiftung zum Fememord: Glück und Ende des Nationalsozialisten Bell,* published—apparently 1934—camouflaged as a propaganda pamphlet for a vacuum cleaner "Elektrolux." Generally about Bell see Aretin, *op. cit.*, pp. 88-89, 111, 114, 120, 127, 129, 146; *Berlin Diaries, op. cit.*, pp. 14, 165-66, and *The Berlin Diaries,* vol. II (London, 1935), pp. 185-86; *Brown Network, op. cit.*, pp. 64-66; Roberts, *op. cit.*, pp. 257, 298-99, 303, 310-20; Johannes Steel, *The Second World War* (New York, 1934), p. 98.

29. Rasche, *op. cit.*, p. 139. The San Francisco Chamber of Commerce informed the writer by letter, November 23, 1953, that in 1936 the average price for platinum was in the United States $41.76 per ounce, in the United Kingdom £10.15s. per ounce.

30. Ewan Butler and Gordon Young assert in their biography of Göring, *Marshal without Glory* (London, 1951), p. 189, that among Sir Henri Deterding's gifts to Göring "were a number of pictures, including a Rembrandt valued at 500,000 marks (£25,000)."

31. Aretin, *op. cit.*, p. 89. Gerlich was for many years editor-in-chief of the *Münchner Neueste Nachrichten*. As a far-sighted and most courageous warner of Hitlerism he was admired by Nazi opponents. Johannes Steiner collected some of his writings in the book *Prophetien wider das Dritte Reich* (München, 1946).

32. *Op. cit.*, pp. 144-45. A German statesman who had a leading share in those elections estimated that the Nazis must have spent at least 20,000,000 marks for Hitler's candidacy (letter to the writer, July 24, 1952).

33. Rasche, *op. cit.*, p. 141. The NSDAP Office for Foreign Affairs reported in October 1935, that it took up "closer contact" with Sir Henri Deterding and his circle, *Trial of the Major War Criminals before the International Military Tribunal,* 42 vols. (Nuremberg, 1947-1949), vol. XXV, pp. 17-18. (This publication hereafter referred to as *IMT.*)

34. Roberts, *op. cit.,* p. 322.
35. Dodd, *op. cit.,* p. 186.
36. Louis P. Lochner, *Tycoons and Tyrant: German Industry from Hitler to Adenauer* (Chicago, 1954), pp. 110-11, records as generally believed that Deterding helped Hitler "in a big way," and that allegedly "he gave as much as ten million marks in the course of the years." Lochner was unable to find concrete evidence for proving this point.—Dr. Alhard Gelpke, Zurich 38, has investigated the foreign financing of the NSDAP since 1930. He informed the writer and permitted him to state here (letters of January 12 and of February 8, 1956) that he is in possession of evidence showing that Deterding supplied the Hitler movement until the middle of 1932 with £1,500,000, that is, roughly with RM 30,000,000. In a book on which he is at present working, Dr. Gelpke will publish details about Deterding's subventions.
37. *Hitler: A Study in Tyranny* (London, 1952), p. 219. Münzenberg, *op. cit.,* p. 234, stated that in 1932 the NSDAP had to supply the SA with 15,000,000 marks a month. This does not contradict Bullock because the SA had various sources of income.
38. Information given by Harry Schulze-Wilde, Munich, on the basis of apparently reliable statements by a former auditor of the Reich Treasury, letters of June 23, 1952, July 31, 1952, and January 6, 1954.
39. Letters to the writer, June 25, 1952, and January 13, 1954. Professor Prochnik lectures at Georgetown University on European diplomatic history.—J. Tchernoff, *Les Démagogies contre les Démocraties* (Paris, 1947), p. 138, asserts that Nazi debts totalled 640,000,000 marks in 1932. According to George W. F. Hallgarten, *Why Dictators?* (New York, 1954), p. 219, the debts of the Party "amounted to 70 to 90 million reichsmarks" at the end of 1932.
40. John W. Wheeler-Bennett, *Wooden Titan: Hindenburg in Twenty Years of German History* (New York, 1936), p. 414, speaks, for November 1932, of the great German industrialists "and certain individuals abroad" as suppliers of funds. George W. F. Hallgarten, "Adolf Hitler and German Heavy Industry, 1931-1933," *Journal of Economic History,* vol. XII, No. 3, p. 246, states one cannot say that industry "made" Hitler's movement. Edward Norman Peterson, *Hjalmar Schacht: For and Against Hitler* (Boston, 1954), declared, p. 116: "Only a small minority [of German industrialists] were actively concerned to get Hitler into power."
41. Letter to the writer, May 31, 1952. Thyssen told Mr. Reves repeatedly that the political and moral aid Hitler received from foreign governments and statesmen who visited him and signed treaties with him, greatly encouraged him [Thyssen] and other German industrialists to give financial aid to Hitler. This applies, of course, to the years when Hitler was in power.
42. Letter by Baron Kurt von Schröder to the writer, January 26, 1954. Karl Billinger, *Hitler Is No Fool* (New York, 1939), p. 127, alluding to the excellent connections of the Schröder Bank,

J. H. Stein, with the London "City," wrote: "English influence may have played a much greater role in Hitler's appointment than the world knows." L. I. Ginzberg stresses British and American material aid to Hitler in a lengthy article "Die Beziehungen der reaktionären Kreise der USA und Englands zur Hitlerpartei (1930-Januar 1933)" in *Sowjetwissenschaft, Gesellschaftswissenschaftliche Abteilung*, Jahrgang 1955, Heft 6, Dezember 1955, pp. 834-44. Apart from Lord Rothermere and Sir Henri Deterding, Ginzberg implicates especially the banking houses Schroeder in England and America, and he insinuates Mr. John Foster Dulles' involvement. See Postscript to Appendix, section 2.

43. Letters to the writer from Dr. Kurt von Schuschnigg, the former Chancellor, March 2, 1952, and from Dr. Anton Klotz, formerly of the official Press Buro in Vienna, March 11, 1952. Cf. the brochure *Hakenkreuzjudas und seine Silberlinge* (Wien, 1933), signed by the Socialist official Hans Philipp.

44. *Earth Could Be Fair: A Chronicle* (New York, 1946), Book Find Club edition, pp. 473-74.—In the pre-Hitler years Berlin government circles received information that Polish and Czechoslovak heavy industry made financial contributions to the NSDAP.

45. *Brit. Docs.*, Secd. Series, vol. I, No. 323, p. 510. Besedovski had refused to return to Russia.—Maurice Laporte, *Sous le Casque d'Acier: Six Semaines avec Hitler et les Bolcheviks* (Paris, 1931), pp. 310-20, pretends to show that Nazi agents told the Russians in July 1930, they would need at least 8,000,000 marks for the coming elections, and that they did receive some millions. Laporte gives the names of well-known Nazis and describes meeting places in Bavaria. His story smacks of J. G. Schoup's hoax which is exposed in the Appendix.

46. *Op. cit.*, pp. 401-02, 415. See also Martha Dodd, *Through Embassy Eyes* (New York, 1939), pp. 327-30, 353.

47. *What About Germany?* (New York, 1942), pp. 42-43.

48. Galtier-Boissière and Lefebvre, *op. cit.*, pp. 55, 57-60, 79-80; Pierre Lazareff, *Deadline: The Behind-the-Scenes Story of the Last Decade in France* (New York, 1942), pp. 28, 55, 93-94; Martha Dodd, *op. cit.*, pp. 327-30, 353; Franklin L. Ford in *The Diplomats, 1919-1939*, ed. by Gordon A. Craig and Felix Gilbert (Princeton, 1953), pp. 460-61. Very critical of François-Poncet's activity in the Ruhr is Paul Wentzcke, *Ruhrkampf. Einbruch und Abwehr im rheinisch-westfälischen Industriegebiet*, 2 vols. (Berlin, 1930, 1932), vol. II, p. 104; cf. pp. 416, 428, 441.

49. Richard D. Challener, in *The Diplomats, op. cit.*, p. 61.

50. Lazareff, *op. cit.*, p. 28.

51. *Op. cit.*, p. 462.

52. *Op. cit.*, p. 395. About Ambassador Dodd see Ford, *op. cit.*, pp. 447-60.

53. Based on inside information given to the writer. In German government circles there was anxious recollection of the French separatist endeavors undertaken at a time when the Ruhr occupation "served the interests of the *Comité des Forges* marvelously," Galtier-Boissière and Lefebvre, *op. cit.*, p. 58.

54. Tchernoff, *op. cit.*, p. 134. Cf. *Crapouillot*, July 1933, p. 62.
55. Francis Delaisi, *La Révolution Européenne* (Bruxelles-Paris, 1942), p. 201.
56. Sir Horace Rumbold to The Marquess of Londonderry, as reported by the latter in *Wings of Destiny* (London, 1943), p. 195.
57. *Op. cit.*, p. 462.
58. *Blood and Banquets: A Berlin Social Diary* (Garden City, N. Y., 1944), p. 79. Cf. Fabre-Luce, *Révolution, op. cit.*, pp. 96-97. On November 23, 1931, Captain Göring, in the presence of a member of the British Embassy and of the American Embassy in Berlin, complained that the French journalists wrote "poisonous articles" about the Party. He could understand their attitude the less, he said, "because of the very definite advances which the new French Ambassador, M. François-Poncet, had made since his arrival in Berlin," *Brit. Docs.*, Secd. Series, vol. II, *1931,* No. 302, p. 347.
59. *Souvenirs d'une Ambassade à Berlin, Septembre 1931-Octobre 1938* (Paris, 1946), p. 8. According to *Ciano's Diplomatic Papers,* ed. by Malcolm Muggeridge (London, 1948), p. 249, François-Poncet said to Count Ciano in November 1938, "that in Germany he had been particularly friendly with members of the Party and that this had helped him greatly to carry out his diplomatic activities."
60. *Les Evénements Survenus en France de 1933 à 1945*, Assemblée Nationale (Paris), No. 2344, vol. III, pp. 761-62. (This publication hereafter referred to as *France 2344.*)
61. *Op. cit.*, p. 79.
62. *France 2344,* vol. III, pp. 761-62.
63. Dodd's *Diary, op. cit.*, pp. 34-35; see also pp. 148, 230. Cf. Elisabetta Cerruti, *Ambassador's Wife* (New York, 1953), pp. 119, 129.
64. Bertrand de Jouvenel, *D'Une Guerre à l'Autre,* vol. II (Paris 1941), p. 393.
65. Ford, *op. cit.*, p. 462.
66. Galtier-Boissière and Lefebvre, *op. cit.*, pp. 82-83; Albert Norden, *Lehren deutscher Geschichte: Zur politischen Rolle des Finanzkapitals und der Junker* (Berlin, 1947), p. 116. Cf. Heinz Pol, *Suicide of a Democracy* (New York, 1940), pp. 70-76, "The Iron Agreement"; George Seldes, *Iron, Blood and Profits* (New York-London, 1934), pp. 251, 293. Concerning British-French opposition to this plan see Stanton B. Leeds, *These Rule France* (Indianapolis-New York, 1940), p. 215.
67. An author in *Fortune,* March 1934, p. 120, stated: "The leading munitions makers not only in Germany but in France united in their support behind the one man most capable of stirring up a new outbreak of international anarchy in Europe." Cf. Robert W. Desmond, *The Press and World Affairs* (New York-London, 1937), p. 167.
68. *Op. cit.*, vol. II, p. 396.
69. André Simone, *J'Accuse! The Men Who Betrayed France* (New York, 1940), p. 76; B. Fromm, *op. cit.*, pp. 31-32.—Students of

the armaments industry have considered François-Poncet's role in the *Comité des Forges* sufficiently important to reproduce his picture alongside with that of the Schneiders, the de Wendels, the Krupps, etc., although towards the end of the row—see Galtier-Boissière and Lefebvre, *op. cit.*, p. 55, and *Fortune, op. cit.*, p. 56. G. E. R. Gedye, *The Revolver Republic: France's Bid for the Rhine* (London, 1930), pp. 80-150, described the role of the *Comité des Forges* in the Ruhr action. Cf. John Gunther, *Inside Europe*, rev. ed. (New York-London, 1940), pp. 169-74.

70. *Op. cit.*, vol. II, pp. 396-97. See in vol. I, chapt. xxv, "Le Franc Controle l'Europe."

71. Elizabeth R. Cameron, *Prologue to Appeasement: A Study in French Foreign Policy, 1933-1936* (Philadelphia, 1942), pp. 177-78; see also pp. 23, 152.

72. Friedrich Siegmund-Schultze, *Die Deutsche Widerstandsbewegung im Spiegel der ausländischen Literatur* (Stuttgart, 1947), p. 11. Siegmund-Schultze signed the writer's *Appeal*, see pp. 149-51.

73. Statements in the present writer's possession by friends of Dr. Etscheit, March 24, 1952, and August 2, 1952. In an Affidavit, published in *IMT*, vol. XXVIII, p. 238, Raymond H. Geist, former United States Consul in Berlin, mentioned Dr. Etscheit as "a prominent Berlin lawyer." See also Kurt Sendtner, "Die deutsche Militäropposition im ersten Kriegsjahr," *Aus Politik und Zeitgeschichte* (Berlin), B X/55, March 9, 1955, p. 146.

74. Simone, *op. cit.*, p. 73.

75. Engelbrecht-Hanighen, *op. cit.*, p. 245; Philip Noel-Baker, *The Private Manufacture of Armaments* (New York, 1937), vol. I, p. 195; Simone, *op. cit.*, p. 77. Cf. Gustav Winter, *This Is Not the End of France* (London, 1942), p. 45.

76. On September 12, 1952, M. Pierre-Etienne Flandin transmitted to me a letter which M. André François-Poncet had written to him on September 8th on the subject of Ambassador Dodd's and Mr. Lochner's assertions. On September 30, 1952, I asked M. François-Poncet for permission to make public use of his refutation in my projected book. As there was then no answer I repeated my request on January 6, 1954.—With regard to the seventh paragraph of M. François-Poncet's published letter, I informed the Ambassador on January 6, 1954, that I would *not* use a story told by the late Juan Gildemeister, Peruvian Minister to Berlin, according to which he once appeared in SA uniform at a party given by Ernst Roehm, because I would consider this to have been a masquerade's joke—if true at all, then someone made himself up as the Ambassador.

77. Letter to the writer, January 20, 1954.

78. Victor Gollancz reproduced one of the advertisements in *Shall Our Children Live or Die? A Reply to Lord Vansittart on the German Problem* (London, 1942), and rightly pointed out, pp. 83-84, that the Versailles Treaty forbade the import by Germany of any kind of war equipment or material.

79. *The Road to War: An Analysis of the National Government's Foreign Policy,* by a small group of experts, Preface by the Rt.

Hon. C. R. Attlee (London, 1937), pp. 101-02. The speech is quoted by several American and British authors as authentic.

80. Richard N. Current, *Secretary Stimson: A Study in Statecraft* (New Brunswick, New Jersey, 1954), p. 68, records that Montagu Norman, Governor of the Bank of England and friend of Hjalmar Schacht, said to Henry L. Stimson in April 1931, that in Europe "Russia was the very greatest of all dangers."

81. *History of the War,* vol. I, *The Cause of the War* (London, 1939), p. 27. Marquess of Londonderry, *Wings, op. cit.,* p. 160, states that in February 1936, he wrote to Lady Oxford: "After all we forced democracy on the Germans."

82. *The Second World War * The Gathering Storm* (Boston, 1948), p. 11.

83. *The Rebel Prince. Memoirs of Prince Louis Ferdinand of Prussia* (Chicago, 1952), p. 41.

84. *The Forrestal Diaries,* ed. by Walter Millis (New York, 1951), p. 80.

85. *Op. cit.,* p. 41. Cf. Gerhard Ritter, *Carl Goerdeler und die Deutsche Widerstandsbewegung* (Stuttgart, 1954), pp. 235, 257, and in the symposium, *The Third Reich* (London, 1955), p. 397.

86. Londonderry, *op. cit.,* pp. 195-96. In an introduction to John Maynard Keynes, *Two Memoirs* (London, 1949), David Garnett stated, pp. 7-8: "The continuance of the blockade was most effectively exploited by Hitler, and most useful to him in building up his position by propaganda against the Treaty and the Treaty-makers of Versailles."

87. *Unfinished Victory* (London, 1940), pp. 26-27. Speaking of the undernourishment period, Bryant observed: "It makes intelligible much that is otherwise unaccountable in Nazi Germany—the hysteria, the emotionalism and the lack of proportion."

88. Max Sievers, *Unser Kampf gegen das Dritte Reich* (Stockholm, 1939), p. 23.

89. *The German Crisis* (New York, 1932), p. 206. Cf. King-Hall, *op. cit.,* p. 30. R. H. Bruce Lockhart in *Guns or Butter* (Boston, 1938), p. 404: "It is a commonplace that Nazi-ism is a youth movement. Its appeal is addressed to youth. It relies mainly on youth for its support."

90. *Bliss, Peacemaker* (New York, 1934), pp. 402-03.

91. *Black Record: Germans Past and Present* (London, 1941), p. 16.

92. *The Between-War World* (London, 1947), p. 147.

93. *Germany under Hitler.* World Affairs Pamphlet No. 8 (New York-Boston, 1935), p. 6. Cf. the same author's excellent study *The Pan-German League, 1890-1914* (New York, 1924).

94. *Op. cit.,* pp. 8-9. Cf. *The Struggle for Democracy in Germany,* ed. by Gabriel A. Almond (Chapel Hill, North Carolina, 1949), p. 30: "It would be wrong to conclude that Nazism grew inevitably from the German past." On the other hand, Louis F. Snyder, *German Nationalism: The Tragedy of a People* (Harrisburg, Pennsylvania, 1952), p. xii, stated: "A century of extremist nationalism was behind the triumph of National Socialism." Edmond

Vermeil in *The Third Reich*, pp. 3-111, overstresses Pangermanism. Cf. Bullock, *op. cit.*, p. 737.
95. *The Origins of the War* (Oxford, 1940), p. 22.
96. *Der Friede von Versailles und die Gegenwart* (Zürich, 1947), pp. 35, 92.
97. *Failure of a Mission* (New York, 1940), p. 27.
98. Co-author of *World Outlook* (London, 1939), p. 120.
99. *This House Against This House* (New York, 1945), pp. 27-29; cf. pp. 48-49.
100. *The German Octopus* (New York, 1938), pp. 2-5, 26. Cf. Thomas A. Bailey, *Woodrow Wilson and the Lost Peace* (New York, 1944), pp. 167-68; Sherwood Eddy, *The Challenge of Europe* (New York, 1933), p. 20; Major-General J. F. C. Fuller, *The Second World War, 1939-45* (London, 1948; New York, 1949), pp. 17-18; Calvin B. Hoover, *Germany Enters the Third Reich* (New York, 1933), p. 213; Frederick Palmer, *op. cit.*, pp. 401-03.
101. *Face à Hitler* (Paris, 1934), p. 8. Cf. M. Baumont in *Third Reich, op. cit.*, pp. 456 ff.; Alfred Fabre-Luce, *Le Siècle prend Figure* (Paris, 1949), p. 105; Sisley Huddleston, *France: The Tragic Years, 1939-1947* (New York, 1955), pp. 7-8; G. Ritter, *Goerdeler, op. cit.*, p. 161.
102. *Brit. Docs.*, Secd. Series, vol. IV, No. 268, p. 474.
103. *War and the Psychological Conditions of Peace* (London, 1942), p. 139. Cf. Sir Arthur Salter, *Security: Can We Retrieve It?* (New York, 1939), pp. 20, 22.
104. Paul Birdsall, *Versailles Twenty Years After* (New York, 1941), p. 255; Raoul de Roussy de Sales, *The Making of Tomorrow* (New York, 1942), pp. 176-77; Arthur Salter, *The Dual Policy* (Oxford, 1939), p. 24.—"That damnable War Guilt Clause" is used by Pares, *op. cit.*, p. 120; see also his book *Russia* (New York, 1941), pp. 163-64. The great significance of Article 231 for Hitler's rise is stressed, among others, by C. E. Black and E. C. Helmreich, *Twentieth Century Europe* (New York, 1950), p. 126; Collin Brooks, *Can Chamberlain Save Great Britain?* (London, 1938), pp. 122-23; Mr. John Foster Dulles, Foreword to Philip Mason Burnett's study *Reparation at the Paris Peace Conference from the Standpoint of the American Delegation*, abridged ed. (New York, 1940), p. xi, as quoted in chapt. I of the present book, pp. 25-26; Sisley Huddleston, *Popular Diplomacy and War* (Rindge, New Hampshire, 1954), p. 97.—H. Schacht, *76 Jahre meines Lebens* (Bad Wörishofen, 1953), pp. 562-63, states that the Versailles policy of defamation drove the German people into a mood of desperation which provided Hitler with the power he wielded.
105. Vernon Bartlett, *Intermission in Europe* (New York, 1938), p. 171; Fuller, *op. cit.*, p. 23; Harold Nicolson, *Why Britain Is at War* (Harmondsworth, 1939), pp. 21-22; Sheean, *op. cit.*, p. 8; Esmé Wingfield-Stratford, *The Harvest of Victory, 1918-1926* (London, 1935), p. 316; Kurt Assmann, *Deutsche Schicksalsjahre* (Wiesbaden, 1950), p. 29. James Murphy, *Adolf Hitler*

(London, 1934), p. 29, points out that Clemenceau proved the salvation of the German militarists.

106. *Let the People Know* (New York, 1943), p. 27. Cf. Churchill, *op. cit.*, pp. 12, 54; Bernadotte E. Schmitt, *From Versailles to Munich* (Chicago, 1938), p. 36.

107. H. E. Barnes in *Modern World Politics,* ed. by Thorsten V. Kalijarvi (New York, 1943), pp. 347-48; Glenn S. Dumke in *The Origins and Consequences of World War II,* ed. by Floyd A. Cave (New York, 1948), pp. 186-87; James T. Shotwell, *What Germany Forgot* (New York, 1940); Richard Lewinsohn (Morus), *Geschichte der Krise* (Leipzig-Wien, 1934).

108. Paul Einzig, *Appeasement Before, During and After the War* (London, 1942), pp. 36, 61-62; Sir Victor Wellesley, *Diplomacy in Fetters* (London-New York-Melbourne-Sydney, 1944), p. 54.

109. King-Hall, *op. cit.,* p. 21.

110. Frank P. Chambers, Christina Phelps Harris and Charles C. Bayley, *This Age of Conflict: A Contemporary World History, 1914-1943,* rev. ed. (New York, 1950), p. 393.

111. Adam Buckreis, *Politik des 20. Jahrhunderts: Weltgeschichte 1901-1936* (Nürnberg-Altenburg, 1942), pp. 522-23, 535, 553.

112. Francis Delaisi, *op. cit.,* pp. 202-03. Cf. Maurice Baumont, *Peuples et Civilisations,* vol. XX, *La Faillite de la Paix* (*1919-1939*) (Paris, 1945), p. 409. Evelyn Anderson, *Hammer or Anvil: The Story of the German Working-Class Movement* (London, 1945), pp. 135-38, 150, stated that actually between eight and nine million wage and salary earners were out of work. Friedrich Lütge in *The Third Reich, op. cit.,* pp. 433-34: "At the end of 1932 the number of officially registered unemployed was over 6 million, and non-registered unemployed probably totalled another million."

113. *I Fight to Live* (London, 1947), pp. 99-100 (German ed. *Europa vor der Entscheidung,* Düsseldorf, 1951, pp. 131-33). Cf. E. Alexander Powell, *Thunder over Europe* (New York, 1931), p. 29.

114. Evelyn Anderson, *op. cit.,* p. 135; Norman Angell, *For What Do We Fight?* (London-New York, 1939), p. 180; M. Baumont in *Third Reich, op. cit.,* p. 477; F. Lee Benns, *Europe since 1914,* rev. ed. (New York, 1934), pp. 433-34; Hugh Dalton, *Hitler's War Before and After* (Harmondsworth, 1940), pp. 39, 41 (endorsing the view of Sir Arthur Salter); R. C. K. Ensor in *The Background and Issues of the War,* ed. by H. A. L. Fisher (Oxford, 1940), pp. 90-91; C. W. Guillebaud, *The Social Policy of Nazi Germany* (Cambridge, 1941), p. 44; Calvin B. Hoover, *op. cit.,* pp. 30-31; King-Hall, *op. cit.,* pp. 125-26; Fritz Hesse, *Das Spiel um Deutschland* (München, 1953), p. 20. In general see also the recent contributions of Louis R. Franck, of Friedrich Lütge, and of Arthur Schweitzer in *Third Reich, op. cit.,* pp. 417-36, 539-94.

115. Reynaud, *op. cit.,* vol. I, pp. 65, 67, 243, and in *France 2344,* vol. I, pp. 84, 88; S. William Halperin, *Germany Tried Democracy* (New York, 1946), p. 406; Broadus Mitchell, *Depression Decade from New Era through New Deal* (New York-Toronto,

1947), pp. 11, 396. Cf. Dwight E. Lee, *Ten Years: The World on the Way to War* (Boston, 1942), p. 39.—Bartlett, *op. cit.,* pp. 175-76, asserts that American financiers did almost as much as M. Poincaré to put Hitler in power because they hurried their capital back from overseas, with the result that in the space of a month or two Germany again fell from apparent prosperity to terrible poverty.

116. *Roosevelt in Retrospect* (New York, 1950), pp. 19-20. Cf. Lee, *op. cit.,* p. 39.

117. *The Truth about the Peace Treaties,* 2 vols. (London, 1938), pp. 1410-11.

118. *Op. cit.,* p. 176. See also Captain Russell Grenfell, *Unconditional Hatred: German War Guilt and the Future of Europe* (New York, 1953), pp. 221-22.

119. *Why Another World War?* (London, 1941), p. 66. Cf. Herbert Hoover and Hugh Gibson in *Prefaces to Peace* (New York, 1943), pp. 269-70; Wellesley, *op. cit.,* p. 73.

120. *The Psychology of Dictatorship* (New York, 1950), pp. 265, 296. Cf. Alan Bullock in *Third Reich, op. cit.,* pp. 350 ff.; Henry M. Pachter, *ibid.,* pp. 710-41; Gerhard Ritter, "Vom Ursprung des Einparteienstaates in Europa," *Historisches Jahrbuch,* 74. Jahrgang (Freiburg-München, 1955), pp. 570-73.

121. *Germany, op. cit.,* p. 15.

122. Werner Bross, *Gespräche mit Hermann Göring während des Nürnberger Prozesses* (Flensburg-Hamburg, 1950), p. 108; Hermann Mau, "Die Zweite Revolution—Der 30. Juni 1934," *Vierteljahrshefte für Zeitgeschichte,* 1. Jahrgang 1953, 2. Heft, April, p. 126. About the size of the SA see *IMT,* vol. XXI, pp. 126, 165-66; vol. XLII, pp. 135-53.

123. *Von Weimar zu Hitler* (New York, 1940), p. 5.

124. Edwin D. Schoonmaker, *Democracy and World Dominion* (New York, 1939), pp. 225, 319.

125. Adolf Hitler, *Libres Propos sur la Guerre et la Paix* (Paris, 1952), No. 155.—For a complete translation of *Mein Kampf* see the fully annotated edition by John Chamberlain, Sidney B. Fay, John Gunther, Carlton J. H. Hayes, Graham Hutton, Alvin Johnson, William L. Langer, Walter Millis, Raoul de Roussy de Sales, and George N. Shuster (New York, 1939).

126. *Brit. Docs.,* Secd. Series, vol. IV, No. 227, Report of January 25, 1933, p. 390; No. 258, Report of March 7, 1933, p. 443. In support of Von Papen, Evelyn Anderson, *op. cit.,* p. 137, may be quoted: "As for the intellectuals, National Socialism found its recruits in the "academic proletariat," among the sons and daughters of an impoverished middle class."

127. *Die Revolution des Nihilismus* (Zürich-New York, 1938), p. 25.

128. *The Foreign Policy of Soviet Russia, 1929-1941,* 2 vols. (London-New York-Toronto, 1947), vol. I, p. 64 n. 3. Cf. Knickerbocker, *op. cit.,* pp. 169, 177; Joseph S. Roucek in Cave, *op. cit.,* p. 441.

129. Friedrich Meinecke, *Die Deutsche Katastrophe* (Wiesbaden, 1946), p. 97; Wilhelm Roepke, *Die Deutsche Frage,* 2nd enlarged ed. (Erlenbach-Zürich, 1945), p. 23.

130. *Op. cit.*, p. 644. The German Jan Valtin (pseudonym for R. J. R. Krebs) differs from Ruth Fischer. In *Out of the Night* (New York, 1941), pp. 360 and 385, he declared: "We all knew that we were not strong enough to make a revolution. . . . We had no illusions about the overwhelming virility of the Nazi Party's military organization. . . ."

131. *The Accused* (New York, 1951), p. 497. C. L. R. James, *World Revolution, 1917-1936* (London, 1937), p. 329, also stated: "This political crisis would end in a dictatorship either of the Right or of the Left."

132. Colonel E. Alexander Powell, *The Long Roll on the Rhine* (New York, 1934), pp. 34-35, 42, 238-41, and chapt. xx-xxii; Spectator, *Deutschlands Erwachen, von einem Ausländer Gesehen* (Genf, 1933), p. 98. Cf. Salvador de Madariaga, *The World's Design* (London, 1938), p. 206, and section "World Revolution," pp. 200-15.

133. Mowrer, *op. cit.*, p. 388; Roucek, *op. cit.*, p. 441.

134. Ev. Anderson, *op. cit.*, pp. 144-48; Nikolaus Basseches, *Stalin: Das Schicksal eines Erfolges* (Bern, 1950), pp. 282, 285; F. Borkenau, *The Communist International* (London, 1938), pp. 342-43, 383; Alan Bullock in *Third Reich, op. cit.*, pp. 509-14; David J. Dallin, *Russia and Postwar Europe* (New Haven, 1943), pp. 60-61, and *The Real Soviet Russia*, rev. ed. (New Haven, 1947), p. 57; R. Fischer, *op. cit.*, pp. 655-56; James, *op. cit.*, chapt. xii, and especially pp. 330-35, 344-46, 350-51; Eugene Lyons, *Stalin: Czar of All the Russians* (Philadelphia-London-Toronto-New York, 1940), pp. 258-59; John Scott, *Duel for Europe* (Boston, 1942), pp. 22, 49; Henry C. Wolfe, *The Imperial Soviets* (New York, 1940), p. 116; Walter Görlitz and Herbert A. Quint, *Adolf Hitler: Eine Biographie* (Stuttgart, 1952), p. 369. Valtin records in *op. cit.*, p. 202, that Georgi Dimitrov, Director of the Comintern for Western Europe, told him in 1931, that the Social Democrats were traitors and "the most dangerous enemies of the workers." It was therefore the Communists' foremost task to liquidate their influence. "Afterwards," Dimitrov declared, "we'll sweep Hitler and his *Lumpengesindel* [riffraff] into the garbage-can of history." Cf. *ibid.*, pp. 190-93, 201-02, 251-52. John Flournoy Montgomery in *Hungary the Unwilling Satellite* (New York, 1947), p. 19: "The Soviets regarded Hitler as their icebreaker who would destroy democracy, prosperity and freedom to their final advantage."

135. Friedrich Stampfer disclosed this at a Party meeting in Nuremberg on August 3, 1947, adding that he memorized Vynogradov's words and could confirm them by oath. Report on the meeting in *Neue Zeitung* (München), August 8, 1947. In a letter to the writer, December 7, 1953, Herr Stampfer reaffirmed the accurateness of the report. Vynogradov's frankness had naturally amazed him.—Dallin, *Russia, op. cit.*, pp. 60-61, gave a less detailed account of the abortive negotiations. Alan Bullock in *Third Reich, op. cit.*, records other efforts made by Social Democrats in 1932 to persuade Communist leaders to join them and the Centre

against the NSDAP, pp. 513, 518; cf. Konrad Heiden, *Fuehrer, op. cit.,* pp. 551-52. See also Gustav Hilger and Alfred G. Meyer, *The Incompatible Allies* (New York, 1953), p. 112; James, *op. cit.,* p. 351. Valtin, *op. cit.,* p. 351, stated: "In the spring of 1932 a working alliance between the powerful Socialist and Communist Parties of Germany would have dammed the tide and thereby changed the course of world history. This conviction grows out of my experience as an active participant in one of the embattled armies. . . ."

136. "Ypsilon," *Pattern for World Revolution* (Chicago-New York, 1947), pp. 161-64, 369. Cf. John W. Wheeler-Bennett, *The Nemesis of Power* (London-New York, 1953), pp. 225, 384.

137. Ev. Anderson, *op. cit.,* pp. 144-48; Basseches, *op. cit.,* pp. 248, 285; Borkenau, *op. cit.,* pp. 347, 379; Alan Bullock in *Third Reich, op. cit.,* pp. 510-20; Ruth Fischer, *op. cit.,* p. 638; Harold H. Fisher, *The Communist Revolution: An Outline of Strategy and Tactics* (Stanford, 1955), p. 20; Ossip K. Flechtheim, *Die Kommunistische Partei Deutschlands in der Weimarer Republik* (Offenbach a. Main, 1948), p. 226; Heiden, *Fuehrer, op. cit.,* p. 461; James, *op. cit.,* pp. 334, 344; G. Ritter, *Goerdeler, op. cit.,* p. 96; A. Rossi, Preface to *Les Cahiers du Bolchevisme pendant la Campagne 1939-1940* (Paris, 1951), pp. xxiv-xxv; Hugh Seton-Watson, *From Lenin to Malenkov: The History of World Communism* (New York, 1954), pp. 107-10; Tchernoff, *op. cit.,* p. 141; Weissberg, *op. cit.,* pp. 146-47, 259. Cf. Allen Welsh Dulles, *Germany's Underground* (New York, 1947), pp. 97-98; Hilger and Meyer, *op. cit.,* p. 252. Sir Horace Rumbold, *Brit. Docs.,* Secd. Ser., vol. IV, No. 265, p. 462, reported that in the elections of March 5, 1933, the six million Communists "were more anxious to fight Social Democracy than Hitlerism."

138. *Op. cit.,* p. 61 n. 1; cf. 62, 66. Alan Bullock in *Third Reich, op. cit.,* p. 521, states: The Communists "did all they could to weaken the opposition to Hitler and to help the Nazis into power. Their contribution was considerable. . . ."

139. For instance Ludecke, *op. cit.,* p. 338; Ernst Mueller-Meiningen, Jr., *Die Parteigenossen* (München, 1946), pp. 56-57; Bernhard Schwertfeger, *Rätsel um Deutschland, 1933 bis 1945* (Heidelberg, 1947), p. 496 (Schwertfeger signed the writer's *Appeal,* see pp. 149-51); Sievers, *op. cit.,* p. 51; Karl Stroelin, *Verräter oder Patrioten?* (Stuttgart, 1952), p. 22; Kurt von Tippelskirch, *Geschichte des Zweiten Weltkrieges* (Bonn, 1951), p. 691. In *IMT,* vol. IX, p. 440, Hermann Göring's statement is recorded: "The dictate of Versailles was such that every German could not help being in favor of its modification." Cf. Bullock, *op. cit.,* p. 286.

140. *After Seven Years* (New York-London, 1939), pp. 384-85.

141. E. H. Carr, *Britain: A Study of Foreign Policy from the Versailles Treaty to the Outbreak of War* (London-New York-Toronto, 1939), p. 153; Joan and Jonathan Griffin, *Lost Liberty?* (New York, 1939), p. 229; C. B. Hoover, *op. cit.,* pp. 42-43; Gilbert Murray in *The Intelligent Man's Way to Prevent War,* ed. by

Leonard Woolf (London, 1933), pp. 144-45; W. L. White, *Report on the Germans* (New York, 1947), p. 40; Gerd Tellenbach, *Die deutsche Not als Schuld und Schicksal* (Stuttgart, 1947), p. 41. Count Kurt Bluecher von Wahlstatt, *Know Your Germans* (London, 1951), p. 144, declared: "Versailles made Germany dishonest, disloyal to old treaties and mistrustful of new ones." Harold Nicolson, *op. cit.*, p. 45, wrote on the strength of intimate knowledge of the situation: "The nerves of even the most stolid nation would have cracked under the long ordeal to which the German people were exposed between 1914 and 1933."

142. *Germany and the Rhineland,* The Royal Institute of International Affairs (London, 1936), p. 67.

143. *Op. cit.,* p. 70. Similar opinions are recorded in Chapt. I and II. The Marquess of Londonderry, *Ourselves and Germany* (London, 1938), p. 14, wrote: "The treatment of Germany since the Great War deserves the severest criticism and is responsible to a very large extent for the present unhappy international situation." Cf. W. Arnold-Foster in *Intelligent Man's Way, op. cit.*, p. 408. Alfred Fabre-Luce, *Journal de la France* (Paris, 1941), p. 74, commented on Hitler's advent: "We have manufactured that gambler."

144. *IMT,* vol. X, pp. 79-90; vol. XVII, pp. 551-54; vol. XIX, p. 437. A valuable work explaining Hitler's rise to power is the symposium—repeatedly referred to in this chapter—*The Third Reich,* published under the auspices of the International Council for Philosophy and Humanistic Studies and with the assistance of UNESCO (London, 1955). The more notable contributions in it for the present book are Chapter 1 by Edmond Vermeil, "The Origin, Nature and Development of German Nationalist Ideology in the 19th and 20th Centuries"; Chapters 8 and 14 by Alan Bullock, "The Political Ideas of Adolf Hitler," and "The German Communists and the Rise of Hitler"; Chapter 9 by Gerhard Ritter, "The Historical Foundations of the Rise of National-Socialism"; Chapter 10 by Friedrich Lütge, "An Explanation of the Economic Conditions which contributed to the Victory of National-Socialism"; Chapter 12 by Maurice Baumont, "The Role of Foreign Policy in the Success of the National-Socialist Party"; Chapter 16 by Louis R. Franck, "An Economic and Social Diagnosis of National-Socialism"; and Chapter 21 by Henry M. Pachter, "National-Socialist and Fascist Propaganda for the Conquest of Power." In Chapter 12 Maurice Baumont demonstrates the use Hitler and his henchmen were able to make of "Versailles."

PART TWO

1. Burton J. Hendrick, *The Life and Letters of Walter H. Page,* 2 vols. (Garden City, N. Y., 1922), vol. II, pp. 162-63.

2. *An Ambassador of Peace,* vol. I, *From Spa (1920) to Rapallo (1922)* (London, 1929), p. 1.

3. Alma Luckau, *The German Delegation at the Paris Peace Conference* (New York, 1941), Docs. 16, 21, pp. 188, 208. Cf. Adam

238 GERMAN-FRENCH UNITY

Buckreis, *Politik des 20. Jahrhunderts. Weltgeschichte 1901-1936* (Nürnberg-Altenburg, 1942), p. 415.

4. Luckau, *op. cit.,* Doc. 29, p. 221. See pp. 49, 91-92 above.
5. Luckau, *op. cit.,* Docs. 51, 53, 56, pp. 272, 288, 305. See pp. 48, 49 of the present book.
6. Luckau, *op. cit.,* Doc. 60, p. 442. Article 227 is printed on p. 93 of the present book.
7. See p. 90 of the present book.
8. Quoted by Arnold J. Toynbee, *Survey of International Affairs, 1920-1923* (Oxford, etc., 1925), p. 87.
9. English ed. published in Berlin, 1924. German ed. *Fair Play für Deutschland: Ein Aufruf an das Britische Volk* (Berlin, 1924). Article "Die Schuldfrage in der öffentlichen Meinung Englands. Das Echo auf 'An Appeal to British Fair Play,' " *Archiv für Politik und Geschichte* (Berlin), 3. (8.) Jahr, Heft 3, März 1925, pp. 249-89. Gustav Stresemann welcomed the publication of the *Appeal* in view of the official step he intended to take at the forthcoming conference in London.—Margarete Gärtner calls attention to the *Appeal,* and a number of its signers, on pp. 192-93 of her memoirs, *Botschafterin des Guten Willens* (Bonn, 1955).
10. *Gustav Stresemanns Vermächtnis,* ed. by Henry Bernhard, vol. I (Berlin, 1932), pp. 524-25; C. A. Macartney and Associates, *Survey of International Affairs, 1925* (Oxford-London, 1928), vol. II, p. 12, with reference to German Press of August 30, 1924. Cf. Buckreis, *op. cit.,* p. 488.
11. *Le Matin,* August 31, 1924. See p. 85 of the present book.
12. *Vermächtnis, op. cit.,* pp. 561-69; cf. pp. 499-501, 570, 591-92.
13. *Ibid.,* vol. II (Berlin, 1932), pp. 177, 185; *Deutscher Geschichtskalender,* ed. by Friedrich Purlitz and Sigfrid H. Steinberg, 41. Jahrgang, II. Band, Inland (Leipzig), pp. 18-20.
14. Macartney, *op. cit.,* pp. 47-48; *Geschichtskalender, op. cit.,* pp. 78, 141. Cf. Viscount D'Abernon, *op. cit.,* vol. III, *The Years of Recovery, January 1924-October 1926* (London, 1930), p. 190 and n. George Glasgow, *From Dawes to Locarno* (London, 1925), pp. 120-21, reproduces the German proclamation and the British answer.
15. Chief German Press, October 3rd and 4th, 1925.
16. *Vermächtnis, op. cit.,* vol. III (Berlin, 1933), p. 36.
17. *Geschichtskalender, op. cit.,* 43. Jahrgang, II. Band, Inland, p. 9.
18. *Vermächtnis, op. cit.,* p. 201.
19. *Geschichtskalender, op. cit.,* 45. Jahrgang, Inland, p. 99.
20. Franz von Papen, *Memoirs* (London, 1952), pp. 176-83; Dr. Paul Schmidt, *Statist auf Diplomatischer Bühne, 1923-45* (Bonn, 1950), pp. 245-46. See also *Documents on British Foreign Policy, 1919-1939,* Secd. Series, vol. III, *1931-2,* ed. by E. L. Woodward and Rohan Butler (London, 1948), Nos. 151, 173-77, 179, 182, 185, 191.
21. *Grey of Fallodon* (Boston, 1937), p. 398.
22. Gilbert Murray in *The Intelligent Man's Way to Prevent War,* ed. by Leonard Woolf (London, 1933), pp. 83, 147.

23. *Twenty-Five Years, 1892-1916,* 2 vols. (London, 1925), vol. II, p. 29.
24. *Lord Grey und der Weltkrieg* (Berlin, 1927), pp. 268-70; *Lord Grey and the World War* (London, 1928; New York, 1928), pp. 332-34.
25. *The Memoirs of Cordell Hull,* 2 vols. (New York, 1948), p. 537.
26. *Op. cit.,* vol. 23 (London-New York, 1929), pp. 347-57.
27. The votes for the Nazis declined from 13,745,781 in July, 1932, to 11,737,010 in November, 1932. Though they lost more than 2,000,000 votes in November they obtained comparatively more seats because of the smaller electorate.
28. *Documents on British Foreign Policy, 1919-1939,* Secd. Series, vol. IV, *1932-3,* ed. by E. L. Woodward and Rohan Butler (London, 1950), No. 243, p. 427.
29. *Annales de la Chambre des Députés,* 12ᵐᵉ Législature, *Débats Parlamentaires,* Tome II (Paris, 1923), pp. 752, 761. Alfred Fabre-Luce deals in his *Histoire de la Révolution Européenne* (Paris, 1954), pp. 16-27, 182-32, with Poincaré's role before and after the First World War.
30. Luckau, *op. cit.,* Doc. 60, p. 414.
31. *The World's Design* (London, 1938), p. 159.
32. *La Victoire* (Paris, 1924), p. 247. Italics in the original.
33. Robert H. Ferrell, *Peace in Their Time: The Origins of the Kellogg-Briand Pact* (New Haven-London, 1952), p. 17. Cf. Paul J. Ferdonnet, *Face à Hitler* (Paris, 1934), p. 309; *Allemagne: Bulletin d'Information du Comité Français d'Échanges avec l'Allemagne Nouvelle* (Paris), 4ᵉ Année, No. 20-21, August-November, 1952, p. 6. It may be recalled that in 1927 Ferdinand Buisson, President of the *Ligue des Droits de l'Homme,* was awarded the Nobel Peace Prize jointly with the German pacifist Professor Ludwig Quidde.
34. Quoted in *Time,* September 13, 1954, pp. 29, 30.
35. *Le Siècle prend Figure* (Paris, 1949), p. 197.
36. *Bulletin de la Société des Professeurs d'Histoire et de Géographie de l'Enseignement Public,* 41ᵉ Année, No. spécial 130 bis (Paris), March 1952, pp. 3-38; *Deutschland-Frankreich-Europa: Die Deutsch-Französische Verständigung und der Geschichtsunterricht,* ed. by Professor Dr. Georg Eckert and Dr. Otto-Ernst Schüddekopf (Baden-Baden, 1953), pp. 15-54; *Internationales Jahrbuch für Geschichtsunterricht,* ed. by Arbeitsgemeinschaft Deutscher Lehrerverbände, Georg Eckert, vol. I (Braunschweig, 1951), pp. 44-67, 167-69; vol. II (Braunschweig, 1953), pp. 78-109; *Deutschland und Frankreich im Spiegel ihrer Schulbücher,* ed. by Internationales Schulbuchinstitut, Kant-Hochschule Braunschweig (Braunschweig, 1954), pp. 7-8, 13-15; *Deutschland-Frankreich,* ed. by Deutsch-Französisches Institut Ludwigsburg (Stuttgart, 1954), pp. 43-96. Dr. Theodor Heuss, President of the West German Federal Republic, is a co-founder and a Director of this Institute.—Noteworthy are also the recommendations of a Belgian-German conference of historians in 1954, and the recommendations of an English-German conference of historians in 1955,

published under the title *Deutschland-Belgien 1830-1945,* and *Deutschland und England 1904-1914,* respectively, both reprints from Internationales Jahrbuch für Geschichtsunterricht 1955 (Braunschweig, 1955). The English-German historians agreed, under IX: "In 1914 German policy was not directed at bringing about a European war. It was primarily directed by the alliance obligations to Austria-Hungary . . . The Russian general mobilisation of July 30th necessarily brought about a German decision to mobilise. From July 31st the attitude of the German government, as of other continental powers, was determined by military considerations. . . ." Reference to the French-German joint conclusions of 1935 was made by D. W. Brogan, *The Development of Modern France* (London, 1949), pp. 688-89; and by Philip Mason Burnett, *Reparation at the Paris Peace Conference from the Standpoint of the American Delegation* (New York, 1940), p. 144.

37. *Op. cit.,* p. 231.

38. *Op. cit.,* p. 80. On pp. 153-54 he wrote: "The real obstacle to collective security is the lack of a truly collective spirit in the nations of the world."

39. *Germany between Two Wars: A Study of Propaganda and War-Guilt* (London-New York-Toronto, 1944), pp. iii, 63; cf. p. 65.

40. *Ibid.,* p. 54. Cf. Sisley Huddleston, *Popular Diplomacy and War* (Rindge, New Hampshire, 1954), pp. 97-98.

41. Published by the Independent Labour Party (London, 1922). German ed. *Das Gift, das Zerstört* (Frankfurt a. M., 1922).

42. Published by Methuen & Co. (London, 1932), pp. vii-x.

43. *Op. cit.,* p. 83; cf. pp. 87, 147.

44. *Britain and the Dictators: A Survey of Post-War British Policy* (Cambridge, 1938), pp. 76-77, 416-17. Seton-Watson's other criticisms were: "(1) . . . our refusal to admit enemy representatives to the discussions at Paris was unworthy and humiliating on the moral side, and tactically a grave blunder. (2) . . . the linking of the League Covenant with the Treaties . . . was . . . a blunder, in that it led large sections of German opinion to regard the League as a mere instrument of ruthless victors, bent upon perpetuating an unjust peace . . . (4) . . . the convenient thesis of Germany's unfitness to administer colonies is as untrue as it is insulting, and should be recanted. (5) Above all . . . the economic clauses of the Treaty were a defiance of plain common sense . . ."

45. Quoted by Charles Callan Tansill, *Back Door to War: The Roosevelt Foreign Policy, 1933-1941* (Chicago, 1952), p. 253.

46. Illuminating is Hjalmar Schacht's interrogation as described in his Memoirs, *76 Jahre meines Lebens* (Bad Wörishofen, 1953), pp. 586-88.

47. *Politics, Trials and Errors* (Chicago, 1950), p. 69. See also Montgomery Belgion, *Victor's Justice* (Hinsdale, Ill., 1949), and F. J. P. Veale, *Advance to Barbarism,* Foreword by the Very Rev. William Ralph Inge, Dean of St. Paul's (Appleton, Wisconsin, 1953).

48. *Op. cit.,* pp. 240-41. Cf. Hans Kohn, *ibid.,* pp. 248-49; Hermann Lutz, *ibid.,* p. 235.

49. Quoted from an article in *La Revue des Deux Mondes* by *Time,* November 22, 1954, p. 39. Cf. Huddleston, *op. cit.,* pp. 179-80. Arnold J. Toynbee, *Survey of International Affairs, 1936* (London, 1937), pp. 391-92, envisaged already at that time an economic German-Russian partnership for the development of Eurasia.

50. *Current History, op. cit.,* pp. 241-42. Cf. Hans W. Gatzke, *ibid.,* pp. 221-22.

51. *Time,* November 22, 1954, p. 23. Cf. Loewenstein, *op. cit.,* p. 241.

52. *Realities of American Foreign Policy* (Princeton, N. J., 1954), pp. 27, 65. *The New York Times* wrote in an editorial, October 10, 1954: "At stake is the fate not only of Germany but also of Europe and the whole free world . . . literally confronted with the dictum: unite or perish. . . ." The paper concluded that the "battle for Germany" was "a battle also for German loyalties." Hans Kohn, *op. cit.,* pp. 247-48, declared: "The closest Atlantic union is not only necessary to contain Russian communism: it is equally indispensable for winning the Germans to the West." Cf. Hermann Lutz, *ibid.,* p. 235.

53. *Time,* November 1, 1954, p. 29.

54. General Günther Blumentritt, a well-known collaborator with Americans, pointed out these facts in a series of instructive letters to the author from August 1951 onward. He repeatedly underscored the necessity of treating the German soldier in moral respects as an equal with his partners. B. H. Liddell Hart, *The German Generals Talk* (New York, 1948), paid a warm tribute to Blumentritt.—Noteworthy is Carol L. Thompson's article "The German Military Tradition" in *Current History, op. cit.,* pp. 200-04.

55. *Time,* October 4, 1954, p. 30.

56. *The Great Globe Itself: A Preface to World Affairs* (New York, 1946), p. 170; cf. p. 215. See also Mr. Bullitt's article "The Tragedy of Versailles," *Life,* March 27, 1944, p. 116.

57. *Op. cit.,* pp. 351, 537, 1625, 1627, 1729, 1733.

58. *Where Are We Heading?* (New York-London, 1946), pp. 363-68, 389.

59. *The New York Times,* September 18, 1953, commenting on Mr. Dulles' Address to the United Nations Assembly on September 17th. Cf. *Time,* September 28, 1953. Stanley High, "The Momentous Aim of John Foster Dulles," *The Reader's Digest,* January 1955, pp. 63-68, under the headline: "The U. S. Secretary of State, by his indomitable faith in the triumph of moral ideas, wields a unique power in world affairs."

60. *The Twenty Years' Crisis, 1919-1939* (London, 1939), p. 126.

61. *Op. cit.,* pp. 445-46. Morality is also stressed by J. F. C. Fuller, *The Second World War* (London, 1948; New York, 1949), p. 398; G. M. Gathorne-Hardy, *A Short History of International Affairs, 1920-1939,* 4th ed. (London-New York-Toronto, 1950), pp. 505-06; Murray, *op. cit.,* p. 150; *Wartime Correspondence between President Roosevelt and Pope Pius XII,* Introduction by Myron C. Taylor (New York, 1947), pp. 1, 15, 52; Arnold J. Toynbee, "A Turning Point in History," *Foreign Affairs,* vol. 17, No. 2,

January 1939, pp. 319-20; Sir Victor Wellesley, *Diplomacy in Fetters* (London-New York-Melbourne-Sydney, 1944), p. 162.

62. In this searching study (Paris, 1925), Professor Renouvin refuted some main charges made at Versailles against Germany.

63. *Evénements Survenus en France de 1933 à 1945. Témoignages et Documents Recueillis par la Commission d'Enquête Parlamentaire,* Assemblée Nationale (Paris), No. 2344, vol. II, pp. 487, 499. Dobler was Consul General at Cologne from 1931 to 1938. Speaking German fluently he had many ties with leading Germans.

64. *Deutschland-Frankreich, op. cit.,* p. 46; *Geschichtsunterricht: Brücke zwischen den Völkern,* ed. by Internationales Schulbuchinstitut, Kant-Hochschule Braunschweig (Braunschweig, 1954), pp. 6, 10-13, 20, 29-37, 45; *Internationales Jahrbuch, op. cit.,* vol. I, pp. 203, 220; vol. II, p. 109; vol. III (Braunschweig, 1954), pp. 92-93, 148, 169, 192, 229, 231, 238, 263, 265, 330, 336, 337, 339, 341-45.

65. In his *Histoire de la Révolution Européenne* (Paris, 1954), Alfred Fabre-Luce sets forth the arguments for a united Europe, "the great revolutionary theme of our epoch" (p. 350). He rightly says that all conditions for an intimate *rapprochement* between France and Germany are already given, and he contends, p. 347, that the greatest obstacle to their reconciliation "is the lack of civic courage of French leaders." When M. Fabre-Luce heard that the writer intends to advocate neutral commissions he wrote him on December 1, 1952: "Nothing could be more useful for the future preservation of peace."

66. Impartial tribunals were favored by Herbert Adams Gibbons, *Europe since 1918* (New York-London, 1923), p. 602; Arthur Berriedale Keith, *The Causes of the War* (London-Edinburgh, etc., 1940), pp. 63, 129; Arthur Salter, *The Dual Policy* (Oxford, 1939), p. 24. Cf. George F. Kennan, *American Diplomacy, 1900-1950* (Chicago, 1951), p. 56. Francis Neilson properly called the fight against the war guilt charge "Duty to Civilization," *Unity,* April-August 1921, reprinted in book form, 1921. In *The Makers of War* (Appleton, Wisconsin, 1950), pp. 154-55, Neilson drew once more attention to the evil consequences of that charge. On pp. 39-40, he justly declared: "There will never be peace in Europe until the lie that Germany was solely responsible for the First World War is cleared out of the minds of the people of Britain, France, and America."

APPENDIX

1. Paul Scott Mowrer, *The House of Europe* (Boston, 1945), pp. 617-18. Cf. Edgar Ansel Mowrer, *Germany Puts the Clock Back,* rev. ed. (New York, 1939), pp. 144-46.

2. Published by Wishart & Co. (London, 1933), pp. ix-xii. Steel's Foreword is dated "London, June, 1933."

3. School of Economics, letter, October 16, 1952; Lawrence & Wishart Ltd., London, letter, June 9, 1952.

4. *The Second World War* (New York, 1934), p. 203.

5. Letter from *Auswärtiges Amt,* Bonn, December 12, 1952; letters from the *Institut,* München, August 2, 1952, and December 10, 1952. Herbert von Dirksen, German Ambassador to Tokyo from 1933 to 1938, wrote in the same sense, July 27, 1952.
6. *World War, op. cit.,* pp. 203 ff. Cf. Glyn Roberts, *The Most Powerful Man in the World: The Life of Sir Henri Deterding* (New York, 1938), pp. 269, 317.
7. *Op. cit.,* pp. xiv, 53.
8. *Ibid.,* chapt. II, pp. 20-54. The passages quoted are on pp. 21, 26-28, 29-31.
9. Letters of December 16, 1953, and February 1, 1954.
10. Letters of November 20, 1953, and December 17, 1953. Cf. *Trial of the Major War Criminals before the International Military Tribunal,* 42 vols. (Nuremberg, 1947-1949), vol. XXXII, p. 543, where Schacht's statement is printed: "I didn't get all the devisen because the Nazi Party for instance never brought any devisen to me when they collected foreign money outside of Germany, never offered these devisen to me. And therefore, I asked Hitler to vest the devisen authority with Goering."
11. *Op. cit.,* pp. 37-38.
12. *Ibid.,* pp. 31-35.
13. *Ibid.,* p. x.
14. *Facts and Fascism* (New York, 1943), p. 122, and pp. 135-38, section "Ford and Early Hitler Money."
15. E. A. Mowrer, *op. cit.,* p. 144.
16. *The New York Times,* February 8, 1923. The present writer knew Erhard Auer, leader of the Social Democrats, personally well enough to vouchsafe that he would not have made such a statement unless he was convinced of its truth.—In 1924, Auer signed the writer's *Appeal,* see pp. 149-51.
17. Konrad Heiden, *Der Fuehrer: Hitler's Rise to Power* (Boston, 1944), p. 369.
18. *I Knew Hitler. The Story of a Nazi Who Escaped the Blood Purge* (New York, 1937), pp. 193, 315.
19. *Adolf Hitler: Das Zeitalter der Verantwortungslosigkeit* (Zürich, 1936), p. 263. Some authors disputed that Ford gave money, for instance Walter Görlitz and Herbert A. Quint, *Adolf Hitler: Eine Biographie* (Stuttgart, 1952), p. 184; Emil Lengyel, *Hitler* (New York, 1932), p. 201.
20. *The Flivver King* (Pasadena, 1937), p. 109.
21. The brackets are in the letter.
22. Harry Bennett, *We Never Called Him Henry: As told to Paul Marcus* (New York, 1951), p. 120. Upon inquiry as to Upton Sinclair's statements, Mr. Liebold replied by letter, March 2, 1954, "there is no truth whatever" to either of them.
23. *Op. cit.,* pp. 121-22.
24. *Frankenstein, op. cit.,* pp. 42, 47, Steel mentions the Swedish Bofors Ordnance and Dry Dock Co., closely linked with Krupps, and the Polskie Zaklady Skoda, a subsidiary of the Skoda Works in Czechoslovakia. On pp. 96-101, Steel reproduced a letter from the Nazi "Agent V. N.," who had fled to Paris, and declared, p.

97: "I was instrumental in bringing about many contributions to the Hitler purse. Two million dollars went through my hands within three years, and found their way ultimately into the Hitler cash box."

25. *Op. cit.,* pp. 98-100. On p. 210 Steel related with regard to the attitude of French armaments firms toward Hitler's advent that in 1932 he asked a prominent member of Schneider-Creusot's in Paris, whether there was any truth in Paul Faure's statement in the *Chambre des Députés,* quoted in chapter IV. The reply was, according to Steel: "A Hitler Government in Germany will frighten the French people into more armaments. That means business for us. Hitler will be a boon to the French armament budget. So what's astounding about the affair?"

26. Letter from the Dutch publishers to the writer, April 9, 1952; further details given by the Netherlands State Institute for War Documentation, Amsterdam, May 2, 1952, based on an interview with Van Holkema & Warendorf, published in *De Telegraaf,* November 23, 1933.

27. *De Geldbronnen van het Nationaal Socialisme. Drie Gesprekken met Hitler door Sidney Warburg. Vertaald door J. G. Schoup.*

28. This summary is taken from the German translation which René Sonderegger deposited in 1947 with the Swiss State Library in Berne.

29. Letter of his son, Henri Schoup, to the writer, April 23, 1952. The State Institute, mentioned in note 26, established the following facts contained in a letter of May 2, 1952: According to Dutch newspaper reports J. G. Schoup was sentenced in 1915 for having stolen Belgian relief goods; in 1932 he was accused of financial fraud and of falsely assuming the title of Dr., pleading guilty to both charges; finally, the weekly *De Haagse Post* revealed that in the files of the British Intelligence Service there was a note about Schoup stating: "Tries to make himself interesting by telling all sorts of lies." The *Haagse Post* was at that time edited by Mr. S. F. van Oss, a family relation of the British Military Attache at The Hague.

30. Letter from Van Holkema & Warendorf to the writer, October 30, 1951. The Amsterdam daily *Het Volk* of January 30, 1934, reported that the publishers had decided to destroy all copies of *De Geldbronnen van het Nationaal Socialisme.*

31. Letter from the Chamber of Commerce, New York, to the writer, July 1, 1952.

32. This refers especially to a supposed Mr. "Deutzberg," Mayor of Munich; to a financial collaborator of Hitler, "Herr von Heydt"; to a Nazi quarter in Berlin, actually in Jewish hands. The publishers might have been particularly puzzled by the fact that Hitler had become Chancellor on January 30, 1933, though at the time of the Reichstag fire, February 27, 1933, he was not yet all-powerful.

33. Alexander Werth, *The Destiny of France* (London, 1937), p. 38. Cf. Bertrand de Jouvenel, *D'Une Guerre à l'Autre,* vol. I (Paris,

1941), chapt. xxv, "Le Franc Controle l'Europe"; Gustav Winter, *This Is Not the End of France* (London, 1942), p. 22.

34. Sir Victor Wellesley, *Diplomacy in Fetters* (London-New York-Melbourne-Sydney, 1944), p. 90.

35. Letter of his son to the writer, April 23, 1952. Mr. Henri Schoup did not reply to the conjecture that the Nazis killed his father.

36. *Spanischer Sommer* (Affoltern a. A., 1948), p. 180; 2nd ed. (Buenos Aires, 1952), pp. 145-46, both published under the pseudonym Severin Reinhard.

37. Letter from the *Institut für Zeitgeschichte,* München, to the writer, January 18, 1952. In the files of Mr. James P. Warburg, New York, appears the version that Sonderegger was approached by a member of the Austrian Secret Service, and that the booklet was given to him by a high official of the Austrian Government, mentioning Minister of Information Adam: see Mr. Warburg's Statement and Affidavit, July 15, 1949, printed as Appendix I in Franz von Papen's *Memoirs* (London, 1952), p. 592.—Sonderegger's brochure *Finanzielle Weltgeschichte: Das III. Reich im Dienste der Internationalen Hochfinanz* (Zürich, 1936), gave the gist of the Dutch booklet.

38. Letters to the writer from Dr. Kurt von Schuschnigg, March 2, 1952; from Theodor Hornbostel, formerly Chief of the Political Department of the Foreign Office, May 28, 1952; from the Austrian Embassy, Washington, June 2, 1952, in behalf of the Federal Chancellery; from two former members of the Press Bureau, March 11, 1952, and June 17, 1952; and from Dr. Otto Strasser, February 17, 1953.

39. *Hakenkreuzjudas und seine Silberlinge,* signed by a Socialist Official, Hans Philipp (Wien).

40. Letter from Dr. Anton Klotz, formerly of the Press Bureau, now editor-in-chief of the *Tiroler Tageszeitung,* Innsbruck, to the writer, March 11, 1952; similarly Dr. Kurt von Schuschnigg in a letter, March 2, 1952.

41. In *Spanischer Sommer,* 1st ed., p. 179; 2nd ed., p. 145, Sonderegger stated: "What could not be withdrawn by a Jewish lawyer in Amsterdam, evidently by order of the Warburg family, was hunted up by the Secret Police of the Hitler movement in Holland." With the "Jewish lawyer," Sonderegger aimed at Dr. Hans J. Meyer, in 1933 partner of Warburg & Co., Amsterdam, who later worked with the firm E. M. Warburg & Co. Inc., New York. His role in 1933 was merely to inform the Amsterdam publishers that they had obviously been the victim of a fraud: letter from Dr. Meyer to the writer, May 4, 1953.

42. Letter to the writer, October 30, 1951. Cf. note 30.

43. *Weltgeschichte, op. cit.,* pp. 22-23.

44. The *Schweizerische Landesbibliothek,* Berne, obligingly loaned their relevant material to the Hoover Institute and Library, Stanford University, for the writer's research work.

45. *Sommer, op. cit.,* 1st ed., pp. 174-94, 296-300; 2nd ed., pp. 142-56, 231-34, deals with the Dutch publication and with Sonderegger's

"proof" for the identification of James P. Warburg with "Sidney Warburg."—Henry A. Wallace had been Secretary of Agriculture.

46. *Op. cit.*, pp. 592-93, 596.

47. Letter, June 16, 1952. The reader will notice that Sonderegger's exploitation of Mrs. Bruggmann's answer is the "unintentional, frank testimony of an American lady of very high position," which he misused already in 1936.

48. Letter to the writer, May 10, 1952.

49. *Op. cit.*, pp. 593, 596.

50. *Ambassador Dodd's Diary, 1933-1938,* ed. by William E. Dodd, Jr., and Martha Dodd (New York, 1941), p. 145. From Martha Dodd's book *Through Embassy Eyes* (New York, 1939), pp. 312-13, it appears that the Dodd family had some—though incorrect—knowledge of the Schoup-Warburg booklet.

51. *Die letzte Frage,* privately printed, also under the pseudonym Severin Reinhard (Zürich, 1949), p. 25.

52. *Op. cit.,* p. 280.

53. *Frage, op. cit.,* p. 31.

54. *Sommer, op. cit.,* pp. 296, and 231 respectively. Cf. *ibid.,* pp. 182-83, and 147-48 respectively, and *Frage, op. cit.,* pp. 24-26.

55. *Liebet eure Feinde* (Thielle/Neuch., 1948), pp. 73-79, chapter "Hitler's geheime Geldgeber" [Hitler's secret financial supporters]. Recantation in *Freisoziale Presse* (Lüdenscheid-Hagen), February 27, 1953, and in Zimmermann's magazine *Drei-Eichen-Blätter* (München), April 1, 1953.

56. *Op. cit.,* pp. 593, 595.

57. *Frage, op. cit.,* pp. 19, 25. After having been an ardent anti-Nazi, Sonderegger changed his attitude completely when the Second World War broke out. In 1940 and 1941 he published several brochures which glorified Hitler to such an extent that the Swiss Government suppressed them. Early in 1953 Sonderegger expatriated to Spain.

Bibliography

Ambassador Dodd's Diary, 1933-1938. Ed. William E. Dodd, Jr., and Martha Dodd. New York, 1941.

Angell, (Sir) Norman. *Must It Be War?* London, 1939.

———— *For What Do We Fight?* London-New York, 1939.

Armstrong, George Gilbert. *Why Another World War? How We Missed Collective Security.* London, 1941.

Bailey, Thomas E. *Woodrow Wilson and the Lost Peace.* New York, 1944.

———— *Woodrow Wilson and the Great Betrayal.* New York, 1945.

———— *The Man in the Street: The Impact of American Public Opinion on Foreign Policy.* New York, 1948.

Bartlett, Vernon. *Intermission in Europe: The Life of a Journalist and Broadcaster.* New York, 1938.

Beloff, Max. *The Foreign Policy of Soviet Russia, 1929-1941.* 2 vols. Secd. impr. London-New York-Toronto, 1949.

Birdsall, Paul. *Versailles Twenty Years After.* New York, 1941.

Black, C. E., and E. C. Helmreich. *Twentieth Century Europe: A History.* New York, 1951.

Boothby, Robert. *I Fight to Live.* London, 1947.

Braun, Otto. *Von Weimar zu Hitler.* New York, 1940.

Brooks, Collin. *Can Chamberlain Save Great Britain?* London, 1938.

Brown, William. *War and the Psychological Conditions of Peace.* London, 1942.

———— *Oxford Essays on Psychology.* London, 1948.

Bryant, Arthur. *Unfinished Victory.* London, 1940.

Bullitt, William C. *The Great Globe Itself: A Preface to World Affairs.* New York, 1946.

Bullock, Alan. *Hitler: A Study in Tyranny.* London, 1952.

Burnett, Philip Mason. *Reparation at the Paris Peace Conference from the Standpoint of the American Delegation.* New York, 1940.

Carr, Edward Hallett. *The Twenty Years' Crisis, 1919-1939.* London, 1939.

———— *Britain: A Study of Foreign Policy from the Versailles Treaty to the Outbreak of War.* London-New York-Toronto, 1939.

———— *Conditions of Peace.* London, 1942.

———— *International Relations between the Two World Wars (1919-1939).* London, 1948.

Cave, Floyd A., and Associates. *The Origins and Consequences of World War II.* New York, 1948.

Churchill, Winston S. *The Second World War * The Gathering Storm.* Boston, 1948.

Clark, R. T. *The Fall of the German Republic: A Political Study.* London, 1935.

Dallin, David J. *The Real Soviet Russia.* Rev. ed. New Haven, 1947.

Dalton, Hugh. *Hitler's War Before and After.* Harmondsworth, 1940.

Dawson, William Harbutt. *Germany under the Treaty.* London, 1933.

Deutschland-Frankreich-Europa: Die Deutsch-Französische Verständigung und der Geschichtsunterricht. Ed. Professor Dr. Georg Eckert and Dr. Otto-Ernst Schüddekopf. Baden-Baden, 1953.

Deutschland und Frankreich im Spiegel ihrer Schulbücher. Ed. Internationales Schulbuchinstitut, Kant-Hochschule Braunschweig. Braunschweig, 1954.

Documents on British Foreign Policy, 1919-1939. Secd. Ser., vol. IV, *1932-3.* Ed. E. L. Woodward and Rohan Butler. London, 1950.

Eddy, Sherwood. *The Challenge of Europe.* New York, 1933.

Fabre-Luce, Alfred. *La Victoire.* Paris, 1924.

——— *Le Siècle prend Figure.* Paris, 1949.

——— *Histoire de la Révolution Européenne.* Paris, 1954.

Fay, Sidney Bradshaw. *The Origins of the World War.* 2 vols. New York, 1928.

Ferdonnet, Paul Joseph. *Face à Hitler.* Paris, 1934.

Fischer, Ruth. *Stalin and German Communism: A Study in the Origins of the State Party.* Cambridge, 1948.

François-Poncet, André. *Souvenirs d'une Ambassade à Berlin, Septembre 1931-Octobre 1938.* Paris, 1946.

——— *De Versailles à Potsdam.* Paris, 1948.

Fraser, Lindley. *Germany between Two Wars: A Study of Propaganda and War-Guilt.* London-New York-Toronto, 1944.

Fuller, J. F. C. *The Second World War.* New York, 1949.

Gathorne-Hardy, G. M. *A Short History of International Affairs, 1920-1939.* 4th ed. London-New York-Toronto, 1950.

Geschichtsunterricht: Brücke zwischen den Völkern. Ed. Internationales Schulbuchinstitut, Kant-Hochschule Braunschweig. Braunschweig, 1954.

Gibbons, Herbert Adams. *Europe since 1918.* New York-London, 1923.

Görlitz, Walter, and Herbert A. Quint. *Adolf Hitler: Eine Biographie.* Stuttgart, 1952.

Gollancz, Victor. *Shall Our Children Live or Die? A Reply to Lord Vansittart on the German Problem.* London, 1942.

Gooch, George P. *Germany.* New York, 1925.

——— *Recent Revelations of European Diplomacy.* 4th ed., rev. and enlarged 1940. London, 1940.

Grenfell, Captain Russell. *Unconditional Hatred: German War Guilt and the Future of Europe.* New York, 1953.

Gustav Stresemanns Vermächtnis. 3 vols. Ed. Henry Bernhard. Berlin, 1932, 1933.

Halperin, S. William. *Germany Tried Democracy: A Political History of the Reich from 1918 to 1933.* New York, 1946.

Heiden, Konrad. *Der Fuehrer: Hitler's Rise to Power.* Boston, 1944.

Hilger, Gustav, and Alfred G. Meyer. *The Incompatible Allies*. New York, 1953.

Hoover, Calvin B. *Germany Enters the Third Reich*. New York, 1933.

Hoover, Herbert. *The Memoirs of Herbert Hoover: Years of Adventure, 1874-1920*. New York, 1951.

Huddleston, Sisley. *War Unless——*. Philadelphia, 1934.

—— *In My Time: An Observer's Record of War and Peace*. New York, 1938.

Internationales Jahrbuch für Geschichtsunterricht. Ed. Arbeitsgemeinschaft Deutscher Lehrerverbände, G. Eckert. Vol. I. Braunschweig, 1951. Vol. II. Braunschweig, 1953. Vol. III. Braunschweig, 1954.

Jackson, J. Hampden. *The Between-War World: A Short Political History, 1918 to 1939*. London, 1947.

James, C. L. R. *World Revolution, 1917-1936*. London, 1937.

Keith, Arthur Berriedale. *The Causes of the War*. London-Edinburgh-Paris-Melbourne-Toronto-New York, 1940.

Kennan, George F. *American Diplomacy, 1900-1950*. Chicago, 1951.

—— *Realities of American Foreign Policy*. Princeton, N. J., 1954.

Keynes, John Maynard. *The Economic Consequences of the Peace*. New York, 1920.

King-Hall, Stephen. *History of the War*. Vol. I. *The Cause of the War*. London, 1939.

—— *Our Own Times, 1913-1939*. London, 1940.

Langer, William L. *European Alliances and Alignments, 1871-1890*. New York, 1931.

—— *The Diplomacy of Imperialism, 1890-1902*. 2nd ed. New York, 1951.

Lansing, Robert. *The Peace Negotiations: A Personal Narrative*. Boston-New York, 1921.

Lee, Dwight E. *Ten Years: The World on the Way to War, 1930-1940*. Boston, 1942.

Les Evénements Survenus en France de 1933 à 1945. Témoignages et Documents Recueillis par la Commission d'Enquête Parlamentaire. Assemblée Nationale, No. 2344. 9 vols. Paris.

Lichtenberger, Henri. *The Third Reich*. New York, 1937.

Lloyd George, David. *The Truth about the Peace Treaties*. 2 vols. London, 1938.

Lochner, Louis P. *What About Germany?* New York, 1942.

—— *Tycoons and Tyrant: German Industry from Hitler to Adenauer*. Chicago, 1954.

Londonderry, Marquess of. *Ourselves and Germany*. London, 1938.

—— *Wings of Destiny*. London, 1943.

Luckau, Alma. *The German Delegation at the Paris Peace Conference*. New York, 1941.

Ludecke, Kurt G. W. *I Knew Hitler: The Story of a Nazi Who Escaped the Blood Purge*. New York, 1937.

Mackintosh, John. *The Paths That Led to War: Europe 1919-1939*. London-Glasgow, 1940.

Madariaga, Salvador De. *The World's Design*. London, 1938.

Millis, Walter. *Viewed without Alarm: Europe Today*. Boston, 1937.

Montgomery, B. G. De. *Versailles: A Breach of Agreement*. London, 1932.

Mowrer, Edgar Ansel. *Germany Puts the Clock Back*. Rev. ed. New York, 1939.
Murphy, James. *Adolf Hitler*. London, 1934.
Nevins, Allan. *Henry White: Thirty Years of American Diplomacy*. New York-London, 1930.
Nicolson, Harold. *Peacemaking 1919*. New ed. New York, 1939.
———— *Why Britain Is at War*. London, 1939.
Nitti, Francesco S. *The Wreck of Europe*. Rev. ed. Indianapolis, 1922.
Palmer, Frederick. *Bliss: Peacemaker*. New York, 1934.
Papen, Franz von. *Memoirs*. London, 1952.
Powell, E. Alexander. *Thunder over Europe*. New York, 1931.
———— *The Long Roll on the Rhine*. New York, 1934.
Prefaces to Peace. A symposium by Wendell L. Willkie, Herbert Hoover and Hugh Gibson, Henry A. Wallace, Sumner Welles. New York, 1943.
Renouvin, Pierre. *Les Origines Immédiates de la Guerre*. Paris, 1925.
Ritter, Gerhard. *Carl Goerdeler und die Deutsche Widerstandsbewegung*. Stuttgart, 1954.
———— "Vom Ursprung des Einparteienstaates in Europa," *Historisches Jahrbuch*, 74. Jahrgang. Freiburg-München, 1955.
Roberts, Stephen H. *The House That Hitler Built*. New York-London, 1938.
Rothermere, Viscount. *Warnings and Predictions*. London, 1939.
Roussy de Sales, Raoul de. *The Making of Tomorrow*. New York, 1942.
Salter, Sir Arthur. *Security: Can We Retrieve It?* New York, 1939.
Schmitt, Bernadotte E. *The Coming of the War*. 2 vols. New York-London, 1930.
———— *From Versailles to Munich, 1918-1938*. Chicago, 1938.
Schuman, Frederick L. *Germany since 1918*. New York, 1937.
———— *International Politics: The Destiny of the Western State System*. New York-Toronto-London, 1948.
Seton-Watson, Hugh. *From Lenin to Malenkov: The History of World Communism*. New York, 1954.
Seton-Watson, R. W. *Britain and the Dictators: A Survey of Post-War British Policy*. Cambridge, 1938.
Sheean, Vincent. *This House Against This House*. New York, 1946.
Shotwell, James T. *On the Rim of the Abyss*. New York, 1936.
———— *What Germany Forgot*. New York, 1940.
Simonds, Frank H. *How Europe Made Peace Without America*. Garden City, New York, 1927.
Smuts, J. C. *Jan Christian Smuts*. London, 1952.
Sontag, Raymond James. *European Diplomatic History, 1871-1932*. New York-London, 1932.
Spectator. *Deutschlands Erwachen, von einem Ausländer Gesehen*. Genf, 1933.
Tansill, Charles Callan. *Back Door to War: The Roosevelt Foreign Policy, 1933-1941*. Chicago, 1952.
The Diplomats, 1919-1939. Ed. Gordon A. Craig and Felix Gilbert. Princeton, N. J., 1953.
The Intelligent Man's Way to Prevent War. Ed. Leonard Woolf. London, 1933.

The Road to War: An Analysis of the National Government's Foreign Policy, by a group of experts. Preface by C. R. Attlee. London, 1937.

The Third Reich. Publ. under the auspices of the International Council for Philosophy and Humanistic Studies and with the assistance of UNESCO. London, 1955.

Trevelyan, George Macaulay. *Grey of Fallodon.* Boston, 1937.

Trial of the Major War Criminals before the International Military Tribunal. 42 vols. Nuremberg, 1947-1949.

Valtin, Jan. *Out of the Night.* New York, 1941.

Vansittart, Sir Robert. *Black Record: Germans Past and Present.* London, 1941.

Vansittart, Lord. *Lessons of My Life.* New York, 1943.

————— *Bones of Contention.* New York, 1945.

————— *The German Octopus.* London-New York-Melbourne-Sydney, 1945.

Welles, Sumner. *The Time for Decision.* New York-London, 1944.

————— *Where Are We Heading?* New York-London, 1946.

Wellesley, Sir Victor. *Diplomacy in Fetters.* London-New York-Melbourne-Sydney, 1944.

Wertheimer, Mildred S. *Germany under Hitler.* New York-Boston, 1935.

Wheeler-Bennett, John W. *Wooden Titan: Hindenburg in Twenty Years of German History, 1914-1934.* New York, 1936.

————— *The Nemesis of Power: The German Army in Politics, 1918-1945.* London-New York, 1953.

White, W. L. *Report on the Germans.* New York, 1947.

Wilson, Hugh R. *Diplomat between Wars.* New York-Toronto, 1941.

Wingfield-Stratford, Esmé. *The Harvest of Victory, 1918-1926.* London, 1935.

Wolfe, Henry C. *The German Octopus: Hitler Bids for World Power.* New York, 1938.

Ypsilon. *Pattern for World Revolution.* Chicago-New York, 1947.

Name Index

Subject Index

Alsace-Lorraine, 12, 20, 22, 75, 88-89, 160

Armaments industry: Comité des Forges, 113, 120-21, 123, 126, 228 n. 53; Schneider-Creusot, 113, 125, 225 n. 17, 244 n. 25; Skoda Works, 113, 225 n. 17, 243 n. 24; Vickers-Armstrongs Ltd., 127-29

Armistice negotiations, 1918, 31, 34, 36-37, 45-46, 55, 69, 71, 91

Austria, Republic, 102, 120-21

Austria-Hungary, 10, 14, 17, 20-21, 23, 48, 53, 57, 60, 67-68, 89, 163

Belgium, 17, 20-22, 42, 49, 53, 69-70, 73-74, 88, 91-92, 164

Bolshevism, see Communism

Britain, see Great Britain

Communism, 66, 106, 112, 115, 125-28, 130, 138-41, 158, 181, 191, 234 n. 126, 235 n. 130, 241 n. 52

Depression, Great, see Economic Crisis

Disarmament problem, 1919-1933, 102-03, 113, 120-21, 127, 136

Economic Crisis, 1929-1933, 100, 102-04, 112, 123, 132-33, 135-38, 141, 192, 233 n. 112

France, 5-7, 9-10, 12, 14, 20-22, 44, 63, 73, 81, 121, 123, 136, 159, 163, 175; attitude towards Germany, 9-10, 12, 16, 21, 63, 68, 84, 87, 102-04, 108-10, 125, 152, 155, 160, 172-73, 223 n. 35; collaboration with German historians, 13, 161-64, 175, 177; collaboration with German industry, 123-24; reconciliation with Germany, xi-xii, 9, 29, 81, 159-60, 173, 242 n. 65

Franco-Prussian War, see War of 1870-71

Germany, until 1919, 3-7, 9, 14-17, 20-23, 32-33, 36-37, 48, 52-59, 61, 79, 83; accused, 39-40, 46, 53-56; belief in defensive war, 17, 42, 48, 58, 84; betrayed, 1919, 31, 78-79, 81, 97, 134, 168; blockade of, 64, 70-71, 91, 131-32, 231 n. 86-87; colonies, 65, 72-74, 88, 207 n. 4, 214-15 n. 119, 215 n. 126, 240 n. 44; crimes committed by, 18, 42, 53, 56-57, 65, 69-70, 79, 91, 93-94, 148; "criminal nation," 14, 24, 28, 61, 67, 87, 141, 151, 172; defeated, 1918, 79, 104, 132-33, 141, 157, 165; punishment of, 41, 46, 52, 56, 77; requests for impartial investigation, 38, 42, 49, 62, 70, 81, 91-92, 147-48, 153-54, 168; responsibilities for First World War, 3, 7, 18-20, 23-26, 38-39, 42, 46, 48-49, 53-63, 68, 77, 79-82, 84, 87-88, 94-95, 148, 155, 159, 163-64, 166-67, 208 n. 7, 240 n. 36; revolution, 1918, 36, 54, 56, 58-59, 96

Germany, Weimar Republic, 33-34, 38, 44-46, 50-52, 61, 63-64, 77, 87, 96-105, 130-31, 141, 158, 220 n. 8, 222 n. 21, 223 n. 33, 237 n. 141; at Paris Peace Conference, 30, 37-88; elections, January, 1919, to March, 1933, 58-59, 96, 98, 101-03, 112, 118, 134-35, 137-38, 140, 158, 239 n. 27; inflation, 1923, 99-101, 103, 108; Reichswehr, 86, 116, 139-40, 168; Ruhr occupation, 1923, 99-101, 108, 110, 120, 228 n. 53; separatist movements, 99, 108-09, 220 n. 13, 228 n. 53

Germany, Third Reich, 4, 134, 164-65, 167, 179-80; National Socialism, financing of, 107-18, 180-89; "purge," 1934, 113, 115, 117, 124, 126; Reichstag fire, 115, 122, 191; support from abroad, 105-30, 141, 179-80

256